READ WHAT OTHERS ARE SAYING ABOUT
THE EXPERT WITNESS HANDBOOK:

🐓 *More and more businesspeople and professionals are discovering a new place to sell their expertise: acting as advisors to attorneys in complex legal cases.* — BUSINESS OPPORTUNITY DIGEST

🐓 *This handbook will tell you how to get started and how not to fall apart in the courtroom.* — RAINBO ELECTRONIC REVIEWS

🐓 *There is good reason to feel intimidated by the court system, but most everything you, as a potential witness, need to know to demystify it is contained in this book.* — JOURNAL OF GROUND WATER

🐓 *The chapter on what to expect at trial is, by itself, quite helpful, full of "nuts and bolts" techniques for being an effective expert witness, handling difficult or tricky questions, etc. The style is direct and informative.* — CALIFORNIA DUI REPORT

🐓 *The book tells how to perform the job professionally—and successfully.* —THE WELDING DISTRIBUTOR

🐓 *A reference for the seasoned litigation consultant and a valuable introduction for the neophyte expert witness.* — AMERICAN CONSULTING ENGINEERS COUNCIL NEWS

🐓 *This is definitely one book you will want to read.* — VETERINARY AND HUMAN TOXICOLOGY

🐓 *Full of ideas and resources,* The Expert Witness Handbook *is chock-full of sample forms and letters, checklists, guidelines and advice.* — INSTITUTE FOR PROFESSIONAL COMPETENCY

🐓 *Read the book and/or hire the author to put on a seminar for you.* — CONSULTANTS NEWS

🐓 *(EWH) will suggest many pointers that will save a lot of trouble down the road.* — BULLETIN OF THE AMERICAN ACADEMY OF PSYCHIATRY LAW

EXPERT WITNESS HANDBOOK

TIPS AND TECHNIQUES FOR THE LITIGATION CONSULTANT

DAN POYNTER

- *Advice*
- *Explanations*
- *Guidelines*
- *Checklists*
- *Examples*
- *Resources*

PARA PUBLISHING
SANTA BARBARA, CALIFORNIA

EXPERT WITNESS HANDBOOK

TIPS AND TECHNIQUES FOR THE LITIGATION CONSULTANT

by Dan Poynter

Published by:

 Para Publishing
Post Office Box 8206
Santa Barbara, CA 93118-8206 USA
Telephone: (805) 968-7277; Fax: (805) 968-1379
Web site: http://www.ParaPublishing.com
e-mail: Orders@ParaPublishing.com

First edition 1987
Second edition 1997, completely revised

Library of Congress Cataloging-in-Publication Data
Poynter, Dan.
Expert Witness Handbook: tips and techniques for the litigation consultant / Dan Poynter. — 2nd ed., completely rev.
        p. cm.
        Includes bibliographical references and index.
        ISBN 1-56860-027-5 (hardcover)
        1. Evidence, Expert—United States. I. Title.
KF8961.P69 1997
347.73'67—dc20
[347.30767]

TABLE OF CONTENTS

ABOUT THE AUTHOR

 **DAN POYNTER** has been a practicing expert for more than 20 years; he counsels and testifies in parachute cases. He has served as litigation consultant throughout the U.S. and in five other countries, so far. This book is full of the inside nut-and-bolts tips only a *participant* could know.

Dan Poynter has also been a *participant* in parachutes and skydiving since 1962. With 1,200 jumps and every license, rating and award, he has written six books on the subjects. Two books have been translated into other languages. Politically active in the sport and industry, he has served on virtually every committee and has been elected Chairman of the Board of the U.S. Parachute Association and President of the Parachute Industry Association. His credibility as an expert witness is verified by his experience in the sport and leadership in the industry.

Dan Poynter has a BA and two years of post-graduate work in law. The author of more than 500 magazine articles, ten audio tapes and more than 70 books, he is an author and publisher first and a technical expert second. His work as an author since 1962 has allowed him to study his subjects in detail while validating his expertise.

Dan Poynter's seminars have been featured on CNN, his books have been pictured in *The Wall Street Journal*, and his story has been told in *U.S. News & World Report*. The media comes to him because he is the leading authority on how to succeed as an expert witness. He has participated in many National Forensic Conferences as a featured speaker, breakout leader and keynoter. He is a Fellow of the National Forensic Center. Dan is an active member of the National Speakers Association.

The author was prompted to write this book because so many people approached him for information on litigation consulting. He lives in Santa Barbara, California.

INTRODUCTION

Whether you are a seasoned veteran or a newcomer to the expert witness business, this book will be your constant reference. It tells you how to get started, how to decide whether or not to accept a case, how to conduct yourself at a deposition or in court, what to charge, how to collect payments, and much more.

Of course, experience is the best teacher. Your own expertise will grow with every case you work on. But this book will help you get started. To increase your knowledge and effectiveness, you will also want to attend expert witness conferences, talk to other experts, and keep on reading. (You will find a suggested reading list in the resource section of the Appendix of this book.)

Because laws differ from jurisdiction to jurisdiction and every case is unique, I offer the following caveats:

Different attorneys handle cases in different ways. It is up to them to deal with the differences and exceptions. Always clear *good ideas* with your client-attorney before proceeding.

Each state and the federal courts have differing rules on whether experts have to be named, whether experts can be deposed by the other side, if acceptance of the risk, signing of a waiver or contributory negligence is a valid defense, etc. Some specialties, such as medicine, have exceptional rules. This book cannot possibly list all of the differences and exceptions but it does provide the best general interpretation of most topics of interest to the expert.

Throughout this text, examples of lawyer-witness exchanges are presented for illustrative purposes. Several peer reviewers of the manuscript commented that these questions and answers were one of the most interesting and valuable parts of the book. These exchanges are not necessarily correct, proper or suggested by the author as answers to the questions. Since every case, court setting and opposing attorney is different, some replies may be appropriate while others are not. They are offered here to educate, stimulate and provoke thought. All have been used by experts—with varying degrees of success.

If you have any questions concerning any of the statements in this book, your client-attorney or other qualified professional is the best source for a complete answer.

Welcome to the challenge of litigation consulting.

Dan Poynter
Santa Barbara, California

FOREWORD

When my old friend Dan Poynter sought my advice about the first edition of this book, I gave it promptly: don't publish this book, for two reasons:

1. It will haunt you. Cross examiners will read it back to you, to your detriment.

2. There are too many dubious experts and too much appalling junk science in our courts already. This book will encourage more, and make slicker phonies.

Several years later, and many thousands of copies sold, Dan is happy he didn't take my advice. I don't know how he has fared with respect to reason number 1, but I have come to realize that reason number 2 was out of control long ago and only the Courts can correct that.

I still think the first two rules of being a successful expert witness are:

☞ *Be a real expert. Stick to what you know.*

☞ *Tell the truth. You deserve to be nailed if you don't, and your client doesn't deserve to win if you can't.*

Litigation purports to be, and certainly should be, a truth-seeking process. If you take the stand as an expert, you should be prepared for your adversaries to take that principal seriously—unless they hate the truth, which is often the case. They won't hesitate to do anything that may discredit you, in any event. If you can't handle that, don't offer your services as an expert. If you are willing to abide by these two rules, you can prosper as an expert and I wish you well. If not, you'd better hope your adversaries aren't very smart or haven't done their homework.

Logan L. Donnel, P.E.
Boulder, Colorado

ACKNOWLEDGMENT

My deepest thanks to the following for their contributions to this book:

To my peer reviewers: maritime expert Kirk Greiner; business management expert George Arneson; vocational rehabilitation expert Marjorie Cockrell; Steven Babitsky, Esquire, of SEAK, Inc.; Betty Buchan, Ph.D. of Final Analysis; economist Bryan Conley, Ph.D.; Richard Saferstein, Ph.D., author of *Criminalistics*; arboriculture expert Jack Siebenthaler; premises security expert Chris McGoey; mechanical engineering expert Heinz Bloch, P.E.; vehicular accident reconstruction expert Joe Thompson; arboriculture expert Walter Barrows Sr.; Richard Jacobs, P.E.; Logan Donnel, P.E.; Bernard Hale Zick of the International Society of Speakers, Authors & Consultants; document analyst M. Patricia Fisher; bicycle expert John Forester; aircraft accident reconstruction expert Ira Rimson; media analyst Marilyn Lashner, Ph.D.; land use expert Eugene Wheeler, AICP; litigation (patent) attorney Harvey Jacobson Jr., Esquire; litigation (family law) attorney Sterling Myers, Esquire; litigation (aviation) attorney J. Scott Hamilton, Esquire; litigation (personal injury) attorney Joseph T. Mallon, Esquire; and Professor Oliver C. Schroeder Jr. of Case Western Reserve University. Other help and materials were contributed by Mike Ravnitzky and Edward J. Monahan.

To Gail Kearns for fact checking and copyediting and Chris Nolt for book design, typesetting and layout.

To Betty Lipscher and the National Forensic Center for hosting the annual expert witness conferences. Her conference introduced me to dynamic people, bolstered my enthusiasm for litigation consulting and gave me the idea for this book.

I sincerely thank all these fine people and I know they are proud of the part they have played in litigation consulting as well as in the development of this book.

WARNING

This book is designed to provide information in regard to the subject matter covered. It is sold with the understanding that the publisher and author are not engaged in rendering legal, accounting or other professional services. If legal or other expert assistance is required, the services of a competent professional should be sought.

It is not the purpose of this manual to reprint all the information that is otherwise available to the expert witness but to complement, amplify and supplement other texts and sources. For more information, see the many references in the Appendix.

Every effort has been made to make this manual as complete and as accurate as possible. However, there may be mistakes both typographical and in content. Therefore, this text should be used only as a general guide and not as the ultimate source on the subject. Furthermore, this manual contains information on the subject only up to the printing date.

The purpose of this manual is to educate and entertain. The author and Para Publishing shall have neither liability nor responsibility to any person or entity with respect to any loss or damage caused or alleged to be caused directly or indirectly by the information contained in this book. When in doubt, ask your client-attorney or your attorney.

Laws and philosophies will change. The author cannot predict what legislatures and courts will decide after this book is printed.

This book is full of typical questions and answers you may encounter at deposition and trial. You will not want to use all the answers provided. Each jurisdiction is different, each expert-witness discipline is different, each situation is different, each client-attorney's strategy is different and each expert is different. Some advice is overstated for emphasis. Your mileage may vary.

If you do not agree with the above, you may return this book to the publisher for a full refund.

DISCLAIMER

CHAPTER ONE

𝕒

WHAT IS AN EXPERT WITNESS AND WHY BE ONE?

If something can break, bend, crack, fold, spindle, mutilate, smolder, disintegrate, radiate, malfunction, embarrass, leach, besmirch, be abused or used incorrectly, infect or explode, you can bet there is someone, somewhere who can explain how and why it happened. These people are often asked to take part in legal actions. There are litigation consultants on jogging, bicycles, dancing, solid waste management, speaking, writing, human bites, coastal planning and even skydiving. These experts investigate and explain to the attorney, and later on they explain or *teach* the subject to the judge and jury.

You do not have to be a forensic scientist or a doctor to be an expert witness, but you do have to be skilled in a particular art, trade or profession or have special information or expertise in a particular subject area.

In court cases, a gemologist may be called in to evaluate jewelry, a toxicologist may explain the affects of alcohol in a drunk driving case, or a retired police officer may describe the

EXPERTS TESTIFY IN SUCH DIVERSE FIELDS AS AEROBIC-DANCE INJURIES AND LAWN-MOWER ACCIDENTS.
—TED GEST IN *U.S. NEWS & WORLD REPORT*

sequence of events in a traffic arrest.

An automobile mechanic may be allowed to testify to the mileage on a vehicle when it does not match the number on the speedometer. He has been under thousands of cars and can tell by the wear and tear about how many miles the car has gone.

There are two kinds of witnesses: lay witnesses and expert witnesses. *Eyewitnesses* to the event may only tell what they saw, heard, felt or smelled; they are not allowed to tell what others have said (hearsay) or say what they think of the case. As a technical witness, on the other hand, you are allowed to express your *opinion* on any relevant issue falling within the scope of your expertise. It doesn't matter that you weren't there when it happened. You're presumed to be an impartial, disinterested witness who is simply explaining why and how things happen.

There are four general reasons why expert witnesses are brought into cases:

1. When required by law. In most jurisdictions, expert testimony is required in cases involving the negligence (malpractice) of a professional. The expert is required to help the court and jury understand whether the professional breached the objective standard of care required of a professional.

2. When required by the facts. When the case concerns complex, technological issues that are beyond the training and experience of a layman. When the subject is sufficiently beyond common experience.

3. To assist the jury. The facts may not be difficult to understand but the opinion of an expert may be of some assistance to the jury.

4. When your client-attorney has a tactical reason for hiring you: if the other side has hired an expert or if the client-attorney feels the jury might be persuaded by you rather than a

---

EXPERT WITNESSES ARE LISTENED TO CAREFULLY. LAY WITNESSES ARE LISTENED TO WITH SKEPTICISM.
—PROFESSOR OLIVER C. SCHROEDER

lay person. Or your client-attorney may wish to use you to get otherwise inadmissible evidence before the jury. Rule 703 of the *Federal Rules of Evidence* (see Chapter Nineteen) says that expert opinion may rely on inadmissible hearsay or evidence that violates other exclusionary rules, so long as the reliance is reasonable. If you testify that the inadmissible evidence supports your conclusion, you are not testifying for the truth of the information source but you may have to support it.

Your client-attorney may suggest you say you relied on a book and that it is a *learned treatise*. If you say relevant portions of the book are reliable authority, your client-attorney won't have to hire the author to come and testify. This is a tactic to get around the hearsay exclusion. On the other hand, he or she may use Federal Rules of Evidence Rule 803 (18).

Rule 702 of the *Federal Rules of Evidence* provides that if scientific, technical or other specialized knowledge will assist the trier of fact (jury) to understand the evidence or to determine an issue, a witness qualified as an expert by knowledge, skill, experience, training or education may testify thereto in form of an opinion or otherwise.

Why would anyone want to be an expert witness?
Five reasons come to mind:

1. To capitalize on your years of education and experience. Serving as a litigation consultant is a way to do more work in the field you enjoy. It enables you to develop a sideline that could lead to a post-retirement career. Sometimes people become experts just because they get tired of doing what they were doing. Perhaps you are already a consultant and are searching for another profit center. Litigation consulting has been called a *prestigious way to moonlight*.

2. To get into the action. To experience the challenge, drama and excitement of dealing with people's lives, large sums of money or even the course of history. It is your chance to

---

THE ROLE OF THE ATTORNEY IS TO BE AN ADVOCATE. THE ROLE OF THE EXPERT IS TO BE OBJECTIVE.

prove or disprove scientific theories. Expert-witness work will put some excitement into your life.

3. To put something back into the system. That is, to help people in your field and to contribute to society. To see that justice is done.

4. To be hired to study. Since you must anticipate every question at deposition and at trial, you will have to conduct research, study and write. This bank of material may later be used in articles and books. Study is fun if you love your subject.

5. To make money. Expert-witness work pays well. It may take up 10% of your time but contribute 20% to your income. There is no inventory investment and the overhead is low. This is a new profit center for your business. You may charge $50 to $500 per hour for work you do at home and $1,000 to $3,000 per day plus expenses when you have to leave town to testify. Serving as an expert can be very rewarding financially. See the *Guide to Experts' Fees*, listed in the Appendix.

Perhaps none of these reasons apply to you. Maybe you work for one of the parties to the suit and are being called to testify about company procedures. This could be the only deposition or trial you attend. If so, you may wish to jump ahead to Chapter Four.

An expert witness or litigation consultant is someone skilled in a particular art, trade or profession or with special information or expertise in a particular subject area. The expert assists the client-attorney in understanding and presenting the technical aspects of the case.

Where and when would you work?

a. Before trial. You may be retained before trial to assist counsel in investigating and understanding the facts. In fact, you could be hired just to investigate and consult rather than to testify.

THE COST MAY BE HIGH TO EMPLOY THE EXPERT, BUT IT MAY WELL BE HIGHER NOT TO EMPLOY ONE. INDEED, COUNSEL WHO CHOOSES TO PROCEED WITHOUT AN EXPERT MAY BE FLIRTING WITH MALPRACTICE. — MELVIN BELLI SR. IN *TRIAL* MAGAZINE

Since some 92% of your cases will be settled out of court, your primary work will be as a consultant. After you investigate the case and make a report to the client-attorney, the attorney may alter the case strategy. You will go to court only when neither side has a clear edge.

Attorneys and courts are relying on expert witnesses more and more to help them understand complex matters or little-known procedures. It is far less expensive for an attorney to call you in for a custom-tailored, *short course* in the subject than to spend months or years trying to learn a new field. The attorney has to know enough about the subject to effectively cross-examine the opposing lay (fact) and expert witnesses.

b. For the judge. Judges may hire a single expert to advise them (Rule 706—see Chapter Nineteen). Your job is easier when you are not expected to take sides. Twenty-two percent of the members polled by the National Forensic Center have been hired by judges for consultation.

Some judges will even sit down with the two experts to try to come to a solution without the lawyers. Many experts will agree it would be easier to come to a settlement this way.

c. To testify in court. You may also be retained by that attorney or the court to educate the jury. You will help the jury understand the technical aspects of the case and will try to persuade the jury to accept your explanation of the technical facts. The judge and jury are looking to you for help in understanding what happened AND what should have happened. They want information.

d. Out-of-court. Experts are often used in out-of-court *alternative dispute resolutions* (ADR), as well. ADR may take the

---

THE USE OF COURT-APPOINTED EXPERTS PRESENTS A LESS
COMBATIVE WAY TO PRESENT EVIDENCE.
— HAROLD FEDER, ESQUIRE

YOU MUST HELP THE JURY TO MAKE A DECISION. JURORS TAKE
THEIR JOB SERIOUSLY. MOST JURORS HAVE FEW OPPORTUNITIES
IN LIFE TO MAKE A DECISION THAT AFFECT OTHER PEOPLE.
— JUDGE HARVEY HALBERSTADTER

form of mediation, mini-trial, arbitration, summary jury trial, etc. Seven percent of all cases filed (20% based on dollar value) wind up in ADR. ADR is less expensive and much faster.

Fifty-one percent of the experts recently polled by the National Forensic Center have performed out-of-court work. The American Arbitration Association offers arbitration and mediation training and casework. The Association currently handles some 60,000 cases annually. To be considered, call the AAA at (212) 484-4000 or contact one of their 36 chapters around the country.

e. Paid by state. Just as the state must provide an *attorney* to the indigent in criminal cases, now those who cannot afford to pay have a right to a state-paid *expert* to support their criminal case.

According to *The Wall Street Journal*, the U.S. Supreme Court has ruled that states must provide indigent defendants with lawyers for felony cases. Other costs considered part of the defense, such as payments to expert witnesses, are also usually covered.

There are many ways to serve as an expert besides testifying in court. There is a lot of work out there for expert witnesses and the demand is expected to grow.

The impact of a technical expert in trial proceedings is three-fold:

1. The expert explains the logic of the mechanism involved, be it a technique, mechanical or medical procedure.

2. The expert gives an authoritative opinion as to causation and fault, if any.

3. The expert, by his or her mere presence, enlarges the importance of the case.

Expert witnesses are put on the stand not only for what they conclude based on the facts in the case but also for what

---

COURT IS A LOSE-LOSE SITUATION. MORE OFTEN BOTH PARTIES WILL BE BETTER SERVED BY RESOLVING THE CASE RATHER THAN GOING TO COURT.

they know about general practices that shed light on the matter at hand.

The expert will help the jury understand the technical aspects of the case and will try to persuade the jury to accept his or her explanation of the technical facts. Many experts are independent consultants. Others work for large *forensic engineering* firms which provide a wide range of services.

What will you do as an expert? Basically, expert witnesses provide four types of services:

1. You will **investigate** the particular scene or event, research everything written on the subject, run tests and then analyze and evaluate your findings. Investigations can be interesting.

2. You will **evaluate** the merits of a potential claim and document your work with a written report on your findings. You will express your opinion about the cause of the problem and merits of the claim.

Most lawyers are good at what they do—lawyering—but they do not have a technical background. They majored in English, economics or history.

3. You will **educate**. You will explain to your client-attorney what happened or what should have happened in the case.

You will analyze the positions of the opposing side and will recommend certain aspects of litigation strategy. You will assist in the discovery process by drafting questions for the opposing expert's deposition. You will serve as part of the litigation team. Your client-attorney may not be suing the right party or all of the parties.

You may know more about the law in this specific area because you tend to collect articles and citations on matters of interest to you. You will suggest other areas to be investigated

FOR AN ATTORNEY TO GO INTO COURT WITHOUT AN EXPERT WAITING IN THE WINGS IS LEGAL MALPRACTICE.
— ROBERT C. STRODEL IN *TRIAL* MAGAZINE

or tested. You probably know the opposing expert and can project the arguments that he or she may use. These recommendations make the expert a valuable assistant to the client-attorney.

You may be able to help your client-attorney locate other experts necessary to the case.

4. You will **testify** in depositions and at trial to explain and then defend the technical conclusions you have reached. The Federal Trade Commission even allows expert witnesses to cross-examine opposing witnesses before an administrative law judge. This is presumably because they know their technical subjects better than the lawyers.

Since most cases never go to trial most expert witnesses' time is spent in investigation and evaluation.

Experts explain to the client-attorney (and later to the judge and jury):

- scientific and technical issues

- issues concerning practice in the trade

- the meaning of certain terminology under trade usage

- damages issues—estimating lost value or profits caused by the defendant's wrongful conduct

Do you have what it takes? To be an expert witness, you must have demonstrated mastery of a subject; that is, have a field of expertise (see Chapter Two) and certain abilities. Attorneys are looking for someone who is:

- **Inquisitive**. Be the type of person who wants to know why things happen. You must enjoy doing library research and running tests. You must have access to reliable sources of information and be able to absorb and evaluate what you

---

OPINIONS; EVERYBODY HAS ONE. SOME PEOPLE ARE AVOIDED FOR THEIR OPINIONS AND OTHER PEOPLE GET PAID FOR THEM. EXPERT WITNESSES ARE CONSULTANTS WHO GET *PAID* FOR THEIR OPINIONS.

learn. According to *Forensic Accounting* magazine, most CPAs do not want to find problems. But forensic accountants love to find them.

☞ **A writer.** You do not have to be a great novelist but you must be able to put your thoughts on paper; to express yourself well. Since you are selling information, your most important tool is your computer.

☞ **A good speaker.** You must have good communication skills and be able to think on your feet so that you can express your opinion and respond quickly to defend your position. You must be able to break down technical topics into examples the jury can relate to. You must be articulate and able to think clearly under the pressure of cross-examination.

(Opposing attorney after continued badgering)

Q: *You haven't told us everything today have you?*

A: *No sir, I haven't told you* **everything**. *It would be impossible to condense 25 years of experience into three hours of testimony.*

☞ **Able to reason.** Can you handle hypothetical questions? Can you think on your feet?

☞ **A teacher.** You need to show counsel, the opposing side, judge and jury why your findings are correct. You should be a good performer; you must be able to persuade. You must be creative enough to provide new perspectives on the case to your client-attorney.

☞ **Mediagenic.** There is a world of difference between honesty and believability. Just knowing your subject is not enough. You must be able to teach it while winning over your

---

READING MAKETH A FULL MAN, CONFERENCE A READY MAN, AND WRITING AN EXACT MAN. — FRANCIS BACON

AN EXPERT WHO DOES NOT SPEAK EFFECTIVELY IS LIKE A MECHANIC WITHOUT A WRENCH.

audience. You have to be likable, exciting and convincing. Some people make good *research* experts while others make good *testifying* experts. Research experts are technically excellent but lack sufficient communication skills. You must *look* like you know what you are talking about. Appearance is vital.

The Wall Street Journal says more and more litigation attorneys are taking acting lessons. Tribeca Lab, a New York acting school, has a course titled "Acting For Lawyers." To most people, it is just a courtroom. To you it must be a platform.

🖙 **Credible.** Credibility comes from expertise in the specific subject required, qualifications such as a degree or title, integrity, knowledge, and speaking/teaching ability. You must be completely objective and honest.

Being a litigation consultant requires all of these. If you don't have these qualities, are you willing to learn them? Are you willing to get coaching in your weak areas?

Other considerations by attorneys might be:

🖙 **Prior experience**. Many attorneys would prefer not to deal with virgin experts. They like experience and track records. But experience in court or at deposition is not a big issue so do not be discouraged.

🖙 **Proximity.** Generally, attorneys like to hire the nearest competent expert to save on transportation costs. Local experts may also be familiar with the standard of care and prevailing local custom in that area. Local experts are also less likely to offend the local jury. On the other hand, attorneys sometimes look for a distant expert to reduce the chance the other side will know of you.

THE MORE YOU APPEAR IN COURT, THE MORE CHANCES YOU GET TO APPEAR AGAIN, PICKING UP WHAT YOU MIGHT CALL FREQUENT TESTIFIER BONUS POINTS.
—WALTER OLSON IN *FORTUNE* MAGAZINE

Can you do it?

Now the question is: Is this your kind of work? Some people rise to the challenge while others do not. Some experts (such as some college professors) get very upset when their opinions are challenged. Many don't like the game being played in court.

Being an expert witness for the first time can be an interesting but frightening experience. You may have heard of colleagues who have experienced brilliant victories or humbling defeats in court. If done properly, the job can be personally satisfying and financially rewarding.

The secret is preparation. Read everything, anticipate every question and be ready with a good answer. Remember, you are being paid to prepare.

Who can be an expert? To qualify as an expert witness, you must have something different to contribute.

Prior to 1993, most Federal courts relied on a 1923 case Frye v. United States. Frye held that proposed scientific testimony be generally accepted by others in the field; that is, be peer-reviewed.

In 1993, Daubert v. Merrell Dow Pharmaceuticals broadened the rule so that any expert that might help the trier of fact (jury) may be heard. The Supreme Court said the Frye Rule had been superseded by the *Federal Rules of Evidence*, especially Rule 702. So if someone with pertinent knowledge, skill, experience, training or education might help the jury to understand the evidence or determine a fact, they may testify. It is up to the judge to make a preliminary assessment of whether the testimony's underlying reasoning or methodology is scientifically valid and can properly be applied to the facts at issue. The court reasoned that it was elitist to insist on paper

BEING AN EXPERT LOOKS EASY, TO SOME IT SOUNDS EASY, BUT DON'T BE MISLED, IT IS AN EMOTIONAL EXPERIENCE THAT SHOULD BE CAREFULLY CONSIDERED BEFORE THE COMMITMENT IS MADE. — RICHARD M. JACOBS, P.E.

credentials before someone could testify. What if someone who got his training from the school of hard knocks turned out to be the next Galileo?

Now experts must be prepared to defend against a *motion in liminie* (motion to limit testimony) by showing what they base their opinion on.

Then the Third Circuit Court of Appeals ruled that a trial judge must make an independent assessment of whether the materials an expert relies on in forming his or her opinion are reliable.

Some states are now adopting a rule requiring that a party need only show that evidence is *scientifically valid and reliable.*

The attorney is looking for someone with good credentials who can develop a plausible theory that supports his case. He may shop around for an expert who will say what he wants.

Expert witness work is not for everyone. Some people rise to the challenge while many find the experience distressing.

Teachers usually make good testifying experts but professors often do not. Many professors do not like to be questioned about their opinions.

Practicing lawyers tend to make bad witnesses, lay or expert. They can be condescending, uncooperative in case preparation, and perceived as untrustworthy. Legal training develops rational patterns of thought rather than scientific ones. This is why legal professionals rarely hire other lawyers to testify as experts. On the other hand, technical experts with law degrees who are not practicing lawyers can be very good witnesses.

Your qualifications may be academic or operational, local or national (even international), general or specific. The hierarchy of competency looks like this:

> ☞ Scientists conduct original research and publish peer-reviewed articles and books. They advance their field of knowledge.

EVERYBODY IS IGNORANT, ONLY ON DIFFERENT SUBJECTS.
— WILL ROGERS

🐦 Specialists are devoted to one kind of work with individual characteristics.

🐦 Practitioners conduct material and informational analysis and interpretation.

🐦 Technicians (criminalists, investigators, supervisors) apply known techniques according to their training.

🐦 Lay people use common sense and life-long experience.

Nearly everyone has an expertise in some field. Almost any skill or discipline will qualify; you do not need a professional or academic degree. Naturally, some skills and disciplines are in greater demand than others. You may be an expert because of your background, experience or knowledge. Since most cases will involve difficult questions, you should be exceptionally competent in whatever field you offer your services. Attorneys, judges and juries will evaluate your ability by your public qualifications. These are the items you will list on your *curriculum vitae.* More specifically they will consider:

🐦 Education, training or practical experience (have you done it?).

🐦 Professional and technical expertise.

🐦 Position and function.

🐦 Recognition by other bodies such as professional associations.

🐦 Awards you have received.

🐦 Publications: books or articles. Have you researched the subject and committed your knowledge to paper to teach others? The public seems to perceive anyone who has written a book as an expert.

JURORS TAKE THEIR JOB SERIOUSLY BUT, GIVEN THE COMPLEXITY OF TODAY'S CASES, THEY HAVE A DIFFICULT JOB. CASES ARE NOT JUST MORE TECHNICAL, THEY ARE LARGER, MORE EXPENSIVE AND MORE COMPLEX.

🐌 Licenses or registrations held. If there are certifications in your field of expertise, you must secure them. Many courts will not admit testimony from unlicensed people. Even if admitted, juries will not give such testimony much weight.

🐌 Memberships in professional societies. What are your levels of membership.

🐌 Accomplishments.

🐌 Research in the field.

—or any combination of the above.

There is a lot of business out there. Each year, 175 accredited law schools in the U.S. turn out thousands of new lawyers; there are 850,000 in all. Some 75% of the world's lawyers are in the U.S and they are filing 18 million law suits annually. There is one lawyer for every 281 people in the U.S. In fact, there are ten times more lawyers than firefighters. All these lawyers are creating a lot of business for the legal industry—and a lot for expert witnesses.

The life of the average civil lawsuit in Federal Court from filing to completion is fourteen months; many run much longer. In state courts, cases run three to nine years. Expert-witness work is a long-term job.

Many expert witnesses find their work to be very rewarding. The challenges are considerable, the technical problems are complex and the money is good. Enlarging your practice to include litigation consulting may be the best decision you could make.

For clarity, the *trier of fact* will be referred to as *the jury* throughout this text. In non-jury *court trials*, the judge is both the trier of fact and the trier of law. (See Glossary)

Beck, Michael J.
534 Deer Park Ave.
Babylon, NY 11702
(516) 587-1924
Specialties: Psychoanalysis; Family problems; Psychological assessments. **Affiliation:** Babylon Consultation Center (Director, Psychological Services). **Degrees and Licenses:** PhD.

Brenner, David
R.D. #1
West Lake Moraine Rd.
Hamilton, NY 13346
(315) 824-1000
Specialties: Marriage; Divorce; Family. **Affiliation:** Colgate University (Assistant Professor, Psychology). **Degrees and Licenses:** PhD.

Bull, Mari
PO Box 279
Claremont, CA 91711-0279
(714) 624-1725
Specialties: Marriage counseling; Spanish-English. **Affiliation:** Private Practice. **Degrees and Licenses:** PhD.

Burg, Gary G.
Located in California
Mailing Address:
The Experts' Link
PO Box 2426
Princeton, NJ 08543
(800) 854-5446, Ext. C106
Specialties: Marriage, divorce & the family; Family law; Career counseling; Social Security evaluations; Life care & disability evaluations; Work evaluations; Personal injury; Wrongful death; Rehabilitation planning; Lost earnings. **Affiliation:** Associated Vocational Experts (Owner, Consultant). **Degrees and Licenses:** MS; CIRS; CVE; CWA; D-ABVE.

Cannon, W. John
1705 Ritchie Rd.
Forestville, MD 20747
(301) 336-1647
Specialties: Psychotherapy; Juvenile delinquency; Diagnostic testing; Marital problems. **Affiliation:** Columbia Union College (Chairman, Dept. of Psychology). **Degrees and Licenses:** PhD.

Chiappetta, Michael F.
DuKane Clinic
1970 Larkin Ave., Suite 9
Elgin, IL 60123
(708) 695-7512
Specialties: Marital family therapy; Decree & post decree; Child custody evaluation; Consultation to courts, attorneys & agencies. **Affiliation:** DuKane Clinic (Director). **Degrees and Licenses:** PsyD; Licensed Psychologist (IL, WI); Approved Supervisor, AAMFT; Certified, Council for National Register of Health Service Providers in Psychology.

D'Alessandro, Gena Joseph
15565 Northland Drive E
Suite 903E
Southfield, MI 48075-5370
(313) 557-1401
Specialties: Marital counseling; Psychological evaluation; Vocational evaluation; Learning disabilities; Special education laws. **Affiliation:** Regional Mental Health Clinic (President). **Degrees and Licenses:** PhD.

Eglash, Albert
1121 Laurel Lane
San Luis Obispo, CA 93401-5822
(805) 543-5808
Specialties: Marriage & family counseling; Psychological evaluations. **Affiliation:** Private Practice. **Degrees and Licenses:** PhD.

Evans, Louise
PO Box 6067
Beverly Hills, CA 90212-1067
(310) 474-1361
Specialties: Clinical psychology; Marriage counseling; Family counseling; Child counseling. **Affiliation:** Private Practice. **Degrees and Licenses:** PhD; ABPP; D-ABCP.

Haya, Avner
16 N. Kings Highway
Cherry Hill, NJ 08034
(609) 779-2529
Specialties: Pension benefit evaluation on divorce; Retirement plans actuarial valuation & certification; Matrimonial pension benefit disputes; Courtroom testimony. **Affiliation:** Independent Consultant. **Degrees and Licenses:** DREcon; FSA; EA.

A collage of two columns of page 226
from the *Forensic Services Directory*

CHAPTER TWO

HOW TO GET STARTED

To get started, you need to do two things: identify your subject area and let the lawyers know you are available.

Selecting a field. Your area of expertise should be obvious to you. Chances are it has to do with your work or the hobbies you pursue. Attorneys seek experts in the following areas:

- Experts on specific areas of activity. For example: skydiving, bicycle safety or horse nutrition

- Experts on the mechanics of injury

- Experts in human factors who understand the plaintiff's inability to recognize a hazard, evaluate the unreasonableness of a risk, or the economy or value (technical or social) of an engineering alternative

- Accident reconstruction experts

- Test experts

- Medical experts

- Economic loss and evaluation experts

- Experts in rehabilitation problems and potentialities

- Researchers for literature searches

- Experts on a standard of care in a particular industry or area of knowledge

Many people know a great deal about something. Use your expertise but do not venture beyond it. Limit your practice to those specific areas in which you are outstanding and where you plan to continue your education. For example, choose helicopters, not aviation. Better yet, choose rotor hubs, if this is your specialty. You cannot be an expert on piloting, navigation, propellers, airframes, and engines, both jet and reciprocating. The narrower your field, the more believable you will be and the less competition you will have. See the Appendix listing of the *Forensic Services Directory* published by the National Forensic Center for a list of specialties.

Marketing yourself. Once you decide to be an expert witness, you must let the legal world know of your availability. Lawyers find experts by asking other lawyers, making a literature search and consulting directories—in that order. So you must contact lawyers, write books or articles, and get listed in directories.

Spread word of your interest wherever attorneys are likely to look: in expert directories, at universities, in professional and technical societies, at other firms in your industry, private consulting firms or other lawyers.

To advertise your availability do some or all of the following:

1. Directory Listings. Send your curriculum vitae (CV) or resume, fee schedule and some promotional literature on your regular line of work to each of the directories and registries listed in the Appendix of this book. (Some experts do not send their fee schedule because they know the prices will change.) See Chapters Twelve and Fifteen on drafting a curriculum vitae and fee schedule.

Once you receive applications from these directories, visit your local *law* library; it is probably in the courthouse. If the county seat is a long way off, a university law school may be more accessible. Ask to see the expert witness directories. Review the areas of expertise listed and photocopy the pages that interest you. Use the photocopies to determine the best place to be listed and to draft a competitive listing.

Brokerages. Some of the resources listed in the Appendix are *expert brokerages*. For example, Technical Advisory Service for Attorneys (TASA) lists more than 24,000 experts in over 6,000 categories of expertise. Once they accept you, they pass your name on to lawyers needing assistance. You work through TASA and they mark up your usual rate.

In contrast, the *Forensic Services Directory* published by the National Forensic Center is a place to list your availability and qualifications. Interested attorneys contact you and contract with you directly.

Some directory listings are free and others charge a fee. List yourself with the free ones for now and consider the others.

Fish, Frederick A.

33 Tributary Road, Suite 333

Big Creek, WY 82999

Tel: (307) 555-1212; Fax: (307) 555-1212

Specialties: Drowning accident reconstruction; Report & deposition interpretation; Data on the sensations of drowning.
Affiliations: Aquatic Safety Experts, USCG Cmdr. (ret.)
Degrees & Licenses: BS, WSI.

Example of directory listing

Code your address when you draft your directory listings. For example, use PO Box 8206-*712* or 48 Walker Street, *Suite 712*. Do not use *department*. This coding is too obvious and many people will not use it. With tracking codes you will know what kind of a return you are receiving from each directory and advertisement. Next year you may alter your advertising to reflect your results.

A THORACIC SURGEON IS NOT QUALIFIED TO TESTIFY ON BRAIN SURGERY.

2. Mailings. Send your curriculum vitae and any promotional literature on your regular line of work with a cover letter to attorneys in your field. For example, if your area of expertise is parachuting, send your packet to aviation lawyers. Do not mail to every lawyer in sight or every litigation attorney in the book. Use the most specific lists possible.

The American Bar Association (ABA) rents its mailing list of 500,000 lawyers by areas of specialization. For information, contact the ABA, (312) 988-5478. Martindale-Hubbell has a list of 800,000 names. Call Cahners Publishing, who handles their mailing lists, at (800) 323-4958 for details. Contact all the associations listed in the Appendix for mailing list information.

December 11, 1998

Ladies and Gentlemen:

I am offering my services as an expert witness in mousetrap technology.

The attached material outlines my experience in this field.

Please place this information on file for future reference.

Sincerely,

Michael J. Maus, R.R.

MJM/mm

Letter offering consulting services

3. Attend meetings in your area of expertise. Most people find courtroom work unpleasant. Let your colleagues know you are open to this kind of work. Tell your national associations and magazine editors. Then when lawyers come looking for an expert, you will not only be referred, you will

---

I KNOW HALF MY ADVERTISING IS WASTED. PROBLEM IS, I DO NOT KNOW WHICH HALF. — WILLIAM WRIGLEY

be recommended.

4. Write articles on your technical experiences and those related to litigation. Spread your name around in magazines. Lawyers will find you through periodical indexes.

5. Take a course in accident investigation. Get to know other experts and lawyers in your field. Lawyers often consult other lawyers first when looking for a particular type of expert. This method makes sense as they can not only find an expert but can ask if he or she is any good. Check local colleges for these courses.

To obtain sample copies of magazines, send a letter like the following:

December 17, 1998

Trial Magazine
1050 31st Street NW
Washington, DC 20007

Ladies and Gentlemen:

Your publication is being considered as an advertising medium for some of our books. Please forward a media package to include:

1. Display advertising rate card

2. Classified advertising rate card

3. Current circulation figures (ABC statement)

4. Schedule of "special editions"

5. Two different sample copies of your publication so that we may determine the best size and placement for our advertising.

Do you provide discounts or special rates for new advertisers?

We would appreciate being placed on file in order to be notified of any future rate or policy change.

Sincerely,

Letter for obtaining sample magazines and ad rates

6. Advertising. If you are in a wide field, such as accounting, and expect most of your cases to be local, advertise in the local *Yellow Pages*. List yourself under *Attorneys' Services* and under *Accountants*. If your area is more narrow and you expect to work in a wide geographical area, try some of the specialized law journals. See the listings in the Appendix, and check the magazines in your local law library. Place your ads where you see ads from other expert witnesses.

Here is a question you may be asked along with answers you may find useful:

Q: *Do you advertise?*

A: *No, sir.*

A: *Only in the Yellow Pages under "Attorney Services."*

A: *No, I am too busy serving my clients to write ad copy.*

7. Speaking. Arrange to be a speaker at a legal seminar. Let the attorneys see and hear you as well as learn about your area of expertise.

8. Write a book. In looking for an expert, lawyers often check for books written in that area of expertise. They simply look in the Subject Guide of *Books In Print* which is available at the reference desk of your public library. It lists all the books currently available on any given subject.

Of course, there are other benefits to authoring a book. The prestige enjoyed by the published author is unparalleled in our society. A book can bring recognition, wealth and an acceleration in one's career. Once you are a published author, many people will consider you to be an expert on that subject.

Start by writing magazine articles and later string them into a book.

IN CIVIL AND CRIMINAL CASES ALIKE, HIRING AN EXPERT WITNESS CAN BE AS IMPORTANT AS HIRING A LAWYER.
— *THE NEW YORK TIMES*

For more information on book writing, see the Appendix for *Is There a Book Inside You?* by Dan Poynter and Mindy Bingham. For more information on book publishing, see *The Self-Publishing Manual* by Dan Poynter. There is an order blank on the last page of this book.

9. Spread the word to your industry and professional societies. Let colleagues know you perform expert-witness work. Then when they are contacted, they will refer you. Contact your own attorney and ask him or her to spread the word for you. Soon all roads will lead back to you.

10. Referrals. As your expert-witness work increases, more and more of your new business will come from referrals. As you become known, as word of your work spreads, people will recommend you.

Now, sit back and wait for the calls—but do not rest. Constantly review your promotion to see where improvements can be made.

TYPICAL QUESTIONS AND ANSWERS ARE USED THROUGHOUT THIS BOOK. THE QUESTIONS ARE SOME OF THE TOUGH ONES YOU WILL HEAR. THE ANSWERS ARE SOME THAT HAVE BEEN USED. THEY ARE NOT THE ONLY ANSWERS AND SOMETIMES THEY WILL NOT BE APPROPRIATE. EACH CASE IS UNIQUE. THEY DO, HOWEVER, MAKE INTERESTING READING.

THE QUESTIONS AND ANSWERS ARE BRIEF. NORMALLY, YOU WILL RECEIVE SEVERAL FOUNDATIONAL QUESTIONS LEADING UP TO THE EXAMPLE QUESTION.

CHAPTER THREE

CONTRACTING TO WORK

It is important to establish a system to formalize the business relationship so that you and your client-attorney both understand precisely who is hiring you, when you are hired and what you are hired for.

There are many things you may be asked to do for the client-attorney besides testifying. You may make literature searches, run tests, build demonstration models for court, advise the client-attorney about the strategy and/or theory of the case, identify issues which may have been overlooked, propose questions for interrogatories and depositions and much more. You may simply read some documents and give an opinion or you may do a lot of hand-holding.

Initial contact. The attorney in search of an expert will either call or write you. If he or she knows (from past experience or attorney referral) you have worked on similar cases, you may receive a copy of the complaint and a cover letter asking if you are interested. If he or she is not sure you are qualified, you will probably receive a telephone call.

The attorney will be searching for the best expert. Remember, that means he or she will be looking for someone with expertise in the specific subject area in which an opinion is needed; who is competent in that field; who has integrity; with the ability to communicate specialized knowledge to lay people; who lives nearby so as to control travel costs. If your area of expertise is very specific, the calling attorney may have to search a wider area but will still be looking for the best but nearest expert witness.

The calling attorney will try to judge your abilities. If he or she has done some homework on the subject, you may be *cross-examined* like an adversary at trial.

Make it clear that until a written agreement has been signed, you do not want any confidential information. Some unscrupulous attorneys will call, give you some details but not hire you so that opposing counsel can't hire you.

Do not give away too much in this initial contact. Ask questions.

You too may wish to investigate the potential client-attorney and case before you sign a contract or engagement letter. It is no fun and it certainly won't help your professional reputation to deal with an incompetent attorney or one without integrity. Part of your decision to accept a case will be based on your judgment of the caller's lawyer-like characteristics. Listen carefully to the telephone voice. Does he or she sound proficient?

Is this a widely-known, well-established firm? Why is this a one-person firm? Is he or she new in the game? Has he or she been unable to attract other good lawyers? Or is the caller part of a small but aggressive firm with a good reputation? Check with other experts and attorneys. Look up the calling attorney in Martindale-Hubbel's *Bar Register of Preeminent Lawyers.* For details, call (800) 526-4902. Call the local bar association to ask if there are any outstanding claims.

A great part of your decision to accept or reject the case should depend on your judgment about the case and how the calling attorney addresses it. Is the caller trying to push you toward a favorable conclusion? Is the caller unreasonable to work with? If, at any time, you realize the client-attorney is incompetent, unreasonable or dishonest, sever the relationship.

A responsible client-attorney wants to know as soon as possible if the case is weak. He or she is relying on the expert to point out both strengths and weaknesses. The expert is providing a screening service. If the case is weak, the attorney will want to cut losses and save money. Plaintiffs may drop cases or not even file them and defendants may be encouraged to settle. Expert witnesses are not hired to bring good news or to draw out cases, they are hired to provide an objective, factual opinion.

Early calls are essential. Too often, experts receive calls from attorneys a week before the trial. Late calls place an undue burden on the expert. The client-attorney should search for and hire an expert as early in the case as possible for several good reasons:

☞ The expert can quickly educate the client-attorney with an inexpensive, background short course on the general subject. No attorney can be an expert in every subject.

☞ The expert needs time to conduct investigations and tests to be able to establish reliable opinions and generate accurate reports.

☞ The expert is a source of information regarding the theories of recovery and who could be pursued. As part of the industry, the expert is in a better position to know of other past or pending cases with similar issues.

☞ The expert may assist in the discovery proceedings. He or she may recommend questions for the other expert, anticipate questions and help prepare witnesses for his or her side.

☞ The expert can assist in answering interrogatories and in preparing deposition questions. His or her information could avoid a summary judgment. Analyzing the opposition's discovery requests may reveal their trial theories.

☞ The expert knows where to find the relevant books, articles, standards and other resource material.

☞ Having an expert on board may enhance the settlement value of the claim. It is less expensive to conclude the case earlier.

🐦 Experts usually take cases on a first-come, first-served basis. So, some attorneys try to tie up the top specialist early in the case to prevent them from working on the other side.

Unfortunately, your initial contact with an attorney in search of an expert will often go like this:

The attorney will call, give a few basic details and say: *Based on what you have heard, what do you think?*

Expert: *I will send you my curriculum vitae and fee schedule. If you like what I send, send me a $500 retainer fee and all the paperwork. I will let you know within a few days if I will take the case.* Do not give an opinion. Instead, tell him or her what additional information and tests you need.

Attorney: *Well are you interested in the case?*

Expert: *I am interested in looking at it. Send the information (complaint, interrogatories, depositions, equipment, police report, coroner's report, witness statements, etc.) and the retainer. I will evaluate them, report to you and will tell you if I am interested in the case and can support your client.* Be firm.

Now, this is the way the call should go:

1. Get full names of plaintiff and defendant, date and place of the incident and the name and firm of the opposing attorney. Make sure you have not been engaged by the other side. Does this attorney represent the plaintiff or defendant?

2. How did they get your name? Were you referred by another attorney, were you found in a directory listing, was it your *Yellow Pages* ad, etc.? You want to know which business promotion is working and which is not.

3. Ask for a brief description of the case. What are the issues? Make sure it is something you can handle. If you cannot, suggest another expert. If you do not like the case, turn it down.

Take notes. Be helpful and concerned. Ask a few intelligent questions or provide some ideas, tips or background to show you know what you are talking about.

When you first talk to the attorney, do not hesitate to reveal your limitations. Make sure he or she understands your background. Do not pretend to be someone you are not. If you are not fully qualified, you will be embarrassed in court.

Skeletons. If you have any conflict of interests or skeletons in your closet, say so. Do you know any of the parties personally? If you have written articles supporting the calling attorney's position, your writing prior to being contacted will add to your credibility. If you have ever taken a contrary position in testimony or publications, how can you argue the change in your position? Opposing attorneys will research your background and may throw any skeletons back at you.

4. Find out whether you will be working for the attorney or client. Clients may be harder to collect from than attorneys. Incidentally, once you have been hired by an attorney, you may be contacted by other attorneys representing clients on the same side of the action. Always tell your client–attorney and obtain permission to cooperate. Open a separate file for the new client–attorney and make sure he or she will be responsible for the bill.

5. Where are they in the discovery process? How many depositions have been taken, were interrogatories answered and do they have any statements? Is there any photography?

6. Who are the insurance carriers and other parties to the case?

7. What is the schedule? Has a court date been set? Is your calendar open? Depositions? What is the Statute of Limitations? Will this case conflict with another you are working on?

8. Close by saying you will send your package (CV, brochures, fee agreement) for review.

Later, you will ask about the opposing attorney and for the local court rules if you have not served there before.

Some experts ask the calling attorney to send only the file for evaluation and ask not to be told which side the calling attorney is on. This approach works especially well in medical cases where there is a file to study. It allows the expert to be more objective.

At this point, you are only agreeing to *evaluate* the case, you are not agreeing to testify. Remain objective. More often than not, as you learn more about the case, you will find it is not as strong as the attorney portrayed it. There are two sides to every story and the opposing attorney will be telling the other side.

February 29, 1998

Hunter and Prey
Daniel J. Hunter, Esquire
1300 North Dos Pueblos
Chumash, CA 93778

<u>Lunch v. Dinner</u>

Dear Mr. Hunter:

Thank you for your letter dated October 14th regarding my availability in the above-referenced case.

Enclosed please find my current C.V., brochure on my major line of work and fee schedule.

Please send me a copy of the complaint, interrogatories, depositions, statements, photographs, reports and any other non-confidential information you may have so that I may form an opinion. Also, please send a check for $500 so I may formally open this file.

After reviewing the materials you send, I will call you with my first impressions and will tell you if I will be able to help you in this case.

Sincerely,

RABBITS UNLIMITED

John Hare Jr.
Owner
JH/pr

Example of cover letter

You may find that you are not hired for some of the cases in which you have been contacted. There are several reasons why this is so. You may not be qualified in the precise area of expertise they need, or perhaps your interpretation of the facts does not support the theory of the case of the calling attorney.

In contracting, be formal, firm and direct. This will instill self-confidence and may scare off the irresponsible callers. Your client-attorney wants to deal with a professional who solves problems, not an amateur who creates them.

Send your curriculum vitae, fee schedule, brochures on your major line of work and cover letter in a flat 9 x 12 envelope. Do not fold them.

Evaluate yourself and the case.

🐾 Are you competent to render an opinion in this particular area?

🐾 Do you need more information?

🐾 What are the weaknesses of the case and can they be diluted or overcome?

🐾 What are the strengths of the case?

🐾 Would more or different tests strengthen your presentation or basic theory of the case?

🐾 Would some demonstrative evidence strengthen the case?

🐾 Do you need some reference materials?

🐾 Can you suggest a reading list to educate the client-attorney?

🐾 Do you have any conflicts of interest?

🐾 Have you ever testified at deposition or trial on this particular question? Does that testimony conflict with what you plan to say in this case?

🐾 Is your client-attorney being candid? If you are not receiving all the information or there is any doubt about the ethical status of the case, you should reject it.

Fees. How much you can charge for your knowledge is discussed in detail in Chapter Twelve. The best way to make sure your client-attorney understands your fees and terms is to give him or her a copy of your fee schedule in writing.

A retainer is an advance payment for future work. It would be more accurate to call this *an advance payment against future billings* but *retainer* is commonly used in the trade. By requiring an advance payment, you formalize the agreement. People who put up money know they are buying something.

Abraham Lincoln once said, *A lawyer's time and advice are his stock and trade.* Many lawyers display these words in their offices as a reminder to clients. This is equally true of the expert witness and lawyers (as well as their clients) must appreciate that.

Some expert witnesses ask for another advance payment when the first runs out and further require a minimum account maintenance balance. This is often the case when they anticipate extensive charges. They do not want to spend scores of hours on a full case workup and then have collection problems because the case has been settled or otherwise terminated. Or they may anticipate collection problems because of the type of client or case.

If you have been hired directly by the attorney's client, he or she may not be as familiar with contracting as an attorney. You may spend small amounts of time or expend small amounts of money anticipating rapid reimbursement but do not extend too much credit. (See Chapters Twelve and Thirteen on fees and collections.)

Estimate what it will cost to read depositions and other materials, perform investigations and run tests. Charge by the hour to read case materials. The client-attorney knows the more material he or she sends, the more time you will spend reading. But only the expert knows what special investigations and tests should be conducted to determine and demonstrate the evidence or your opinion. Do not spend more time on the case until you reach an agreement on the estimate. See the sample letter, which follows:

February 29, 1998

<u>Lunch v. Dinner</u>

Dear My Lyon:

To properly investigate the above-referenced case, I feel we should conduct the following searches and tests. The itemized list below includes estimated time and costs.

1.

2.

3.

We are ready to proceed as soon as we hear from you.

Sincerely,

RABBITS UNLIMITED

John Hare Jr.
Owner
JH/pr

Sample estimate letter

Tell your client-attorney what tests you want to run and what research you feel you should do. Let him or her decide if he wants to spend the money. Cover yourself.

Fees have to be controlled—understood by both sides. With proper communication, the attorney will not have to explain unexpectedly high costs to the client.

The amount an attorney is willing to pay for more research and case preparation will depend on the potential recovery of the case.

Initial conference. Suggest a meeting with the attorney early in the case. You will be able to size up the attorney and he or she will be sizing you up. Your mission is to give information, get information and establish a rapport.

You may have special information such as knowing the

other party to the suit, the other experts, etc. Perhaps you know that no company in the industry carries insurance.

Do not be talked into underperforming or doing less preparation than is necessary.

Client-attorney: *This is a simple case so you will not require a great deal of preparation.*

Expert: *I have not earned my reputation by losing cases and I am not about to begin with yours. If you do not intend to prepare properly, I do not want to go into court with you. I will not go into court unprepared.*

Listing witnesses. Some attorneys will bluff the opposing side by saying they have hired you and that you are prepared to testify in support of their case. If you are well-known in the field, just having you on board may cause the other side to cave in.

Or attorneys may contact every expert in the field in order to tie them up. They may hire the expert to evaluate a case and render a preliminary opinion. If the opinion is adverse, the attorney may decide to keep the expert as a *consultant* on the case. That way, the expert can't work for the other side. His consulting work for the client-attorney may be considered *attorney work product* since he is not scheduled to testify in court. Attorney work product is confidential (not discoverable) as explained in Chapter Eight on discovery of evidence.

Some attorneys will contact several experts, place them on their witness lists and then never use them. Or they may list every expert in the field on their witness list without even contacting those witnesses. This keeps the other side very busy looking for a qualified expert.

Many experts tell the calling attorney they may not disclose them as a witness until a contract has been signed and a retainer has been received.

If an attorney ever involves your name in these ways, you may be entitled to damages for interfering with your ability to make a living. Some experts have a *designation* or *listing fee* on their fee schedule. You should, at least, send him or her a bill.

Multiple experts. You may be working with other experts on this case. They should not duplicate your expertise but should be complementary to your field. Judges view multiple witnesses testifying on the same general subject as being cumulative, an abuse of law and a waste of judicial resources.

Or you may consult with other experts (see Rule 703). Or you may suggest other experts in a multidisciplinary case. Perhaps you are an arborist and you need a weather expert. This is called promoting a *team approach*.

Be sure you have your attorney's permission to contact the other witnesses and then do it. Work with them to coordinate your testimony. Be very clear what areas you are responsible for and be careful about the areas you cover in deposition and at trial.

Pre-deposition conference. You must meet with your client-attorney just prior to your deposition. Often it is an abbreviated breakfast meeting. Here are some of the things you will want to cover:

- Review the case from the perspective of your client-attorney.

- Review the case from the perspective of the other side.

- Evaluate the differences in views and arguments about the case.

- Prioritize the issues of liability or damages.

- Review the subpoena. Was it a *duces tecum?* Do you have all the documents requested?

- List the plaintiff's theories of the case.

- List the defendant's theories of the case.

- Your client-attorney will go through your file and review each document. He or she will remove any attorney work product.

SOME DEFENDANT ATTORNEYS BRING IN MORE EXPERTS IN ORDER TO PROVIDE MORE BILLABLE HOURS.

☿ Review notes of any interviews you conducted.

☿ Discuss the strategy of the deposition testimony. Should you hold back and give short answers or should you educate the opposing attorney.

☿ Tough questions to watch for.

☿ The issues to watch for.

☿ Any points of law to watch for.

☿ What is the opposing attorney like? What is his or her manner or style? How can you expect this deposition to proceed?

☿ Any other suggestions.

Dress well and take any props (see Chapter Nine) you may need. You want to show that you not only know what you are talking about but can demonstrate what happened, or what should have happened, in the case. If you have written books, take them; they make you look professional.

Knowledge is power. You want to be the best-informed person on the case; to know more about the file than the attorneys, the judge and even the clients. With more knowledge, you will be comfortable with your role and able to answer any question to the satisfaction of all. Experienced judges and lawyers who are heavyweights in their own fields recognize heavyweights in specialized fields of expertise by the way they carry themselves. You want to project knowledge, confidence and expertise. So do not cut corners or take shortcuts. There is little demand for expert witnesses who make mistakes.

Accepting the case. To agree to work on a case, you may send a letter like the sample following. A written agreement is the safest way to proceed. Often, you simply accept a case

---

JUST BECAUSE SOMEONE HAS BEEN INJURED, IT DOES NOT MEAN THAT SOMEONE (ELSE) IS AT FAULT.

during a telephone conversation and the client–attorney sends a letter confirming that you are hired.

February 30, 1998

Lunch <u>v.</u> Dinner

Dear Mr. Lyon:

This letter will confirm your retention and assignment of me as an expert to assist your firm in the above-referenced case.

We will accept the case based on our published rate (fee schedule dated January 1997) of $230/hour and $1800/day.

We will perform investigation, testing, report writing and testimony at your direction.

After the investigation, we will issue an oral opinion. This report will be followed by a written opinion if you wish.

Please sign and return this agreement.

Sincerely,

Signed   Accepted

Date: Date:

Sample simple agreement

Contract. Most experienced experts will not work without a full-blown, signed contract. Here is an example from Kirk Griener of Maritime & Aviation Consultants.

CONSULTING AGREEMENT

This agreement is entered into as of the dates set forth at the end of this Agreement by and between (YOUR NAME) (hereinafter "Consultant") and

(hereinafter "Client").

The name or style of the case:

Case number:

Court case filed in:

1. RETENTION

1.1 Consultant will be available to commence work for a Client upon receipt of a retainer.

1.2 Consultant agrees not to work for any other person or party involved in this case on matters relating to this case for two weeks after he is verbally retained, or upon acceptance of the retainer set forth below. Should the two weeks lapse without receipt of a retainer, Consultant is free to accept work from any other party.

2. SERVICES TO BE PERFORMED

2.1 Consultant agrees to perform consulting and/or expert witness services as requested by Client and in connection with such services agrees to perform such investigation, document review, studies and research so as to be able to consult with Client and/or advise Client as an expert witness with respect to Consultant's findings. Consultant agrees to verbally report his facts, conclusions and findings to Client and, if desired by Client, Consultant will prepare a written report and cause it to be sent or delivered to client. Consultant also agrees to assist in trial preparation and to testify as an expert witness in those areas in which he is qualified.

2.2 The full scope of Consultant's work will be determined as the matter proceeds, and will be subject to the needs and requests of Client. Consultant and Client agree that Consultant will be performing services to this Agreement as an Independent Contractor.

2.3 Upon request, Consultant will provide an estimate of the time and costs it will take to perform the work outlined by the Client. If it becomes apparent to Consultant that he will need to exceed the estimates provided to complete his work, he will provide Client with a revised estimate and shall proceed only after being granted permission by Client.

3. CONFIDENTIALITY

3.1 Consultant agrees to retain all non-public information obtained from Client as confidential and agrees not to release or discuss any of such information unless Consultant has obtained the prior consent of Client or is otherwise forced, compelled, or required to disclose this information by operation of law or applicable government authority.

4. COMPENSATION

4.1 Fees are billed to the Client by the tenth of an hour with a minimum charge of .2 of an hour as follows:

4.1.1 Travel time at **ONE HUNDRED dollars ($100.00) per hour.**

4.1.2 Testimony at either trial or deposition at **TWO HUNDRED dollars ($200) an hour.** This rate applies to office or courtroom waiting time as well as actual time testifying.

4.1.3 All other work including research, report preparation and telephone calls, **ONE HUNDRED TWENTY FIVE dollars ($125) per hour.**

4.2 When in the **local area** away from the Consultant's office, time is billed from the time of departure from Consultant's office until the time of return.

4.3 Each full day **away from the local area** (Your city and state) on assignment is billed on the basis of an eight hour day. Where more than eight hours work or travel is performed in one day, the actual time is billed. Day of departure and day of return are prorated.

4.4 A **retainer** of $500 is charged for each case. This amount is a non-refundable minimum fee charged. Billings for services performed or expenses incurred will be charged against the retainer until such time as it is exhausted.

4.5 Permission to use Consultant's name or in any way indicate that he is an expert witness or Consultant for

Client's side of the case, either informally or formally with other parties, is not granted until the retainer has been paid.

4.6 Notwithstanding the Agreement of Consultant to bill Client at an hourly rate in one tenth of an hour increments for services performed, the following minimum fees will be due, whether or not Consultant is required to spend the amount of time necessary to result in these minimum fees if time was charged on an hourly basis. The minimum fees and types of services exclusive of travel to which they apply are as follows:

4.6.1 Attendance at a deposition either to assist client or to testify as an expert witness - $500.00.

4.6.2 Attendance at court to assist Client, testify as an expert witness, or while waiting at court for an opportunity to testify or assist Client in court - $500.00.

4.6.3 The above are minimum billings and if actual time spent results in an amount due which exceeds these minimums, then the actual amount will be due.

4.7 Fees and rates, once established for a job, will not be increased for that job even though fees or rates may increase for new jobs for a period of one year. Twelve months after being retained, fees may be raised to those currently charged other Clients at that time but shall not exceed 10% per year.

5. <u>EXPENSES</u>

5.1 Travel and miscellaneous expenses, including long distance calls, are charged at cost plus ten percent. Travel by car is at the rate of thirty cents a mile. No travel expense is charged in the local (Your city and state) area.

5.2 Travel will be performed by the most economical means compatible with the Client's time constraints except that first class air travel accommodations will be used for all flights of more than four hours duration including cumulative time where connecting flights are required.

5.3 Client may avoid the 10% surcharge on expenses by furnishing travel and lodging which is billed directly to Client by the carrier or hotel.

6. BILLINGS

6.1 Invoices will be tendered after the end of each month. A detailed breakdown is furnished itemizing each charge for the month. Billings from the previous month not paid will be noted as, "Previous Balance". **Payments made out to (Your company)** are due 28 days after the invoice date. Late charges at the rate of 1.5 % per month will be added to bills not paid within 30 days.

6.2 The payment of all fees and expenses is the responsibility of the Client notwithstanding Client's relationship with third parties, contingency arrangements, subrogation, etc. As a convenience, Consultant may agree to prepare separate billing for an attorney taking Consultant's discovery deposition, but the responsibility for payment remains that of the Client. Failure to include a chargeable item in one billing shall not constitute a waiver of the right to assess the charges in a subsequent billing.

6.3 Questions concerning specific billings are welcomed and requests for corrections must be submitted within 30 days after date of billing in question.

7. TERMINATION

7.1 This Agreement may be terminated by Client upon 15 days written notice for any reason. Upon termination of Consultants services by Client, Client shall immediately pay all fees and expenses incurred by Consultant, subject to receipt of an appropriate bill.

7.2 Consultant may terminate this Agreement upon fifteen (15) days written notice if payments are not made within 60 days of the date billing is mailed. This does not relieve Client in any way from payment for services rendered or expenses incurred.

8. DISPUTE RESOLUTION

8.1 The parties agree that any action which is required to be filed to enforce the terms of this Agreement may be filed in (Your) County, State of (Your state) but this shall not preclude either party from bringing an action in any other county which represents the proper venue for such an action.

8.2 In the event that either party is required to retain the services of an attorney to enforce the provisions of this Agreement, then in such case the Client agrees to pay reasonable attorney's fees and all costs and expenses incurred by Consultant including collection costs, provided that Consultant is the prevailing party in said matter either by settlement, litigation or otherwise.

9. <u>GOVERNING LAW</u>

9.1 All actions arising out of the performance of this Agreement shall be governed by the laws of the State of (Your state).

The parties do hereby execute this Agreement at the places set forth below on the date set forth below.

Date: Location:

_____

(Your name), Consultant

Date: Location:

_____

(Attorney's name), Client

Sample contract

Rejecting the case. Before you are retained you can turn down a case for any reason: time, inclination or conflict of interests. You do not want to go to trial for a losing side. You do not even want to appear in court for the winning side in a bad case. Both are bad for your professional reputation.

Be objective and take a case only if you are on the side of right. If the case is a poor one, inform your client-attorney. He probably will not want you to continue on the case. Sometimes, client-attorneys attempt to proceed with an expert who does not support their case. Most experts will drop out in such situations.

Do not accept a case for which you are not qualified. You will probably be found out and embarrassed. The woods are full of rent-an-experts and opposing attorneys love to tear them apart.

If you make your investigation and find you cannot support the client-attorney's position, say so (orally) and recommend that you stop working on the case. Submit your bill but do not send a written report unless it is requested.

If you cannot be wholehearted about your testimony, turn down the case. It is better to turn down a case and lose the business than to do a poor job or lose your self-respect.

February 30, 1998

<u>Lunch v. Dinner</u>
Certified mail - return receipt

Dear Mr. Lyon:

I am unable to serve as an expert witness in the above-referenced case (do not say why) and am returning the documents and the unused portion of the retainer.

Please keep my name on file. I hope you will contact me when you next have a case in my area of expertise.

Sincerely,

List of enclosures:

Example of letter rejecting a case

If the prospective client-attorney appears to be careless, uncooperative or disreputable, reject the case. You want to work with professionals who will enhance your reputation, not sleezebags who will injure it.

If you turn down a case, the file should remain confidential. Return all the materials furnished by the client-attorney by certified mail, return receipt. Keep a list of the items returned. Refund any moneys not expended. Once you reject a case, list the reasons in your folder and file the folder. Then do not talk to anyone else about the case—it is not ethical.

Ethics. The expert witness industry has standards. Several organizations such as the National Forensic Center, the American College of Forensic Examiners and the American Academy of Forensic Sciences have published codes of ethics. Contact them for copies. Addresses are in the Appendix.

Switching sides. If you turn down a case in which you have done more than read the complaint, other public documents and a cover letter, it is not ethical to work for the other side. Some courts have ruled it impermissible to hire an expert previously engaged by the other side.

If you do turn down a case and are then contacted by the other side, tell the calling attorney of your prior involvement in the case. He or she will have to decide whether you are free to switch and how to answer the inevitable questions in court. Make sure the calling attorney wants to hire you—that he or she is not just fishing for information.

It is best to ask only for non-confidential information and to insist on an advance payment and contract before starting work. Until you accept the advance and sign the contract, you are free to negotiate with the other side. If you do not follow these rules, you may be unable to serve either side.

Conflict of interests. There are times when you should not take a case because you are too close to it. Even if you do

---

THE CLIENT (ATTORNEY) DISCLOSES INFORMATION TO THE PROSPECTIVE EXPERT BEFORE RETAINING HIM AT HIS OWN RISK, AND THE EXPERT IS NOT NORMALLY PRECLUDED FROM ACCEPTING WORK FROM THE OPPOSITION ON THE SAME CASE UNLESS HE HAS BEEN RETAINED.
— KIRK GREINER, MARITIME & AVIATION CONSULTANTS

not feel too close, a judge or jury might think otherwise. On the other hand, there are times when similarities in your condition (you have suffered an injury similar to the plaintiff's) or experience may work in your favor. A conflict may also arise if you have done business or have otherwise been associated with (friend, relative, etc.) the plaintiff, defendant, other attorneys or anyone associated with the case. Whenever there is a potential conflict, let your client-attorney know.

Q: *You served on the board of the association for sixteen years, then wouldn't you say you are protective of the association and are inclined to defend the sport and the industry?*

A: *No, sir.*

A: *Yes, I am protective of the sport and industry. I have a reputation for being very straight-laced. Whenever I see misconduct, I point it out to the proper authority. The best way to protect the sport and the industry is to make sure every company is operating with proper quality control.*

Record keeping. As soon as you have been contacted and agree to look into a case, set up a file folder. Write the name of the case and the attorney on the top tab.

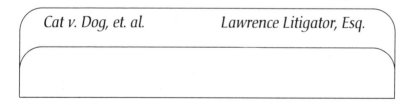

Cat v. Dog, et. al.　　　　*Lawrence Litigator, Esq.*

File folder labeling

YOU HAVE ONLY ONE CLIENT—YOUR PROFESSIONAL INTEGRITY.

Write the attorney's name and telephone number on the inside of the folder so that they will be easy to find. Keep a running time sheet in the folder. Place all correspondence, your narrative (with the case number, attorney names, court, etc.) and documents in this folder. If you receive a large stack of depositions, they may have to be placed in a separate folder and/or stored elsewhere but place a note showing their location in the folder. Some experts like to maintain separate files for time and billing, research, and correspondence. This system separates the administrative material from the opinion material. Another way to handle larger cases is to transfer the contents of the folder to a two- or three-inch accordion file. Some cases may require three-ring binders.

Support documents such as photographs, copies of regulations, position papers, and articles will also go into this file folder.

Keep a log of all documents received.

Keep records of all work. Every time you receive a call from your client-attorney or otherwise spend time on the case, note the following on a fresh sheet of paper: date, time started and stopped, and a brief description of the work. You may use a computer program with a time-slips feature. Your running time sheet and these notes will be the basis for billing the client.

Do not discard the file once the case is complete. Make a brief summary of the disposition of the case and place it in front of the file folder. You may need the information again or you may be asked about it in a subsequent case.

Accounting. Since expert-witness work requires written reports, a word processor is almost mandatory. The computer also enables you to maintain records for your consulting business. Many experts use an accounting program such as *QuickBooks*.

Travel records are most easily kept on a plain #10 envelope. Take a standard business envelope, cut open the end and seal the top flap. As you travel to depositions and trial, note all your expenditures on the outside of the envelope. Write down what you spend each day for meals and lodging, air and other fares, travel expenses such as cabs and tips and so on. Place any receipts you receive in the envelope. When you return home, you will have a detailed record of every penny spent and you will be ready to bill the client and enter the information into your own ledger.

Continuing correspondence. Every six months or so, review all your open cases and write to the client-attorney. Ask if the case is still active, if a court date has been set and if you should keep the file open.

Follow-up correspondence. Sending a letter to a client-attorney after a case has been resolved is just good public relations. Obviously, the letter is easier to write if your side won. But if you lost, he or she feels bad, too. Your letter could cheer up the client-attorney. In any case, this attorney may have business for you in the future or may recommend you to fellow attorneys. Build bridges, do not burn them.

Disengagement. If you decide to stop work on a case, send a termination letter. Put it in writing and send it by certified mail. Be aware, however, that your client-attorney has time and money invested in you and may not be happy.

Liability. You can be sued for doing a bad job. The National Forensic Center reports that 6% of the experts polled have been subjected to a lawsuit.

Expert witness have been sued by the opposing side claiming defamation, negligence, misrepresentation an even intentional infliction of emotional distress. When you are in court, your testimony is privileged. It is not in the public interest to have people afraid to testify. So you are safe here.

You may also be sued by your side—your client-attorney or the client—for (allegedly) doing poor job or making a mistake. It is called *negligence* or *malpractice*. Most cases deal with poor research and reports, not with a situation of being caught without an answer on the stand.

Insurance. From time to time we hear of insurance for forensic errors and omissions. Check with the various expert witness associations for current availability. Always read a policy closely and consider and exclusions.

According to a 1996 survey of experts run on the Internet by the Legal Research Network, eight of the 44 experts who responded have errors and omissions (E&O) insurance. Most were paying premiums of $1,000-$2,000 annually.

While insurance is expensive, the cost of legal defense can put your assets at risk.

CHAPTER FOUR

OPINION FORMING

As a technical expert witness you are not retained to give a favorable opinion. You are hired to arrive at an objective opinion after thorough investigation. This is a subtle but essential difference.

Q: *When did you form your opinion on this case?*

The opposing attorney may try to trap you by asking when you formed your opinion. He or she may try to show you agreed to testify before studying the case adequately. In reality, opinions begin to form (or suspicions begin to be confirmed) as you read documents, conduct research and interview witnesses. It is a process where your preliminary thoughts and opinions evolve.

Defending yourself will be easier if you can show you read every applicable document (the complaint, interrogatories, depositions, test reports), ran tests, inspected the equipment, visited the site, performed library research, and spoke with witnesses and other experts in the process of shaping your opinion. Similarly, new facts discovered as the case progresses may change your opinion.

The expert *interprets* scientific and technological facts and *renders* scientific and technological opinions based on the facts. Opinions must be based on a reasonable interpretation of the facts and scientific probability. Do not give opinions unless you can identify facts to support them.

The facts on which an expert's opinion is based should come from:

1. Evaluation of the facts including those facts in dispute. Whatever you learned in your investigation, testing and/or analysis.

2. Personal knowledge of the particular field. What you have learned through education, training and experience.

3. Assumed facts supported by evidence.

As a technical expert, you have a duty to research the field and right to rely on reports, professional texts, etc. You may not offer opinions on *questions of law*; those are for the court to decide.

Do your best to get all the facts, whether they support your case or not. You want to see the entire file on the case. Be persistent and continue to request any information you need to form an opinion. Some attorneys may hold back on evidence damaging to their case. Your opinion may change (on the stand) when presented with omitted facts on cross-examination. It is better for all concerned if you have all the facts before the trial begins.

One reason your client-attorney might hold back information is because the other side might find it in your file during discovery. Your files are open, the attorney's are not.

You can't get too much information. Once you read over the complaint and interrogatories, draft a list of questions for which you need answers. List the tests you must run and the research you must do. Many times, experts do not form opinions until the case is well underway.

Client-attorneys usually do not know as much about your field of expertise as you do. They do not even understand the relevance of some of the file material they have. Make sure you get to see everything, even information they think is not important.

AN EXPERT'S OPINION IS ONLY AS GOOD AS THE DATA UPON WHICH IT IS BASED. — JUANITA R. BROOKS

Limit the scope of your testimony. Form an opinion on what you know and do not venture out of your area. Lawyers often attempt to convince experts to go as far as possible. It is far better to limit your testimony or even to refuse the assignment than to represent yourself as an expert in unknown territory.

Forming your opinion. Once you have studied the file, run your tests, made a site inspection, questioned the parties, etc., you are ready to finalize an opinion. You must decide what happened or what should have happened and why. You must thoughtfully develop your opinion and identify each and every fact on which you base your opinion. For example, go through the depositions and/or research and extract passages to support your opinion.

Your role is that of a teacher. Although each and every element of your opinion must be scientifically and factually supportable, your report should be crafted in a way that is simple and instructive. Avoid ambiguous and technical nomenclature.

Make sure you are thoroughly prepared to support your opinion.

Second thoughts. If you learn during your evaluation that your opinions will not support the client-attorney's theories, tell (orally, not in writing) the attorney. Your participation may be changed from *testifying expert* to *consulting expert*. They certainly do not want to turn you loose as you could be contacted by the other side.

Remember, you are not being retained to bring good news; your job is to render an objective opinion. You have a duty to point out the weaknesses in the case so your client-

---

IT IS NORMALLY MUCH SAFER TO ENTER AN ENGAGEMENT AS A CONSULTANT AND THEN TO CHANGE YOUR STATUS TO EXPERT AFTER IT IS DETERMINED THAT YOUR OPINION AND THE ATTORNEY'S GOALS ARE COMPATIBLE. SWITCHING FROM EXPERT TO CONSULTANT CAN STILL SUBJECT YOUR WORK PRODUCT TO DISCOVERY.   — ROY CORDER, CPA

attorney can better assess the technical merits of the case and the possible settlement value. Following this advice will foster a reputation as being a straight shooter and not being an advocate for either side.

Your client-attorney is working for himself and secondly for his client; he certainly is not working for you. He wants to win. Consequently he may push you on the range of your opinion or the scope of your expertise. You must protect your reputation. Do not get emotionally involved in the case. You did not create the problem and you are not here to solve it. You are simply making an objective evaluation of the case or of the portion with which you are involved.

Practice saying your opinion over and over until you can clearly state your opinions and the basis for each one without hesitation or confusion.

When did you form your opinion? One line of questioning went as follows:

Q: *When did you form your opinion?*

A: *I finalized my opinion the day before yesterday.*

Q: *The day before the trial started?*

A: *Yes. The problem was that the plaintiff would not allow me to inspect the subject equipment. This forced me to run many, many tests to try out several theories. After the September 28th visit to the factory and the tests performed there, I had a fairly firm impression as to the cause. I could not confirm that theory until I saw the equipment on January 12th. Yes, this would have put the defendant in a very difficult position if I had not seen what I thought I would see.*

Before going to a deposition or into court, review your notes to refresh your memory concerning when your opinion was actually formed. It may be helpful to write out a time/event schedule similar to the one which follows. With this

---

YOUR CLIENT-ATTORNEY IS AN ADVOCATE FOR THE CLIENT. YOU ARE AN ADVOCATE FOR YOUR OPINION.

time-line to refresh your memory before you go into court, you will be able to rattle off the dates of each event.

When I formed my opinion

January 26, 1997: Levin called me. He also mentioned the case a couple of times at national conventions. He wanted to tie me up (preferably on his side).

May 13, 1997: John Moore of Moore and Moore called me.

May 15, 1997: I sent my CV, rates, etc. to Moore.

August 31, 1997: Jones contacted me. See my deposition, page 11.

September 1-8, 1997: I conducted research. Read depositions to date, used own library and called other experts.

September 8, 1997: Memo to factory regarding tests to be run.

September 13-14, 1997: Trip to the factory to see the quality control system, discover paperwork in files, and run tests.

September 15, 1997: I wrote Jones asking to investigate the equipment.

September 28, 1997: Trip to the factory to run tests, etc.

January 12, 1998: Inspected equipment for first time and confirmed suspicions.

Formed final opinion.

February 16, 1998: I was deposed.

Opinion-forming chronology

CHAPTER FIVE

CASE PREPARATION

WORKING WITH THE CLIENT-ATTORNEY
ORAL AND WRITTEN REPORTS

Your client-attorney is in charge of the case. While you are a member of the team, he or she calls the plays. It is not your job to change a play or take control. You could be doing something not in the game plan. Remember: you do not win or lose cases. You assist attorneys who win or lose cases.

Your job is one of *service*. Do not tell the client-attorney your problems. He or she wants to know what information you can offer, and is paying you to solve problems. He or she wants your best opinion based on your knowledge, experience, research and tests.

You specialize in *objectively* analyzing failures and advising attorneys so they may prepare their case. They may point out important information or angles to you, while you may alert them to topics they shouldn't address.

Keep the relationship with your client-attorney on a professional level to avoid becoming an advocate.

Your role before the trial. You are a consultant to your client-attorney. Before the trial, you may assist in:

🐾 Educating the client-attorney

🐾 Suggesting sources of evidence

🐾 Helping draft interrogatories and interpreting answers

🐾 Investigation and testing

🐾 Preparing deposition questions

🐾 Helping prepare the other witnesses

🐾 Preparing (advising and consulting) exhibits and demonstrative evidence

🐾 Suggesting case strategy

A case calendar could possibly look like this:

1. Attorney calls expert, determines qualifications, briefly describes case, asks if the expert is interested and requests a first impression.

2. Expert mails curriculum vitae, fee schedule and other materials with a cover letter to attorney.

3. Attorney writes expert a letter enclosing a copy of the complaint, witness statements, photographs and a check. A cheque for the retainer fee is enclosed. Expert opens a file on the case.

4. Expert reviews materials, drafts narrative and calls attorney with a preliminary opinion and requests more information and documentation. Expert may have several questions.

5. Expert writes attorney requesting authorization to conduct further research and tests. Costs are estimated.

6. Attorney sends requested materials to expert.

7. Attorney authorizes research and tests.

8. Attorney asks expert to draft some interrogatories to be sent to the opposing side, for both the opposing expert and the other opposing parties.

9. Attorney asks expert to help answer interrogatories received from the opposition. Expert drafts a formal written opinion.

10. Attorney informs expert he will be deposed by the other side. They discuss the case, anticipate difficult questions and attend the deposition.

11. Attorney asks expert to attend the deposition of the opposing expert to counsel attorney. This rarely happens.

12. Attorney asks expert to attend a settlement conference to advise him or her. This rarely happens.

13. Attorney and expert prepare for the trial. Demonstrative evidence in the form of models and charts are constructed. Both review testimony and anticipate difficult cross-examination questions. Courtroom demonstrations are rehearsed for clarity and flow.

14. Expert testifies at trial.

15. Expert writes follow-up letter to attorney and closes file.

Maintain close contact with the client-attorney. Call him or her periodically to check on the status of the case. Inform each other of what you find and what you learn. Work with your client-attorney to schedule depositions and the trial around your calendar.

Be professional. Your image as an expert is affected by: your promotional materials and advertising, your initial meeting with the attorney (he or she is sizing you up), how you brief the client-attorney on your findings, the appearance and tone of your written report, and your testimony

Witness list. In most jurisdictions, expert witnesses must be named before the trial. The amount of time may be at least 70 days before the trial starts but at least ten days after the setting of the trial date. Rules vary from jurisdiction to jurisdiction. Witnesses not on the list are barred from testifying. This window of time is necessary to make the expert witnesses available for depositions.

To notify the opposing side that you are on the case, your client-attorney will write them a letter. The letter will list your name, address, a brief statement on your qualifications and the general substance of your anticipated testimony.

Investigating the opposing expert witness. The starting point to undermining the opposing witness is an investigation into his or her background. The opposing side will send a similar witness list to your client-attorney. Your side will want to know who the opposing expert will be and what his or her opinion is going to be. You will study the position of the opposing expert and advise your client attorney on courses of action. Normally you will be in a better position to investigate and evaluate an opposing witness than your client-attorney. If your field is narrow, you will probably know the opposing expert.

Both you and your client-attorney will want to know:

☞ The length of time he or she has worked as an expert witness.

☞ The number and identity of cases in which he or she was involved. Ask the witness to produce copies of his or her depositions. It is also possible to get copies from deposition services.

☞ His or her balance of cases. How many times has he or she worked for the plaintiff and defense. Is this expert really objective or does he or she favor one side?

☞ Did any of these previous cases involve the same issues? How many and which ones?

☞ Has this expert ever worked for this law firm before?

☞ Has this expert performed litigation consulting for this client before?

☞ Has this expert ever worked for his or her client in any other (regular) capacity?

☞ What percentage of the expert's time is spent in the field and what percentage as a litigation consultant?

🐦 Request a copy of the expert's curriculum vitae. What is his or her background?

🐦 What has the expert published? Where can copies be obtained?

🐦 Does the expert have any experience particularly relevant to the subject?

Some of the above questions will be answered through your investigation. Others will require interrogatories or depositions. Advise your client-attorney that you need answers to the above questions. Litigators have discovered fudged credentials and have revealed them with devastating results on cross-examination.

What do you know about the opposing experts? How are they perceived by your peers? Have they been involved in any controversies? Are their any skeletons in their closet? Is there anything that might tarnish their reputation? How can they be expected to react to certain questions?

Narrative. A narrative is a summary of what happened. It includes the names of the parties, date and place of accident, basic events, weather, injuries, relative historical data, etc. Every time you discover new material, update or correct it. Review the narrative and all the written material in your file before you give a deposition or go to trial. Second readings of the file will reveal ideas and facts overlooked in your initial reading. Some areas will become clearer. Add to the narrative. Start building a narrative, listing only the facts (no opinion) of the case on your word processor. As you read depositions and other materials, add to the narrative.

The narrative is kept on top of your file folder. It may be used for quick review any time you need to refresh your memory on the case.

Unless you have misunderstood a material fact, it does not hurt to let the opposition discover your narrative. But make sure your client-attorney has reviewed it for accuracy.

The layout of narratives will vary depending on the type of case. Some accident cases may follow this outline:

Plaintiff: Name, age, height, weight, marital status, dependents, employer, job title, name of attorney, firm and city.

Defendant: Name, age, height, weight, marital status, dependents, employer, name of attorney, firm and city.

Date and place of accident:

Weather conditions:

Training/experience:

Equipment:

Events:

Injuries:

Allegations:

Defenses:

Schedule for depositions, trial, etc.:

Questions:

Example of case narrative outline

Attorneys often call with questions about the case when you haven't looked at the file for several months. These calls can result in embarrassment and even a lost client if you forget the facts and which side you are on and start supplying arguments which do not support this attorney's case. Just say: *I am busy with (a client, etc.), let me call you back in fifteen minutes.* Then go read the file and narrative before returning the call.

A narrative also proves you have done your work. It can be matched to time sheets should you ever have to justify a billing to your client-attorney.

Investigate and report findings. Keep written correspondence to a minimum. Once you have agreed to testify, your entire file becomes discoverable. (See Chapter Eight)

Oral reports. Preliminary reports should not be in writing because the questions have yet to be firmed up. Your initial report to your client-attorney will probably be oral. If you are in the same town, the report may be made in person. If you are some distance apart, the report will be made over the telephone. Many attorneys ask their expert not to submit a written report until all the facts of the case have been discovered. They do not want the expert's opinion to be impeached by a report based on antiquated or false information. Further, he or she does not want your opinion committed to paper until he or she knows what it is.

Orally list the strengths and weaknesses of the case. Tell the client-attorney where you think the case stands.

Written reports. Your client-attorney may request a brief letter on the cause of the accident, an expanded *letter of advice* explaining your opinion or a full-blown lengthy report in a report cover. Since 1993, written reports have been required in Federal Court.

The purpose of your report is to persuade, so sequence your facts and evidence to lead to a conclusion. In some states, a written report is not only required, it is supplied to the jury.

Your client-attorney will ask for a thorough report if the intent is to settle the case and a simple report if the intent is to go to court. In the latter case, he or she will not want to give away your position completely.

The formal reports notify the attorneys on both sides of the expert's opinion. It is assumed that trial testimony will be the same. It is possible, however, that new information will cause an expert to alter his or her opinion. If you find yourself in this situation, you should notify your client-attorney immediately and probably draft a superseding report.

Before drafting your report, get the entire case file, ask your client-attorney for an outline of desired testimony with questions to be addressed and review the case strategy with him

---

MANY EXPERTS WILL NOT SEND THE REPORT UNTIL THEY ARE PAID TO DATE.

or her. You must include all facts, sources and conclusions because what you put in those pages will dictate what you are allowed to testify to in court. If you do not list an important journal article, you may not be able to bring it up in court. If you send a draft of a report to your client-attorney, mark it *draft*. You do not want readers to think, or be able to say, it is a final opinion.

Always discuss the probable contents of your written report with your client-attorney before committing your opinion to paper. Understand the purpose of the report and what is necessary to it. Many adverse parties may see your work before the case is eventually closed.

Since some 92% of the cases never go to trial, your written report could cause the plaintiff to drop the case or the defendant to settle. Your written report is also the cornerstone of your courtroom presentation.

The longer you wait to prepare it, the more information you will have. Opinions and positions can change in light of new information. Additionally, some experts find it emotionally difficult to retreat from an earlier conclusive position.

Your report should be impartial, objective and thorough. Avoid statements the other side could pretend to misinterpret in court. When proofreading your report, ask yourself "How does this sentence sound if it is read independently or out of context?" Your report must be consistent with your previous reports and testimony in other cases.

List other experts, articles, sources, documents and books you consulted. Cite all scientific tests that support your conclusion. List the machinery, test equipment, gauges, standards and test methods used. Render technically correct statements in all communication. All your written documents will be compared. Make sure interrogatories, depositions and written reports agree. Do not misrepresent the facts upon which you base your opinion. You will be caught.

AN EVALUATION IS ONLY AS CREDIBLE AS THE VALIDITY OF THE INFORMATION ON WHICH IT RELIES.

Your report should look professional. Use a laser printer and good paper.

The *full-blown lengthy report* should have a cover sheet with a title, citing the case, your name and address and the client-attorney's name and address. Then add paragraphs on the following to answer the questions Who, What, Where, When and Why?:

🖛 Your qualifications: education, training, professional affiliations, publications, etc. Make a very brief statement and append your curriculum vitae. Append a list of all articles and books you have written over the past ten years.

🖛 List all the materials sent to you for review.

🖛 The name and full address of the client (Plaintiff or Defendant).

🖛 The name and full address of your client-attorney.

🖛 Generally describe the subject of your assignment from the client attorney.

🖛 State the objective of the assignment.

🖛 Describe your general methodology.

🖛 Summarize your conclusions. Include a complete statement of all the opinions to be expressed along with their basis and reasoning. You will be cross-examined on this.

🖛 State the various hypotheses under investigation.

🖛 Describe your exhibits: Diagrams, charts, maps, photos or photocopies should be appended.

🖛 List the investigative reports incorporated into your report.

🖛 Provide the specifics of your investigations.

🖛 List the tests, site visits and calculations you performed. What equipment did you use?

🖛 What other experts or sources did you consult with?

☞ State the findings on your physical inspection/examination.

☞ If you performed any corrective action, what methods were followed? Doctors can do this, many other experts cannot.

☞ You may be required to state your compensation for this study.

☞ Append a list of all the cases in which you gave deposition or trial testimony for the past four years.

☞ State the investigations and testing you still want to make. (To cover yourself.)

☞ Include a statement reserving the option to supplement the report as additional information becomes available. (To cover yourself.)

See amended Rule 26 of the *Federal Rules of Civil Procedure*. Ask other experts for copies of their reports and use them as examples.

Include a cover letter reciting the transmission of the report. Recheck your calculations and spelling. Proof well. You can be sure the jury will be shown any imperfections.

Write clearly. A non-expert reader must be able to understand what you are saying. Do not send out a report the same day you write it. Sleep on it, review it and revise it as needed.

Your client-attorney will want you to use words such as *reasonable probability* rather than *possibility*. Reasonable probability means there is at least a 51% chance that the result will occur. A *reasonable certainly* is even more compelling. Most experts will not commit themselves this far.

For many types of cases, you will keep the report to four or five pages. Write in tight sentences. The opposing attorney will try to make you eat some of them in court. Additional information such as a list of your publications should be put in the Appendix. Put the report in a report cover or binder. If the report is long, use tabbed dividers. Dress it up and make it look like it is worth what you are being paid for it.

Summary judgments. Expert witness affidavits are being used more and more to support motions for summary judgment. Your written report may move the court to decide or the parties toward settlement. Your affidavit and report will have to be notarized. Check your *Yellow Pages* and know where you can locate a notary on short notice and at odd hours.

CHAPTER SIX

POSITION PAPERS

Writing a position paper helps you review the case and clarify your thoughts. If the opposing attorney asks you to cite the relative merits of the flat circular and conical parachute canopies, you want to be able to rattle off the comparative advantages and disadvantages without hesitation. The faster you can rattle them off, the more credible you will appear and the more uneasy the opposing attorney will feel about cross-examining you.

Researching and writing the position paper helps you get your facts straight and identify any problem areas. Draft the information and put the draft in a file folder with photocopies of all the supporting reference material (magazine articles, military specifications, maps, etc.).

Position papers may also become scholarly answers to important questions in your field. They may be used as the basis for journal reports or magazine articles, thus becoming another source of income while they also validate your expertise and your theory. Then, next time you need the information in court, you may even cite your own article.

Position papers on the same general subject area may be the basis for a book. Books validate your expertise even more than journal or magazine articles.

Often our investigations reveal new challenges. It may be a

part that has never broken before or an accident that has never happened before.

Do not, however, write an article or book on the subject of a case until the case is concluded. Your attorney may not want you to reveal your thoughts. This can create a difficult problem for experts. What if your investigation reveals a safety problem? Shouldn't you spread the word as quickly and widely as possible?

For now, research, write and bank your material. Over the years as the files take shape, you will think of other ways to use the information.

Experts who have not been published in magazines, journals and books are at a serious disadvantage.

Q: *You mean you are not published? None of your theories have been peer-reviewed?*

Q: *And isn't it true that you spend so much time testifying that you do not have time to write?*

Position papers are a product of your research done on billable time. This study makes you a better expert, and the material can be used again. Repackaging the information provides more income while the article, book, video or lecture can be listed in your CV as evidence of your expertise.

WE OPERATE A SECOND-HAND STORE. WE SELL TO CLIENT **B** WHAT WE LEARN WHILE WORKING FOR CLIENT **A**.

CHAPTER SEVEN

MAINTAINING COMPETENCE

It is important to remember that you are a consultant in your field of expertise, not a professional expert witness. Do not let expert witness work overshadow your original line of work. Keep up-to-date on what is happening in your field.

In some areas of expertise (document examination and criminal laboratory work, for examples) you are actually practicing your technical skill when you act as an expert witness. But most experts have to maintain their competence and continue to work in their field because, when testifying, they are evaluating the skills of others rather than honing their own.

Maryland has passed a law requiring that some experts spend a minimum of 80% of their professional time in their area of expertise. Kansas has a 50% rule, and bills are pending in other states. The object of these laws is to make sure witnesses are experts, not just courtroom performers. Check the local rules.

Most attorneys prefer expert witnesses with some courtroom experience. New witnesses may appear less contaminated but they are less predictable. Attorneys like street-wise experts they can count on. These experts are much easier to prepare for deposition and trial.

Opposing counsel may try to show you are a *hired gun*, a

professional expert witness, by asking what percentage of your business comes from being an expert witness. You must answer these questions truthfully but you can turn calculations to your advantage. You may spend 10% of your time on this kind of work while it may constitute 40% of your gross income.

Q: *What percentage of your income is from expert witness work?*

A: *I spend about 10% of my time advising lawyers and educating juries.*

You may spend 10% of your *time* and derive 50% of your *income* from expert witness work.

Q: *When did you race last?*

A: *It has been almost five years. In the last race, I suffered a major accident and was laid up for over a year. I am not able to race now.*

You show you would still be active if you were able and you turn a difficult situation into one where you gain sympathy from the jury.

Attend both expert witness conferences and conferences in your field of expertise. Each year you will pick up new information and, often, previously presented ideas will suddenly become clear. Conferences are a place to get your questions answered.

Q: *When did you last exercise your license to _____ ?*

A: *Two hours ago.*

(At this point he or she may be too cautious to go on.)

Q: *You mean you were out _____ .*

A: *No, the regulations are clear about being current. Working in the field could be working hands-on with the equipment, reading the manual or teaching a class.*

WINNING IS NOT EVERYTHING, MAINTAINING YOUR INTEGRITY IS EVERYTHING.—RICHARD SAFERSTEIN, AUTHOR OF *CRIMINALISTICS: AN INTRODUCTION TO FORENSIC SCIENCE*

There are many ways to measure professional time. You are certainly not on vacation when you attend conferences, write a magazine article or read professional magazines. Since you probably work more than eight hours each day and 40 hours each week, it would not be fair to compute your activity with those numbers.

Q: *When was the last time you packed a parachute?*

A: *About two years ago.*

Q: *Then you are not current?*

A: *Many parachute riggers pack parachutes, some people teach them how and a very few of us teach the teachers.*

Q: *Then you are not currently designing bridges; you are not working as a structural engineer.*

A: *Engineers involved full-time in bridge design do not have the time and opportunities I do to visit many bridges to get an overview of the issues in bridge design.*

Keep all of these views in mind and anticipate the inevitable questions regarding your maintenance of competency.

Q: *Mr. Poynter, you are the author of* The Expert Witness Handbook. *Does that qualify you as the expert's expert? Aren't you a professional expert?*

A: *I have written several books on parachutes and that does not make me the best skydiver. Many expert witnesses are making the history; I just write it down.*

You do not want to become a professional expert witness. If you spend all your time in court, you will establish a negative credential as a full-time expert.

Continuing education. Our society, technology and information base are all evolving rapidly. It is imperative that you maintain your expertise and currency. You must keep up with theories, concepts, methods and equipment.

You must subscribe to, read and save professional literature;

remain active in your field; keep up with certifications; attend continuing education courses and seminars; conduct research, publish and have your work peer-reviewed; teach; consult; and attend professional conferences.

CHAPTER EIGHT

DISCOVERY OF EVIDENCE AND YOUR FILES

Discovery is a formal pre-trial; a procedure by which one party gains information held by another party.

Today, very little detail is given when a suit is filed. The Plaintiff gives the Defendant very little detail as to why the suit was filed. The details come later through *discovery*.

The objectives of discovery are to locate evidence (and preserve all relevant material for use at the trial), preserve testimony, narrow the issues (to avoid spending court time on undisputed facts), remove surprise and promote settlement before trial.

The forms of discovery are:

- Interrogatories

- Production of documents and things

- Requests for admission

- Physical and mental (medical) examinations

- Oral depositions. Taking sworn testimony before a trial

- Requests for admission—designed to eliminate issues from trial

Just as your client-attorney wants to know all your opinions and what you base them on, your opponent-attorney wants to know, too. Opposing counsel will normally use interrogatories and/or a deposition proceeding to determine your opinion. He or she will be asking who your are, what you think and how you got there. Expert witness discovery is covered in Federal Rules of Civil Procedure 26(b) (4).

You will assist your client-attorney in the discovery process to learn as much as you can and to develop a theme for the case. You will help generate questions to be asked of the opposition, advise your client-attorney in responding to the opposition's questions, and you will respond to questions both written (*interrogatories*) and verbal (*deposition*).

Interrogatories are lists of questions drafted by one side and sent to the other. The object of interrogatories is to go fishing for helpful information. Consequently, the other side often may try to answer unimportant questions fully and important questions vaguely. You and your attorney will probably work together on any interrogatories presented to you.

In Federal proceedings, interrogatories are normally used to identify the experts, to reveal the subject matter on which they are expected to testify, and to state the substance of the facts and opinions on which the expert plans to testify. Just knowing the expert's area of expertise (ballistics, psychology, handwriting) can tell you a lot about your opponent's approach to the case.

Attorney-client privilege. New expert witnesses are often shocked to find their files are not private. The *attorney-client relationship* of confidentiality does not protect your files from the opposing attorney. Only the plaintiff or defendant who has hired the attorney to obtain legal advice has this relationship. On the other hand, if the client-plaintiff or client-

---

THE PURPOSE OF DISCOVERY IS TO LEARN AS MUCH AS YOU CAN
AND TO TELL AS LITTLE AS YOU MUST.
— HAROLD FEDER, ESQUIRE

defendant reveals confidential information to the expert in order to help the expert form an opinion to relay to the attorney, there may be an attorney-client privilege.

An expert who is also an employee of the client-plaintiff or client-defendant has been held to be an extension of the client and protected by the attorney-client privilege.

Attorney work product. *Attorney work product* is not discoverable but your work may not be protected by this rule. *Work product* is limited to material prepared by an attorney as an attorney and usually refers only to his or her notes, analysis and trial strategy.

There are two reasons for the work product rule:

1. To encourage counsel to thoroughly prepare both favorable and unfavorable parts of the case and

2. to prevent one attorney from taking advantage of the other's industry and efforts.

Information you record as a consultant *prior* to being retained for the trial is usually considered part of your client-attorney's work product which is not discoverable. This is because your advice is part of his or her research. You must be acting as an associate of the attorney in the preparation of a confidential report to be used by the attorney. This is one reason why many attorneys request that you make your first report orally, over the telephone.

The rules change when you graduate from *consultant* to *witness*. Once you have been retained for the trial, whatever you have in your file is discoverable—even your earlier work. This is because the other side has a right to know your position (*opinion*).

One case held that information given by the expert to the attorney is work product but that any information not given to the attorney is discoverable. Certainly if you are being paid directly by the attorney's client, the work you do cannot be considered attorney work product.

Information communicated by the client-attorney to the expert witness may be privileged if the information is necessary for the expert to do his or her job. If your client-attorney steers your investigation in the proper direction, the communication may not be discoverable.

To obtain maximum protection from the work product rule, the client-attorney should retain you and all your work should be transmitted directly to the client-attorney. If you have already been hired by the client, counsel should write you a letter retaining you directly.

For the sake of confidentiality, attorneys often like to put off naming their experts as long as possible.

Updating responses. If a responding party discovers new information after an interrogatory, deposition, etc., he or she must notify the other side. This is a continuing duty.

Discoverability. Once you are designated a witness to testify at the trial, the work product rule is waived and all earlier communications become discoverable. Many experts do not save documents they do not want discovered. Anything in writing is easily discoverable. Many experts consolidate their files and destroy their notes once they have been declared a witness. They reduce their files to useful reports only.

The best rule is not to commit any thought to paper that could hurt you if read by the other side. While you must always answer truthfully when testifying, you do not have to provide the opposition with a written record of potentially damaging information. You are not obligated to hang on to negative notes or observations you may have made in the process of preparing your case. The less paper you have in your file the better.

Today, many experts keep their information in their computer. Their documents become ever-growing files; they make changes and delete the irrelevant.

Q: *Where are your earlier notes?*

A: *That earlier material was written over. With a computer, you do not save scraps of paper.*

The above interpretations are generalities. Remember that

NEVER WRITE ON DEPOSITIONS AND OTHER DOCUMENTS. THESE NOTES ARE DISCOVERABLE.

lawyers deal in exceptions. When in doubt about attorney-client relationship rules, work product and discoverability, consult your client-attorney. The safest rule is simply to treat everything as potentially discoverable. Anything you have ever written may be discovered, including e-mail and your contributions to Internet listservs. Be careful what you say and write.

Protection. You may ask for a court order to protect sensitive documents in your file (proprietary formulas, income figures, etc.). That is, you will still have to turn them over to the opposing attorney, but he or she may not show them to anyone else.

Some items in your file such as books and magazines may be covered by copyright. When copies are requested, remind opposing counsel that copying them may violate copyright law.

Be careful of the question: *What documents have you reviewed?* Any records, photographs, books, etc. you have seen can be requested by the other side.

Sometimes the opposing attorney tries to harass the expert by using a subpoena duces tecum to request all of his or her files—he or she wants to see every case ever worked on and the expert's entire library. If this happens to you, call your client-attorney to try and have the subpoena modified or withdrawn. If the requesting attorney is firm, quote a price to cover time and photocopying costs. Request payment in advance. You are entitled to do this but you must provide an itemized statement of your work. Faced with a large bill, the attorney may back off.

Record retention. You must retain your files, exhibits and other evidence until the case is completely settled and the appeal term has lapsed. That is until after the time for appeal has expired. Waiting a year after final settlement is usually sufficient, but many experts save everything as they may be able

---

THINK OF YOUR FILE AS A HANDOUT FOR A SPEECH. WHAT DO YOU WANT YOUR AUDIENCE (OPPOSING ATTORNEYS) TO TAKE HOME?

to use the materials again. Consult with your client-attorney before disposing of any materials.

MORE INFORMATION IS NOT THE ANSWER. BUT CONCISE, DIGESTIBLE AND BELIEVABLE INFORMATION IS.
— ALLEN CRENSHAW

CHAPTER NINE

DEMONSTRATIVE EVIDENCE AND PROPS

Demonstrative evidence is an exhibit which supports expert opinion. Properly designed, it shows what your opinion is and how you arrived at it. Props are items you use to enhance your oral testimony. Props are usually used before you trot out the demonstrative evidence.

A verbal description may not have sufficient impact on the jury. They have been listening to words all week and are bored. The jury was raised on television; they require more action to stay alert. What you need to enhance your presentation are photographs, video, diagrams, maps, charts, recordings, enlargements, slides, overheads, models, mock-ups, parts, animation, samples, specimens, graphs, etc. It does not matter if you are discussing accounting or skydiving, the jury will respond more favorably to visuals.

Props. You will use your props to explain the activity before you explain your opinion. Buy your props and set up your dog-and-pony show. Make a basic video. Take the props

WE TALK FAR TOO MUCH. WE SHOULD TALK LESS AND DRAW MORE. I PERSONALLY SHOULD LIKE TO . . . COMMUNICATE EVERYTHING I HAVE TO SAY IN SKETCHES. — GOETHE

to the first meeting with the attorney and use them to demonstrate your (preliminary) findings in the case. He will be impressed and will ask: *Can you do that in court?* which is exactly what you want. Attorneys are readers and talkers and they know the case inside-out. Many do not realize that the jury needs visuals. So take your props to the first meeting and use them.

The author uses a parachute, target, wind arrow and anatomical model; Para-Sail, car, boat, etc. For a deposition in a Para-Sail case, he demonstrated what was supposed to happen and then what actually happened. The case settled the next day. The opposing attorney not only realized the author was right, what was more frightening, he could demonstrate it in court.

Other props might be your books. Take them to the stand and place them on the rail of the witness box. The jury will connect you with the books and be impressed.

Demonstrative evidence (exhibits) can be anything that appeals to the jury's senses: sight, touch, smell, taste, or hearing. It may include models, diagrams, charts, photographs, videos, maps, and so on. Designed to inform, persuade, justify and educate, they can be used to help the jury focus on the critical issues of the case.

Your demonstrative evidence must be fair and accurate or it will be objected to by the other side and excluded by the judge. Be sure to check the demonstrative evidence proposed by the other side. You may be able to have it excluded or limited. Help your client-attorney. You know more about the subject than he or she.

Willie Sutton, the famous bank robber, was being interviewed:

Q: *Willie, why do you rob banks?*

A: *That is where the money is.*

A FUNDAMENTAL PURPOSE OF DEMONSTRATIVE EXHIBITS IS TO ESTABLISH A PICTURE IN THE VIEWER'S MIND.
— STEVEN M. SCHORR, P.E.

Q: *Willie, why do you always use a gun?*

A: *I have found the best way to get your point across is with a few well-chosen words and visual aids.*

Demonstrative evidence must be:

🖛 Relevant. Does this chart have something to do with the case?

🖛 Cumulative. Does it add anything to the expert's oral testimony?

🖛 Unprejudicial. Will it unnecessarily inflame the jury?

🖛 A fair and accurate representation of what it is supposed to represent. Is the video reenactment a fair representation of what happened or is it exaggerated? Has the proper foundation been laid for its admission?

Your presentation must also be:

🖛 Short. Juries will like you for not wasting their time. Thirty seconds of a demonstration are more effective than 30 minutes of words.

🖛 Simple. Do not make it hard to understand. Do not overdo the exhibit. The jury has a lot to remember and you want to leave a lasting impression.

🖛 Sweet. Create empathy.

🖛 Swift. Make it move.

🖛 Substantial. Build the evidence to a solution.

🖛 Smooth. Do a top-notch editing job.

In short, your presentation must be professional. You are being compared with MTV.

A SUCCESSFUL DEMONSTRATION INFORMS THE JURY ABOUT YOUR INFORMATION, COMMUNICATES THE BENEFIT OF YOUR UNDERSTANDING, AND INSPIRES THEM TO ACCEPT YOUR THESIS.
— ALLEN CRENSHAW

Juries need visuals. Remember the maxim among educators: people will remember 10% of what they hear, 20% of what they see, 50% of what they read, and 90% of what they do. Involve your jury! Demonstrative evidence has a wake-up effect. It can be used to refocus the attention of an otherwise bored jury. Studies show they will remember 65% of a demonstrative presentation after 72 hours while retaining only 10% of oral testimony alone. And you can leave the drawings up to make a continuous impression on the jury. Even better, demonstrative evidence goes into the jury room when they deliberate.

Your client-attorney may ask you to obtain models or other demonstrative evidence. You do not have to physically prepare the exhibits yourself but you do have to *direct the preparation*. Since the exhibits are presented to demonstrate your theories, they should be *your* exhibits. The opposing attorney will ask if you *prepared* the exhibits.

Professional exhibit makers. There are firms that specialize in designing and manufacturing courtroom exhibits (see the *Yellow Pages*). They can turn your sketches into professional presentations. One benefit they offer is their expertise. They have prior experience with exhibits.

Another benefit of working with professional exhibit people is that in explaining what you want and working over the development of the exposition, you become much more familiar with your own work. You will learn more about the case and the preparation will help you to focus on your theories and opinions.

Types of exhibits:

1. Photographs can make a case seem more real, especially *before and after* shots. Photographs may be of equipment, the site, or the plaintiff.

You must take the photographs or they must be taken

THE WORST MISTAKE YOU CAN MAKE IN COURT IS TO BORE YOUR JURY.

under your supervision. Photographs taken by the expert carry far more weight than those taken by a professional photographer. Viewers may suspect the professional took the photos in a way that slants the subject. Additionally, your photos show you were there and studied the subject or the site. When you get your developed prints, initial and date one set so you can identify the ones you took, later in court.

Enlarged prints are preferable to slides or overheads. You do not want to risk equipment failure or have to orient the screen and darken the courtroom so everyone can see. Use hard copy when you can.

Photographs need only be an *accurate portrayal* of what they are supposed to represent. The type of camera and film are not important, even though opposing attorneys sometimes try to discount photographs taken with inexpensive cameras. On the other hand, the technical details may become important if the photograph is being used to demonstrate dimensions.

2. Videotape offers the advantage of motion. It can also be stopped and replayed. Jurors are generally comfortable with video today as most use it in their own lives.

Video is being used more and more in the courtroom and as tool to encourage settlement. To be effective, however, it must be a true and accurate representation of something the jury needs to know.

Many attorneys are videotaping depositions, especially when they have reason to believe the witness might not be available to testify at the trial.

If you are using a film projector, slide projector, video player, etc., bring your own and test it in the courtroom before the trial. You can't risk bulb burn out or other failure.

3. Charts and graphs are most effective for clarifying your case or opinion.

It is best to present just one message per chart. Multiple ideas can be confusing.

Some experts like to use Mylar overlays with separating

A PICTURE IS WORTH A THOUSAND WORDS.

sheets of paper. This system allows them to build their presentation saving their conclusion for the finish. Mylar also allows you to write on the exhibit without obliterating it.

Stand on the left side of the easel and do not block it. Encourage the jury to look at your drawing and then let their eyes drift back to you. Make sure the evidence can be seen; consider size and position.

4. Diagrams are most effectively used in augmenting witness testimony. They work particularly well when used in conjunction with other visual aids such as photographs.

Take your own marker pens—several different colors—to court. Do not expect all the equipment to be there. Use the black marker pens first. They are easier to read. If the opposing side has already used black, select a color that is readily distinguishable from theirs. Some experts like to use water-based markers with Handiwipes to allow for erasures.

5. Maps may be used to establish locations and distances.

6. X-rays, medical illustrations and anatomical models can be very useful in injury cases.

7. Three-dimensional models are good for recreating accident sites. Operational models are often useful in patent infringement cases.

8. Courtroom demonstrations of a procedure can backfire, so do not use them unless you are certain of the outcome. Go through the demonstrations several times and get a critique. Your best critic may be a professional court exhibit maker. Make sure your demonstration shows what you want the jury to understand. Committing the experiment to videotape is safer. You can repeat the procedure until you get the results you want.

9. Documents. When letters and other documents are discussed, it is often wise to provide copies for the judge and each juror. Important words or passages may be accented with a highlighting pen. The impact will be greater if each can hold the document in his or her hands. If you want to point to important areas, you may use a blow-up of the letter. Enlargements may appear more important than smaller documents when taken into the jury room.

Do not overdo it. Too much demonstrative evidence can be confusing and may be likened to a three-ring circus. Present the case to the jury in the most graphic way without being overly dramatic.

Do not make your demonstrative evidence look too expensive. Do not trot out huge glossy photographs when simple snapshots will do. Viewers may become suspicious if your side is spending money on exhibits that the case does not appear to warrant.

Attorney resistance. On the other hand, some attorneys are reluctant to spend money on demonstrative evidence. You must explain what you need and counsel against going into court with the second-best models and drawings. Be assertive or creative. Come up with less expensive alternatives.

Check the layout of the courtroom and your distance from the jury. Make your exhibits large enough to be easily seen but small enough to fit through the door. Scout the sizes of the elevators, stairways and entryways.

Keep your drawings and models covered until ready for presentation. Build the jury's curiosity, do not distract them during your earlier testimony.

Make your exhibits *jury-friendly*; show pieces they can pass around, handle and compare. During your demonstration, hand items to the jury. Use models or before-and-after overlays the jury can pass around the box and compare. Involve your jury.

Use a presentation program such as *PowerPoint* to create your demonstration. It will print out your handout for the jury. This is just another presentation. Your presentation has to be slick; your demonstrative evidence has to be superior and you have to be able to perform. You are dealing with juries who were raised on TV. You must testify in sound bites, you must

---

DO NOT SHOW OFF YOUR EXPERTNESS—EDUCATE YOUR JURY; AS IN ANY PRESENTATION, THE AUDIENCE COMES FIRST.

speak clearly and say things that are both understandable and memorable.

Exhibits go with the jury into the jury room. So think carefully about what you want to leave with the jury. Your models and drawings will speak for you long after they forget what you said. Some experts like to use marker pens and large sheets of paper for *chalk talks*, to draw as they explain. But they may be stopped before making their full presentation and their drawings may not be professional. Pre-drawn exhibits are already complete and will give the jury the whole story. Put them on hard board so they will stand up by themselves.

Practice, practice, practice. Get a critique on your presentation. You want to communicate your opinion accurately. The opposing attorney will use your models or drawings against you if he or she can.

To get demonstrative material entered into evidence, have your attorney expose it at a pretrial conference. At trial he or she can say: *But your honor, he saw this three weeks ago and did not object.* Also, try to see the opposing expert's demonstrative evidence prior to trial so that you may check it for accuracy.

Before preparing an exhibit, consider the foundational criteria and its admissibility.

1. Foundational criteria.

   a. Demonstrative evidence must be accurate and to scale. The opposing attorney will ask you about accuracy.

   b. Was it built under your direction and can you verify that it is a correct representation? Have you signed and dated it?

LAWYERS NEED EXPERTS AND EXPERTS NEED EXHIBITS.
— FAUST ROSSI, CORNELL LAW SCHOOL

YOU DO NOT HAVE TO SHOCK THE JURY BUT YOU DO HAVE TO ELECTRIFY THEM.

c. Will it help to explain and verify your verbal testimony?

d. Are you sure it will not mislead the jury?

e. Are you qualified to testify as to the accuracy of the exhibit?

2. Admissibility.

a. The judge will rule on the admissibility of your demonstrative evidence. If your model, drawing, video, etc. will help the jury to understand the problem, the judge will let the jury see it. If the judge feels your design is misleading, he or she will not.

b. Is the exhibit accurate?

c. Is the exhibit relevant and material?

Once admitted, exhibits will be marked for identification by the court stenographer. Normally, exhibits are marked sequentially and are preceded by a "P" or "D" depending on whether they have been introduced by the plaintiff or defendant. Once marked, the exhibit becomes part of the record.

THE ROLES OF A PROFESSOR IN A CLASSROOM AND AN EXPERT IN A COURTROOM ARE SIMILAR. — JAMES P. ROMUALDI, PH.D. & HUGH L. DAVIDSON, PH.D., IN *EXPERTS-AT-LAW* MAGAZINE

Chapter Ten

The Deposition

A deposition is a *discovery* proceeding in the form of *oral* testimony taken by the opposing attorney in advance of the trial. Some experts have declined to make drawings at depositions because they were subpoenaed to give *oral* evidence.

As a Notary Public, the court reporter places the witness under oath so that testimony is given under penalty of perjury. Then as a certified stenographer, he or she records the testimony. Although interrogatories are used to acquire initial information, depositions are used to develop and expand on this information.

Notice of deposition. Both your client-attorney and the opposing attorney will probably call you to arrange a convenient time and place for the deposition. It is not unusual, however, for the opposing attorney to formally *subpoena* you. If you are served, notify your client-attorney immediately.

In many jurisdictions, you may not be compelled to testify without someone agreeing to pay you. Without such an agreement, you may request the subpoena be quashed.

Failure to appear. If you should fail to show up for the deposition, your absence could prove to be expensive—both for you and the other parties. If your failure to appear is willful, you can be held in contempt of court, a charge that could result in your being fined and imprisoned. The opposing attorney will also have a claim against you for out-of-pocket expenses and perhaps even his or her fees for time spent attending the abortive deposition. Further, if you fail to appear for the deposition, the judge will probably bar you from testifying at the trial.

If you do not wish to be deposed, seek advice from your client-attorney. But remember, your client-attorney represents the person paying his or her bill, not you. If this is a sticky situation, or if you have an extraordinary reason for not wanting to be deposed, consult your own personal attorney.

If you have a true emergency, contact your client-attorney as soon as possible. Then the burden will fall on him or her to make the necessary rearrangements.

Document production. You may be ordered to bring certain items to the deposition with you; usually, your entire file. Specific documents and other specific tangible evidence may be ordered with a *subpoena duces tecum*. If you do not understand what they want or if you object to bringing something such as your tax returns, call your client-attorney. Depositions are discovery proceedings. Bring only what you are specifically asked to bring; if they want it, they have to ask for it. Once in the deposition, you may be asked for more documents.

Q: *Will you send me a photocopy of that article?*

A: *We can have one made now.*

A: *Surely you are not suggesting I violate the author's or publisher's copyright. It appeared in the September 17th edition of Newsweek. I am sure you can find a copy.*

The documents the opposing attorney may request are:

🖝 Your curriculum vitae

MANY EXPERTS WILL NOT GO TO THE DEPOSITION UNLESS THEY ARE PAID TO DATE.

- All your publications: books, articles and speeches

- All materials upon which you relied in forming your opinion

- All exhibits and demonstrative evidence you are planning to use to explain your opinion in court

- Transcripts (if you have them) of your prior deposition and trial testimony

- The written results, including raw data, notebooks, computer files and notes, of any tests you may have performed

- Any written opinion you may have rendered

- All time and billing records and/or diaries you have maintained in connection with this case

You will not be deposed in every case. The opposing attorney has to decide if questioning you is worth the time and money.

If you are serving only as a consultant to your client-attorney and have not been declared as an expert (named to testify in court), you will not be deposed. Opinions of, and work by, *consultants* are covered by the attorney work product rule and are generally not discoverable.

Depositions have two main purposes: *discovery* and/or *impeachment*. They also allow the opposing attorney to size you up under conditions less formal but no less important than a trial. The form of the questions will reveal the opposing attorney's major interest. If discovery is the goal, the questions will be broad and the subjects far-reaching. He or she will be looking for new facts. If the questions are tightly focused, he or she is trying to produce admissible evidence for the trial. The object is to force you to commit yourself to a position. Your client-attorney may follow with questions to clarify certain areas.

1. Discovery is a fishing expedition to learn new facts. So do not volunteer information. If you are asked for your name, do not give your address and birth date too. Such an answer would be beyond the scope of the question or *non-responsive*.

The opposing attorney's objective is to get the expert to help in his or her research. He or she wants to know who you talked to, what you read, what tests you ran, what investigations you made, and about your research and findings.

In other words, the opposing attorney is trying to *discover* how you arrived at your opinion in order to see what kind of case your side has. He or she wants to know what work you have done on the case, what you plan to do and what position you are taking. If possible, he or she will try to lock you into a position or set of circumstances that will be difficult for you to maintain at trial.

2. Impeachment is designed to nail down your testimony for use at trial. The opposing attorney wants to find out what you know and what your case will be. The object of the deposition is to reveal and test your opinions and conclusions and pin you down to them.

Be prepared: anticipate questions. Practice saying your opinion aloud with conviction until you sound certain. Be familiar with the facts. Know the dates, places, names, etc. If you make a mistake in the deposition, you will pay for it in court.

At trial, the opposing attorney may read a sentence from your deposition and then ask: *Did you say that?* Then he or she will ask: *Do you still agree with that?* And then he or she will ask you to justify what you said in light of some other evidence. Juries tend not to believe witnesses who change their story.

Q: *Did you lie in your deposition, or are you lying now?*

The opposing attorney should be so well prepared for the deposition that he or she knows the subject of your expertise

---

WHEN I BEGAN EXPERT-WITNESSING, I THOUGHT THAT DEPOSING ATTORNEYS WERE JUST BORN OBNOXIOUS. I STILL THINK CERTAIN PEOPLE ARE BORN OBNOXIOUS, BUT I HAVE SINCE DISCOVERED IT IS POSSIBLE TO OBTAIN TRAINING IN THIS ART.
— RAYMOND SINGER, PH.D.

and is fairly sure of your answers. If the deposition is short, the opposing attorney is good. If it is long and has a number of semi-relevant questions, the attorney has not done his or her homework.

Normally only one deposition is taken of an expert witness. Unless the case is very large, you are not liable to be deposed more than once.

Preparation for the deposition. The opposition has a right to depose you and you cannot be properly deposed unless you are prepared. If you cannot answer the questions, the deposition will be meaningless and the opposition may move to have you barred from testifying at the trial. They may even get a court order making you pay their fees and expenses because you were not prepared for the deposition.

Insist on a conference with your client-attorney in advance of the deposition. Discuss the questions either of you expect the opposing attorney to ask. You must work together and be ready with concisely-framed answers. Too many busy attorneys meet with their experts for only half an hour or so, often over a hurried breakfast. This is not enough time.

If you hear the opposing attorney is a tough examiner, you may wish to read other depositions he or she has taken.

Request a briefing on the law relevant to the action. You want to know how your testimony fits into the case.

You will also be asked about your qualifications. The opposing attorney hopes to expose potential bias or lack of qualifications or experience.

Tell your client-attorney if you have ever expressed a contrary opinion in a previous case, a magazine article or book. How long ago was it? Has thinking, teaching or equipment changed? Is there new information? New technology? How can you justify a change of thought now?

Be prepared and read everything again. Remember, some 92% of the cases never go to trial—the plaintiff gives up or the defendant makes a settlement. Therefore, you must be prepared for the deposition. Be ready to list all the things you did and read before forming an opinion. Do not try to *wing it*. If you are sure of your material, you need not feel threatened.

What to wear. Wear whatever you wear on the job. Be comfortable, be clean and neat. Men should usually wear a suit or conservative jacket and tie. Similarly, women should dress for business. Do not wear expensive jewelry such as a Rolex watch. You want to give the impression that you are a serious, quiet, careful, thoughtful individual. Remember, the opposing attorney will be sizing you up. He or she will be evaluating how you will act in court.

What to take. Remember, a deposition is not your place to volunteer information. Take only what has been requested and supports your opinion. In most cases, this will be your file folder with CV, fee schedule, narrative, time sheets, bills, reports, and backup documents. You should have all facts and data upon which you relied in forming your opinion, but take only what you want the other side to know. Anything in your file is discoverable. Show the file to your client-attorney in the meeting prior to the deposition. He or she will want to filter out all non-discoverable (privileged) information. The opposing attorney may ask the stenographer to photocopy the entire file and attach it to the deposition.

Everything you have in your possession is discoverable. Plan on having the opposing attorney ask to go through your attaché case. Think of your case as a container for your speech handouts. Put things there you want him or her to find.

Before the deposition, go through your voluminous notes and reduce them. Throw out all your early notes, questions, wrong ideas and early "conclusions." You want a smaller, more up to date file that can be reviewed quickly. Do not *sanitize* your files, *update* them.

When you meet with your client-attorney prior to the deposition, he or she will want to look through your file to make sure there are no *work privileged* items in there. Do not bring any items to the deposition without your client-attorney

---

WHEN WORKING ON A CASE, PREPARE YOUR FILE FOR AN
EVENTUAL DEPOSITION. — BRYAN CONLEY, PH.D.

reviewing them first. Now, if you are asked if you saw some attorney work product and if your client-attorney took it back, you must answer truthfully. Let the lawyers argue about producing them.

Take demonstrative evidence such as models or drawings if they will help to explain your case.

Place. Do not allow depositions to be taken at your home or business. Anything you have with you is discoverable and if you are at home, all your files, library and records are open to the opposing attorney. Suggest a neutral site such as a court reporter's office.

Although selecting the site for the deposition is up to the attorneys, you may have to help if you want to keep them off your premises. Get out the *Yellow Pages* and look up some local court reporting services under *Reporters-Court*. Call two or three for a description of services and rates. Keep this list handy so that when an opposing attorney calls to arrange a deposition, you will be ready with a telephone number he or she may call to secure the site.

Who will attend. The deposition will be attended by your client-attorney, the opposing attorney and a stenographer who is usually a notary public. The plaintiff and defendant are allowed to attend and sometimes do. Sometimes the opposing party and/or expert will attend to help the opposing attorney.

The opposing attorney usually begins by asking if you know the ground rules so that you cannot claim at the trial that you did not understand what was going on. Ask the opposing attorney to review the rules even if you have given many depositions. Rules differ from jurisdiction to jurisdiction, and each court changes its rules from time to time. You should not have to research these rules. That is the lawyer's job. You want the record to reflect what he or she told you. Sample deposition instructions are printed at the end of this chapter.

How to act. Make sure the court reporter understands what you are saying. Talk in complete sentences. Remember, one of the most important considerations in your deposition is this: how will your answers look in writing? You are a teacher.

Speak slowly and spell out technical words. When you give your name, spell it out. This is professional and lets the opposing attorney know you have given depositions before. Hand your business card to the court reporter. A card not only insures correct spelling, it lets the reporter know where to send the transcript for review, correction and signing.

Do not overstate your qualifications. If you exaggerate, you may be exposed at trial. Ask for clarifications of technical legal terms. What is *reasonable certainty*? What is the *standard of care*? Make sure you and the questioner are talking about the same thing, Review your own past writings and look for inconsistencies. Do not educate the opposition. If they fail to ask, do not tell. Be firm in defending your opinion. Do not raise doubts about your conclusion. If handed a document, ask what portion you are addressing and then read it and understand it before answering. If you relied on certain tests or texts, be prepared to explain them.

If you have taken any medication in the past 48 hours, tell your client-attorney. He or she will want to know if you are not operating at 100% of your capacity.

Be dignified and polite. This is serious, expensive business and you want to project a serious image. During the deposition, everything you say will be *on the record*, committed to paper. Do not clown around, even outside the deposition room. Do not speak with opposing counsel. The opposing parties may begin to doubt both your sincerity and your testimony.

What you will be asked. Many attorneys today use a deposition checklist.

- Name, address, telephone numbers. You should have given your business card to the stenographer.

- Your curriculum vitae. What is your area of expertise?

- Educational background, beginning with college.

- Employment history including military service.

- Other jobs that provided on-the-job training or assistance.

🐾 Professional society memberships.

🐾 Degrees or certificates.

🐾 Teaching or lecture experience.

🐾 Licenses or certifications. When? Have any of them ever been questioned, investigated, suspended or revoked?

🐾 Have you ever been sued as a result of your professional activities?

🐾 Publications: Have you written any books, journal articles and/or magazine articles?

🐾 Have you conducted any research relevant to this case? Were the results published?

🐾 Have you testified before? Where and when?

🐾 How often? Percentage of time spent testifying as opposed to practicing your profession

🐾 What percentage of your income is derived from litigation-related work?

🐾 The number of cases you have served as a consultant, testified in deposition and at trial.

🐾 What percentage of cases do you work for the Plaintiff? Defendant? Do you have an even balance of cases? If not, you may have a good reason. For example, construction litigation usually involves one plaintiff and several defendants. Since there are more opportunities to work for defendants, an equal split of cases could suggest a plaintiff bias.

🐾 How many prior cases involve the same issue as this case? Name them. If they are too numerous to recall, say so.

🐾 Have you ever worked for this party or law firm before? Are you a close friend of the client? Are you doing him or her a favor? Name the cases and issues involved. Often, you may answer *I do not remember.*

🐝 Do you know the other expert?

Q: *What is (the opposing witness's) reputation in your field?*

(This is a trick. He or she wants you to say the other expert is outstanding.)

A: *She is a fine person.*

A: *Counselor, it is not up to me to qualify your witness.*

A: *She was one of my best students.*

A: *He is the best expert money can buy.*

(It is not likely you will encounter a situation where you can use that one.)

🐝 How did you prepare for this deposition today?

🐝 Do you advertise your expert services? When and where?

Q: *Do you advertise in the* Yellow Pages?

A: *Yes sir.*

Q: *Doesn't that make you a "professional expert"?*

A: *Not at all. I am a professional who spends a few hours a year in court. I do this to help people.*

A: *I advertise that I am available to review cases but I never state I will testify.*

A: (Reaching into your file), *I notice you advertise in the* Yellow Pages. *The headline is INJURED? WE CAN GET THE MONEY FOR YOU!*

🐝 How were you first contacted? Who called you and how did he or she find you? Date of first contact.

🐝 How was the nature of the assignment presented to you? What were you asked to do? Have you ever done this task before?

🐝 Do you have notes of that call? Describe the contact.

🐝 Describe each subsequent contact. Do you have notes?

🐦 When did you receive the materials and when did you read them?

🐦 What is your fee schedule?

Q: *How much do you make each year?*

A: *That is between me, my accountant and, regrettably, the IRS.*

A: *I do not consider that relevant and will only answer if directed by a judge.*

(They should ask about litigation-related income only.)

Q: *How much are you charging for your opinion in this case?*

A: *I do not charge for my opinion. I charge for time on a hourly basis.*

🐦 How much time have you spent on the case? Do you have time sheets?

🐦 Have you ever worked for an (small-firm plaintiff's) attorney where you had to cut your bill when the plaintiff lost?

🐦 Who have you discussed this case with? What did they say? Do you have notes?

🐦 The basis for each of your opinions.

🐦 Have you found any facts, articles or other matter that is inconsistent with each of the opinions you have reached?

🐦 What facts might alter the opinions you have reached in this case?

Q: *What facts might alter the opinions you have reached in this case?*

A: *I can't speculate on that. The question is too broad.*

🐦 What is your assessment of the opinions reached by opposing experts?

🐦 Have you found any *defects*?

🐦 What are the *standards of care*? Does anyone in your field disagree with these standards? Who?

☞ Describe your testing. Did you examine the item? Explain the *chain of custody*. How was it identified? Were photographs or other records made? If the item was similar but not the same, what differences were there? Where and how did you get the similar product? Do you plan further tests?

☞ Was a computer used? What hardware and software? What results? Supply details on disk.

☞ Describe all equipment used in testing and evaluating. Calibration. What were the results? Were they recorded?

☞ Do you plan further research or work before trial?

☞ If you had an unlimited budget, what else would you have done?

☞ Going through your file, identify all the depositions, notes, calculations and records. Where did you get each document? Is this your complete file?

☞ What records were provided to you? Who gave them to you and when?

☞ Do you expect to examine more records? What records?

☞ Were there any records you wanted but could not get?

☞ Have you written any reports for this case?

☞ Will you submit any written reports in the future?

☞ Were there any draft reports before the final one? Who did you send them to?

☞ Have you been told not to prepare a report? By whom?

☞ Have you ever been indicted, convicted, sued, etc.?

☞ Have you done all the work yourself or have you had assistance? What assistance? Were you present during their work?

Q: *Did you discuss this case with your attorney?*

(The opposing attorney is trying to get you to agree your deposition testimony is rehearsed.)

A: *Yes, of course. We reviewed it over breakfast.*

(You are expected to talk to your client-attorney about the case. Do not lie about the meeting.)

🐟 State each opinion reached as a result of your work on this case. Recite the operative facts on which each is based. List any assumptions and their bases.

🐟 When did you initially form your opinion? (Was it before you looked at the file?)

🐟 Are there any other opinions or conclusions you have reached in this case you have not already studied?

Q: *Have you mentioned all your opinions?*

(This is a trap)

A: *All I can think of at this time.*

A: *That question is open-ended. Do you have any more questions?*

🐟 Are you going to testify to anything at trial you have not discussed today?

🐟 Have you misled or mistaken any testimony you want to correct at this time? Beware of this open-ended bombshell.

Q: *Have you misled or mistaken any testimony you want to correct at this time?*

A: *Not that I can think of.*

A: *I will read and sign the transcript at my leisure. I will not be rushed now.*

In summary, the opposing attorney wants to know who you are, what you did, what you know, how you got there, and what your opinion is. You are there to explain what happened or what should have happened.

In answering, follow these three basic rules:

1. Listen to the question and pause before answering.
Pay attention. You cannot tell the truth if you have not heard
and understood the question. Sometimes we assume we know
what the question is and we stop listening in order to formulate
our answer.

The pause permits you to formulate your answer and allows
your client-attorney to object to the question if it is improper.

2. Look directly at the attorney asking the question and
give a responsive answer, but do not volunteer additional
information. Carefully phrase your answers and do not add any
unnecessary detail. Remember, the longer the answer, the
more likely you are to give away unasked-for information or
make an error. Be careful of open-ended questions such as
What happened next?

3. Tell the complete truth. A deposition is sworn
testimony and the transcript can be read into the record at the
trial. It is better to say *I do not know* or *I do not remember* than to
make a guess.

Q: *Did counsel tell you what to say at this deposition?*

A: *No, of course not.*

A: *My counsel told me to tell the truth.*

When your client-attorney objects, listen carefully. He or
she may be making a legal point, may be sending you a
warning or may want to break the questioner's stride.
Whenever your client-attorney starts to talk, stop immediately
and listen.

If your client-attorney directs you not to answer a
particular question, state *I will not answer on advice of counsel.* Let
the attorneys work it out.

Analyze every question. It may be *vague and ambiguous.*

IF YOU DO NOT ANSWER HONESTLY, YOU ARE PROSTITUTING
YOURSELF. YOU ARE COMMITTING PERJURY AND COULD BE FINED
OR SENT TO JAIL. YOU MUST APPEAR HONEST, UPRIGHT AND
WILLING TO COOPERATE.

Make sure you understand all the terms used. Do not hesitate to ask that the question be reworded. Ask to have words defined so that you are both working with the same meaning. If you do not express a lack of understanding, counsel will presume you understood and your answer will be taken as a full and complete response.

If you think the opposing attorney is trying to be tricky, ask him or her to rephrase the question as a delaying tactic. If the question is ambiguous, make your answer clear and specific.

A: *If you mean . . . , then the answer is . . .*

One effective technique for clarifying the question is to include the question in your answer.

Q: *When did you run the tests?*

A: *I ran the tensile strength and tear tests on the fabric on September 17th.*

When a (compound) question has many parts, ask to have it rephrased, one question at a time. Be alert for questions with the words *or* or *and*. Be careful of negative questions; those that start with *is it not true...*

Q: *Don't you agree that . . . (lengthy statement)*

A: (If you can honestly disagree with any part of the lengthy statement) *No.*

The opposing attorney may ask you a question which does not call for new facts. The question is considered *argumentative* if he or she is seeking an explanation of a previous answer. You may answer with *I have already answered that question.* It is up to your client-attorney to object if the question is argumentative.

Do not make assumptions unless they are based on facts

YOU MUST NOT ONLY *BE* HONEST AND INDEPENDENT, YOU MUST *APPEAR* TO BE HONEST AND INDEPENDENT.

THE EXPERT WITNESS IS *NEUTRAL.* YOU DID NOT CAUSE THE INJURY OR DISPUTE. YOU MUST NOT TAKE SIDES.

which are in evidence. *Foundation* must exist or your answer will admit the assumed fact.

If the opposing attorney attempts to summarize your testimony, he or she may be *putting words in your mouth* by suggesting things you did not say. Do not accept this characterization of data, assumptions or descriptions of events. Listen carefully and point out each and every inaccurate statement in the summarization. Clarify erroneous premises in questions before answering.

Be wary of questions including words such as *probable* or *possible.*

Do not talk to opposing counsel during coffee breaks. Pleasantries are okay but should be avoided too. You are not supposed to talk to your client-attorney either but you usually will.

Leading questions are those with a given statement in which you are only asked to agree. If any part of the question is not correct, the answer is *no.* Or, you may say that you *cannot entirely agree.*

Hypothetical questions are almost always signs of a mine field. *Assuming this and that and this, what would you expect a rational person in this area to do?* Keep your eyes open and tread carefully. See hypothetical questions in Chapter Eleven on trials.

Requests to endorse the work of others. The opposing attorney may try to get you to qualify his or her expert or to endorse the writing of another party.

Q: *Have you read Professor Gamble's book?*

A: *Yes.*

Q: *Do you consider it authoritative?*

A: *Some of it. Please read me the part you want me to agree with and I will tell you if I do.*

DON'T LET PAST QUESTIONS WORRY YOU. PERFECTION IS IMPOSSIBLE. — HEINZ P. BLOCH, P.E.

Catch-all questions. Watch out for *overly broad* statements such as *tell us all you know about...* Make your answer accurate and truthful, but be as brief as possible. Cover yourself by ending with *that is all I can think of at this time.*

Q: *What are your opinions in this case?*

A: *One of my opinions is....*

A: *I have many opinions on this case. Please specify which aspect of the case you would like my opinion on.*

A: *I will tell you all I can but more may arise later.*

If you state only a few opinions, the opposing attorney may object to any new opinions expressed at the trial on the grounds that you did not reveal them during the deposition.

Q: *Tell me each and every fact on which you base your opinion.*

A: *Would you like a general summary?*

A: *If you ask me a specific question, I can give you a specific answer.*

Q: *How much experience do you have running a beauty shop in Texas?*

A: *That example is very limiting. My experience is much broader than that.*

Capsulize your testimony down to three concise sentences. Include your study, findings, conclusions and opinion. Then practice and memorize the statement.

Answer questions with *yes* or *no*, not with *un-huh* or a nod of the head. The court reporter will have trouble taking down your response. Do not repeat questions or start sentences with *a....* or *um....* These responses will prove embarrassing when read back in court. Take turns speaking with the attorneys. The court reporter can only record one person at a time.

Yes or no. In some instances, you can be required to give a simple *yes* or *no* answer, but you have a right to explain your one-word reply.

Be very careful in estimating time, speed and distance. Most people cannot do so accurately. The opposing attorney may be trying to trip you up.

Refer to documents by name or number. This makes you look professional. Do not just point.

When relaying conversations, indicate whether you are paraphrasing or quoting word for word.

Here are some expressions you should not use: *honestly, in all candor, to tell the truth,* and *I am doing the best I can.* Do not use *always* or *never.* The opposing attorney will jump on adjectives, exaggerations and superlatives.

Avoid obscenities, racial slurs and other inappropriate language. Remember, every word is being recorded. Snide and contentious remarks may take on a meaning you did not intend, when transcribed. Attempts at humor will not be appreciated by those who are paying for your time.

If at any time during the deposition you become confused, ask for a break to go to the bathroom. Then confer with your client-attorney. Of course, the opposing attorney may ask you about the consultation on the record when you return.

Do not sound argumentative. It is often wiser to answer a question you believe to be leading than to argue the relevance of the question. In other words, never try to out-attorney the attorney.

If you become tired, ask for a break. Many witnesses have given inaccurate testimony because they lost the ability to concentrate on the question.

Your opinion. Normally, the opposing attorney does not want to hear your opinion until the end of the deposition.

Off the record. From time to time the attorneys will agree to talk without the dialogue being recorded. Be careful of what you say. The opposing attorney has the right to question you about what you said while off the record.

You versus the opposing attorney. Remember that lawyers are professionals. They work with words for a living. The opposing attorney may start off by intimidating you. Each has his or her own technique and approach, but here are some standard types to watch for:

☞ **The pal** is an examiner who is disarmingly friendly. *Tell me* *everything, I am your pal.* Remember, depositions are an adversary proceeding. Anyone trying to be your pal is sneaking up on you.

☛ **The freight train** moves at a fast pace. *Come on, come on, let's go!* He or she is trying to make you talk before you think.

☛ **The butterfly** jumps from subject to subject unpredictably rather than pursuing one line of questioning at a time. He or she is trying to confuse you, hoping you will give conflicting testimony. Read your deposition transcript carefully before signing it.

☛ **The cunning linguist** subtly twists your words (usually when you appear exhausted) to ask a trick question so that you give an answer that will be damaging when you hear it read at trial.

A: *The question does not characterize my prior testimony. I did not say your client had stopped beating his wife.*

☛ **The time bomb** saves the difficult questions for the end of the deposition when you are tired.

Harassment. If the opposing attorney becomes overbearing, your client-attorney may come to the rescue by objecting. If you are handling the nastiness, your client-attorney may not object to avoid appearing overly protective on the record. You may wish to defend yourself this way by getting his or her actions on the record.

A: *Counsel, please stop making faces at me and please lower your voice.*

Do not argue or become angry with the opposing attorney. If you feel yourself getting mad, ask for a break. Sarcasm, belligerence and loss of composure may lead to careless testimony and certainly make an adverse impression. Do not undermine your credibility and ability to persuade. Do not

LAWYERS ARGUE; WITNESSES TESTIFY. DO NOT ARGUE WITH THE OPPOSING ATTORNEY. — ROY CORDER, CPA

tempt the opposing attorney to taunt you when you get to court hoping you will blurt out a damaging or poorly-conceived answer.

Your client-attorney may or may not ask a few clarifying questions at the end of the deposition. He or she may want to put some of your qualifications or opinions on the record that cross-examination has not elicited. Your client-attorney is only attending the deposition to protect the client; to defend you from harassment and protest improper lines of questioning by making objections or instructing you not to answer.

Your qualifications. The opposing attorney may neglect to ask you about your qualifications. This is a trick. If for some reason you are unable to appear at the trial, your deposition can be read to the jury only if you have been *qualified*. Your background must be brought out to lay a foundation for your opinion. If the opposing attorney neglects to ask you about your qualifications, your client-attorney should examine you or enter your curriculum vitae into evidence. It will then be attached to the deposition as an exhibit.

Video is being used increasingly in depositions especially when it is known the expert will not be available for trial. If your deposition is being videotaped, be prepared to be cross-examined too. If you do not attend the trial, the deposition is the opposing attorney's last opportunity to examine you. The video camera is not just another recording device. Jurors are used to professional talent on their television screens. You must be aware of the camera and be mediagenic. If you think you may be videotaped, take a course. Many authors take courses to learn how to act on talk shows.

Talk to the camera. Do not fidget or touch your face. Appear relaxed, confident and testify with conviction. Perform for the video audience.

Eight fundamentals for testifying at deposition:

☞ Be a real expert. Stick to what you know

☞ Tell the truth

- Stay alert
- Don't volunteer
- Take your time
- Do not guess
- Speak only for yourself
- Stay cool

Remain after your deposition to debrief with your client-attorney. Ask how he or she perceived your testimony. This evaluation will help you to reflect on your performance and plan for the future. Discuss the weak areas such as the foundation and areas for further research.

Attending your opposing expert's deposition. If your client-attorney is not extremely knowledgeable in the subject, he or she should have you attend the depositions of the other side's key witnesses. You will be able to see problems and suggest lines of questioning. If you do not attend the deposition, questions may go unanswered, making trial preparation more difficult.

There may be a tactical advantage in taking the opposing expert's deposition before yours. It is helpful to know where they are taking the case, what the other expert's opinions are, and what he or she bases them on. On the other hand, your client-attorney may want you to go first to educate the other side and lead to a favorable settlement.

Generally, plaintiff's experts should be deposed first to explain the theory of the case. Defendants should be told why they are being sued and they should not have to explain why they are generally blameless. The defendant's expert should be given the opportunity to criticize the Plaintiff's expert's opinion.

Search for everything the opposing expert has ever written or done on this subject. If the opposing expert has testified previously in a related matter, obtain and study the transcript.

Have the expert identify and categorize each item in his or

her file. Your client-attorney may wish to have each piece marked as deposition exhibits.

The opposing expert should be asked all the questions mentioned in investigating the opposing witness in Chapter Five, along with the following:

1. Has the expert prepared any draft or preliminary reports that are not in the file?

2. If the expert has not produced a written report, was this on instruction of counsel or anyone else?

3. What work has been performed on this case? When was the expert first contacted by the opposing attorney? What is the exact nature of the assignment? What does the expert charge? How many hours have been spent on reading, discussion, tests, site visits?

4. Has the expert been assisted by anyone else and, if so, what type of work was performed? (An assistant could hold an inconsistent opinion.)

5. What additional work does the expert plan to perform on the case? What additional work would the expert like to perform if he or she had an unlimited budget?

6. What is the expert's opinion, tentative or final, on each issue involved in the case? Has the expert arrived at any other opinions not already mentioned?

7. What is the basis or foundation for each opinion? On what facts, assumptions, publications or other factors has he or she relied?

8. Is the expert aware of any opinions, facts or articles which are contrary to his or her own opinion?

9. Take copious notes on the opposing expert's testimony, especially if he or she is not being cogent. You may be the only one in the room who understands that a ridiculous statement has been made. Tell your counsel during a break.

Transcript. The deposition will be sent to you for review and signing. Never waive the reading and signing. It is very rare that you won't find several mistakes.

Make sure the court reporter understood your technical words and did not make any transcription errors. Invite the stenographer to call you if questions arise during the preparation of the transcript. You should read and correct the transcript. Then sign the deposition in front of a Notary Public (when required) as soon as possible and return it.

If you made a mistake during the deposition, say so and correct it. It is far better to clarify the record immediately than to be challenged at the trial. Retain copies of your past depositions so you can always see what you said in an earlier case. Sharp opposing attorneys will dig out these depositions to search for conflicting testimony.

Save the depositions of other experts in your field, as well. You may learn from them and learn about potential questions. You may be able to use their words against them in the future.

Payment. The (opposing) attorney who requested the deposition is responsible for paying you and for the deposition expenses. Charge for the actual time used in the examination. (See Chapter Twelve for the pro's and con's of alternative fee arrangements.) Charge travel time and mileage to your client-attorney. Your client-attorney will pay for copies of the transcript. Charge your client-attorney for the time it takes you to prepare for the deposition and to review the transcript. Sometimes the two attorneys will agree to another type of split.

Preferably, work for and bill your client-attorney for all time and expenses on the case. Let him or her collect from the adversary attorney for your activities that benefit the adversary, such as your deposition.

In some jurisdictions such as California, the opposing attorney must show up with a check to cover the anticipated time of the deposition; the balance, if any, must be paid within five days. It is almost impossible to get paid by opposing

REVIEW THIS CHAPTER BEFORE YOU ATTEND A DEPOSITION.

counsel in a reasonable amount of time after the deposition. (See Chapter Twelve on fees for details.)

Here are sample deposition instructions. You are not likely to have these provided to you but they give you an idea of the ground rules.

Sample Deposition Instructions
From the Opposing Attorney

To The Expert Witness:

This proceeding is known as a Deposition. The person transcribing the proceedings is a Certified Shorthand Reporter, and also a Notary Public who has placed you under oath. During the course of this proceeding, I, and perhaps other counsel present here today, will be asking you questions pertaining to this lawsuit.

Although this proceeding is being held in an informal atmosphere, since you have been placed under oath, your testimony here today has the same force and effect and is subject to the same penalties as if you were testifying in a Courtroom before a Judge. Specifically, you are subject to the penalty of perjury. Perjury is defined as willfully, and contrary to an oath administered, stating as true any material fact which one knows to be false. The penalty for perjury may be imprisonment for not less than one (1) year, nor more than fourteen (14) years. You are advised that an unqualified statement of that which you do not know to be true is equivalent to a statement of that which you know to be false.

If, at any time during the Deposition, you feel that any question is ambiguous or unintelligible, or that you are unable to understand it, or you fail to hear the question for any reason whatsoever, please tell the person asking you the question. If you do not so indicate, it will be presumed that you have heard and have understood each question and that your answer to each question is based upon your

---

complete and full understanding thereof. If, after a question has been posed to you, you have any question yourself relating to what has been inquired about, please tell the person who posed the question before you answer his or her question.

The reporter is only able to transcribe audible responses, so please do not nod your head, shake your head, or say ahha or haah. Further, the reporter can usually record the words of only one person speaking at a time, so please allow time for the question to be completed before you respond. You will normally be allowed to finish each and every answer before a new question is posed.

At the conclusion of this Deposition, the reporter will transcribe these proceedings into a booklet form, and you will have an opportunity to read that booklet and make any changes in your testimony, as it is given here today. I will be entitled to ask you why you made such changes, and comment upon those changes before a Judge or jury trial of this action. Because of that fact, it is important that all of your answers be full, complete, and correct.

If I ask you about any conversation you have had in the past, and you are unable to recall the exact words used in the conversation, you may state that you are unable to recall those exact words, and then you may give me the gist or substance of any such conversation, to the best of your recollection. If you recall only part of a conversation, or only part of an event, you are requested to give me your best recollection of those events, or parts of conversations that you recall. If I ask you whether you have any information upon a particular subject, and you have overheard other persons conversing with each other regarding it, or have seen correspondence or documentation regarding it, please tell me that you do have such information, and indicate the source, either a conversation or documentation, or otherwise, from which you derive such knowledge. In answering, please do not be concerned with whether or not your answer is hearsay or concern yourself with any technical rules of evidence you think may preclude answering.

Our purpose here today is not to trap you, or to trick you in any manner, but simply to ascertain and discover that information about the facts concerning this lawsuit that you have within your knowledge.

At the conclusion of this Deposition, the attorneys present may, by agreement, stipulate that you sign the booklet containing your testimony in the presence of any notary public, rather than the reporter who is here today, taking and transcribing this Deposition. If we do so, it will be upon the expressed understanding, and your promise, that you will, upon receipt of the Deposition, promptly and as expeditiously as possible, read it, correct it if you feel it is necessary, and sign it in the presence of a notary public, and return it to the office from which it was sent to you.

Do you understand everything that you have just read? (Please circle)

YES   NO

Do you have any questions pertaining to either the procedure, or what is about to transpire, insofar as this Deposition is concerned? If so, please ask them of me now.

Please indicate that you have read and understood all of the foregoing, by signing this document where indicated below.

Signature of Deponent

Exhibit #   to the Deposition of   ,

taken on   ,19

SOME OF THE MATERIAL IN THE CHAPTER WILL BE REPEATED IN THE NEXT CHAPTER ON THE TRIAL. THIS IS MEANT TO OFFER FULL COVERAGE OF EACH SITUATION AND MAKE THE MATERIAL EASIER TO REVIEW BEFORE THE DEPOSITION OR TRIAL.

CHAPTER ELEVEN

THE TRIAL

You are hired because you are an authority in your field of expertise but now you are using that expertise in a whole new and different arena. Going to court, you are attending a new game with a strict set of unfamiliar rules. The game is called the *adversary system of justice*.

Many people find the game distasteful but the regular players, the judges and attorneys, love it. They are the professionals who do this for a living and they not only know the rules, they have the home field advantage. The expert witness also has an advantage because he or she knows more about the subject.

IT HAS BEEN SAID THAT PEOPLE CAN BE DIVIDED INTO THREE GROUPS: THOSE WHO MAKE THINGS HAPPEN, THOSE WHO WATCH THINGS HAPPEN AND THOSE WHO WONDER WHAT HAPPENED. THE ADVERSARY SYSTEM OF JUSTICE IS A TEAM SPORT MADE UP OF THE SAME THREE SETS OF PARTICIPANTS:
1. THOSE WHO MAKE THINGS HAPPEN: THE JUDGE AND THE OPPOSING ATTORNEYS.
2. THOSE WHO WATCH THINGS HAPPEN: THE BAILIFF, STENOGRAPHER, CLERK OF THE COURT, JURY, GALLERY, AND WITNESSES.
3. THOSE WHO WONDER WHAT HAPPENED: THE PLAINTIFF AND DEFENDANT WHO ARE PAYING FOR IT ALL.

To the expert witness, testimony is a serious effort to arrive at a fixed and incontrovertible truth. To a lawyer, the trial offers challenge and excitement. Under cross-examination, you will be attacked, your expertise questioned, and your honor impugned. Yet, at the end of the day, your client-attorney and the opposing attorney may leave the courtroom together and go out for a drink.

As an expert, you are not a player, you are a prop. This is not your game; it belongs to the legal profession. It is their game and they make the rules. The courtroom is their territory.

Basically, you will be involved in two types of cases: Civil (between two or more people or companies) and criminal (the government against a person or company).

Preparation is the most important part of presenting effective and persuasive forensic evidence in both civil and criminal cases. The trial is your *final exam* and the passing grade is 100%, not 70%. You may spend five days reading, reviewing and anticipating for what may be two hours on the stand. A well-prepared, attorney-expert witness team is rarely surprised.

How do you prepare?

Draft proposed questions. Write out lengthy answers. Do not just answer *yes* or *no*. Polish your act. You want to do a good job: Get the evidence in and win over the jury. Convey all the pertinent information in as few words as possible. Speak in *sound bites*. The initial attention span of jurors is about 30 seconds. This is when they assess whether or not what you are saying has any value to them. Draft your questions and practice your answers. Drafting your Q&A's for direct is a good way to prepare for court.

If you have worked with the same client-attorney several times, drafting questions may no longer be necessary unless the case is much different.

Send questions with answers to the client-attorney in advance. Script them in groups and suggest an order. Put headings on the groups for quick reference. Ask him what other questions he plans. Get them in writing and rehearse your answers.

Be prepared with lengthy, fact-filled answers to each question. He needs help and will probably welcome your prompting.

In court, all you will need are the questions from the attorney—a cue, then go into your routine. Examples:

Q: *Is skydiving popular in the U.S.?* (You could just answer *yes*, but you don't.)

A: *There are 35,000 active parachutists making 1.9 million jumps, 100,000 students make 500,000 jumps, for a total of 2.4 million jumps per year. Typically, we make four jumps per day. There are 250 drop zones across the country, each making a few thousand to over 90,000 jumps per year.*

Q: *Is auto racing dangerous?*

(The answer could be *yes* and it could be *no*.)

A: *That depends.*

So,

Q: *Is auto racing dangerous?*

A: *If you mean is it dangerous compared to other high-speed sports— no. But if you compare it with watching television on Sunday afternoon—then yes.*

Q: *Is skydiving safe?*

A: *Of course not. If skydiving were safe, the parachute center would not require you to sign a waiver.*

A: *If skydiving were safe, the parachute center would not require us to pay in advance.*

A: *Skydiving probably would not be much fun if it weren't dangerous.*

ONE OF THE REASONS I LIKE EXPERT WITNESS WORK IS THAT YOU CAN ANSWER ALMOST EVERY QUESTION WITH *THAT DEPENDS* AND STILL BE CONSIDERED AN EXPERT.

Now to put skydiving into perspective, you can expect one malfunction every 700 jumps which is why we wear two parachutes. There are 29 fatalities each year; one for every 83,000 jumps. Compare that with 90 people who perish SCUBA diving, 900 who die while bicycling, 7,000 who drown, the 1154 who succumbed to bee stings and the 300 who were hit by lightning. No one will ever tell you skydiving is safe. (But it is exciting). You must weigh the risk and the reward and make a personal decision.

When testifying for the defense, we are trying to show that there are several (29) parachuting fatalities each year. This is just one of them, not the only one. There are more than just a few jumps being made.

You should be provided with all the questions your client-attorney intends to ask you. Work on developing crisp, clear and concise answers.

If you do not have your questions scripted out, you may feel ambushed by your own client-attorney. If you explain yourself in detail, you will make your attorney look good. But do not take your script into court. You do not want to be crucified for having a crib sheet.

For cross-examination, anticipate nasty questions from overbearing attorneys and be prepared to respond without being defensive.

Q: *Doctor, you are using a lot of medical words. What do I have to do to understand what you are saying?*

A: *I am sorry you do not understand but this is the appropriate medical terminology. I will try to explain it again in simpler terms.*

A: *You could start with four years of dental school.*

Q: *Isn't it a fact the deceased skydiver consumed alcohol before boarding the aircraft?*

A: *It was determined there was alcohol present in the deceased.*

A: *What is a fact is he died in the crash when the engine failed on takeoff.*

Subpoenas. If you are subpoenaed by a court, you must appear (if it has jurisdiction over you—generally in the same county, state or a reasonable distance).

If you are hired by a law firm as an expert witness and you do not appear, that firm may sue you since they relied upon your testimony in building their case.

Lay witnesses (performing their civic duty) may be paid as little as $12/day plus mileage while an expert witness (providing a service) may command $1,500/day or more. If you are subpoenaed as a lay witness, do not give away your opinion. For example, if you are a doctor who examined the plaintiff, relay what you did in the examination but do not comment on the meaning of the tests.

A subpoena can work in your favor. It shows you are in court because you are ordered to be there; not because you are doing a favor for the client.

Q: *Aren't you here today because you are making a lot of money?*

A: *I am here today to explain what happened in the accident.*

A: *I am here because I was ordered by the court. I received a subpoena.*

Specific documents and other specific tangible evidence may be ordered to court with a subpoena duces tecum. You may be ordered to bring certain items (such as your file) to court with you.

A good expert witness will:

Know the rules. Read this book, especially the chapters on depositions, trial, and the Federal Rules of Evidence. Review the procedures for the trial and the basic rules of testifying. If you know the rules of the game, you will play it better.

Know the legal issues and the applicable law. Understand the theories of the case (both sides) and the place you occupy in it. Have a clear understanding of your client-attorney's objectives. You must understand the relevancy of your testimony.

Understand legal definitions. You do not want to be trapped by a misunderstanding in cross-examination. Ask for a definition.

Re-read the entire file (every deposition, etc.) in light of what you know about the case today. Underline, take notes, and add to your narrative outline of the facts of the case. You want to refresh your memory on what you said and what everyone else has said so far. In complex cases, you may have to compile an index so that you can locate the material you need quickly.

Base your opinion on legally permissible grounds. Generally, all tests and facts must be entered into evidence.

Review direct examination testimony with the client-attorney. Practice your testimony in the same manner and form you will use at trial. But avoid *sounding* rehearsed.

Some jurors will be hostile. They didn't volunteer, they were drafted. Some will be bored and some will be preoccupied with outside problems. You must gain and maintain their attention and even participation. Help them to understand the scientific aspects of your case. Show them you are a nice person. Persuade them to accept your version of what happened by your manner and demeanor. Look at the jurors' faces. Talk to the ones who are obviously paying attention.

Learn about all the players: opposing attorney, judge, jurors, opposing experts. Decide which jurors to address with each part of your presentation.

Find out if the opposing attorney asks questions in an irritating manner, does a lot of finger pointing or otherwise tries to make a witness feel uncomfortable. If you were deposed by this attorney, think about how you were treated. The

THE CHALLENGE OF THE JURY SYSTEM IS THAT THE EXPERT'S TESTIMONY IS BEING EVALUATED BY 12 PEOPLE WHO ARE NOT SMART ENOUGH TO GET OUT OF JURY DUTY.

questioner who was a gentleman at the deposition may turn into a tiger in court. Discuss these mannerisms and your best counter with your client-attorney.

Ask the client-attorney about the judge's preferences. Will he or she allow you to narrate a string of events in response to a single question or will the judge insist on short answers? At least one federal judge in Oregon requires experts to file their testimony in writing before the trial and allows them only to read from the document verbatim at the trial. Know what to expect.

Suggest and prepare exhibits to illustrate your testimony. They must be large enough to see and clear enough to understand.

Make sure you have done a thorough analysis, run all tests, and so forth.

Anticipate cross-examination questions. Plan your answers. Go over your deposition and formulate explanations for any difficult areas. Research and write out all the facts so you can rattle off your answers quickly if asked. There may be information you want to slip into the answers to other questions. Practice the cross-exam with your attorney. Review all possible questions so you won't be caught off guard on the stand. Make sure you have credible explanations in response to all potential areas of attack. If you are not prepared for 90% or more of the questions, your client-attorney has not done his or her job.

If this is a major case and there is more than one expert witness, coordinate your work with the other experts. Your testimony should be consistent and should not overlap. You do not want the opposing attorney to use you to impeach each other. Read their opinion papers and spend a good deal of time discussing the case. If you get to know the other expert's position and philosophy, you will be able to predict what he or she would say. This preparation is especially important if you are *sequestered* (kept out of the courtroom) and not allowed to hear

THE JURY DECIDES WHICH SIDE HAS THE BEST LAWYER.

the testimony of the other expert. Never disparage the other expert when you are on the stand.

Practice, practice, practice. Anticipate questions and practice the answers. Do not try to wing it.

Going to court. Get a good night's rest. Eat a good breakfast. This is one day it is okay not to stick to your diet. Do not drink alcohol for 24 hours prior to the trial. If you are on medication, tell your client-attorney. You want to be sharp.

Dress to be credible. Project confidence. Look the part and wear regional attire so your jurors will identify with you. If you wear a uniform on the job, wear it to court. Do not overdress or underdress; do not bring undue attention to yourself. Dress for the venue (i.e. dressier when in a big city).

For men, this normally means a suit or conservative jacket and tie. A dark blue pinstripe with a white, plain-collar shirt, and conservative tie is best. Do not wear double-breasted suits; they bunch up when you sit.

Women should wear a conservative dark dress or suit, no pants suits. Wear moderate-height dress shoes. Do not wear a hat, excessive makeup, low-cut dresses or carry a fancy purse. Jewelry should be limited to seven pieces: two earrings (one per ear), two wedding/engagement rings, one watch, one simple necklace and maybe one additional small ring; no bangle or charm bracelets that may rattle as you walk to the stand. You want to look professional, authoritative and bold without being schoolish, homely or provocative.

Be neat. People perceive a sloppy dresser as a person who is also careless in details of testimony. You want to give the impression that you are a serious, quiet, careful individual. You want to look clean, conservative and professional.

Do not wear Rolex watches or expensive jewelry. Do not wear tinted glasses. Jurors may be intimidated. Worse, they may

---

THE CLOSER THE EXPERT BECOMES TO BEING LIKE THE LADIES AND GENTLEMEN OF THE JURY, THE MORE DIFFICULT IT WILL BE FOR THE OPPOSING ATTORNEY TO PORTRAY THEM AS UNETHICAL, HIRED GUNS. — JUANITA R. BROOKS

even think you are a gangster. You want to be respected for your education and knowledge, not your apparent wealth.

Do not wear lapel pins or buttons. A juror may have been kicked out of that organization or disagree with your politics.

Just as clothes make an impression, so do bearing, gestures and tone of voice. Convey a sense of authority with good posture. Restrain gestures. Look like an expert.

Take only your file folder with what you need and no more than your curriculum vitae, fee schedule, narrative, time sheets, bills, reports, and opinion backup documents. Take all facts and data upon which you relied in forming your opinion, but only what you want the other side to have. As in the deposition proceedings, anything in your file is discoverable. Show the file to your client-attorney in the meeting prior to your testimony. He or she will want to filter out all non-discoverable (privileged) information.

Give yourself plenty of time to find a parking place and get to the courtroom. Sit in the spectator section of the courtroom unless witnesses have been *sequestered* (kept out of the courtroom except when testifying).

Watch the judge, jury and opposing attorney and keep score cards on each. Whenever you see any of them writing, note the subject of the testimony at the time. A later check of your notes will reveal the issue they found of interest. Later, you may address these matters in your testimony. You will know the *players* better and this information may provide clues about the outcome of the case.

Pay attention and show respect. Do not read, chew gum, talk or sleep in the courtroom. Jurors feel this is serious business. Do not react favorably or unfavorably to testimony. Jurors may take note of your reactions.

Unless this is a highly technical case where you must continually advise the client-attorney, it is best to stay away from the other people in the trial. Do not pass notes to your

---

YOU WANT THE JURY TO TRUST YOU NOT ENVY YOU.
— BETTY BUCHAN, PH.D., USF COLLEGE OF PUBLIC HEALTH

client-attorney in court. You do not want to appear to be partial to the client in the eyes of the jury. Many jurors do not realize that experts are hired and paid by one side or the other.

In a court trial (no jury) you may be asked to sit with your client-attorney to assist him. Judges are well aware of attorney-expert collaboration. Your counsel will usually know the judge and will know what will or will not offend him or her.

Do not discuss the case in hallways, bathrooms or anywhere you might be overheard. You could be overheard by a juror or give your case away to the opposition.

Do not take family or friends to court to *watch the fun*. Their presence may distract you and cause you to give less than the 100% performance you are being paid for.

You will be examined by both sides: Direct, cross, re-direct and recross. On direct you will get short questions and will supply lengthy answers. On cross-examination, you will receive lengthy questions and try to give short answers.

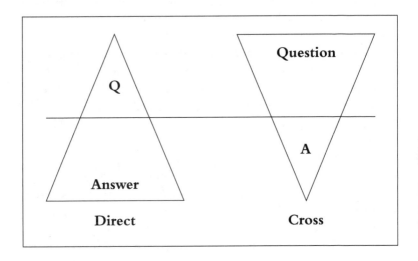

Direct examination. The direct examination is the unfolding of a story told from your side's point of view—and you have an assigned role. Understand the point of your appearance and the part of the overall story you are supposed to supply. You should never have a bad direct examination because you have control over it and a lot of time to prepare for it.

Write down the main points you know you must make. Clear them with your client-attorney. Think: what are we trying to get across? Memorize them. Make sure you get your evidence on the record. If your client-attorney forgets some of them on direct, slip them in on cross. Do not just answer questions, follow a plan.

Direct examinations go better in the morning when the jury is fresh. Cross-examinations are best in the afternoon when the jury is mentally napping. Your client-attorney may try to get you on in the morning and make the direct fairly snappy. Then he or she may try to slow down the afternoon cross in an effort to put the jury to sleep.

Most attorneys prefer that notes not be taken to the stand. But in some cases it is not unreasonable for you to refer to notes in order to be accurate. If your case deals with many figures, for example, you may wish to have these facts with you on the stand. Clear these notes with your client-attorney. Remember, the opposing attorney has a right to see any notes from which you testify.

Also take a clean sheet of paper and a pen to the stand. You may wish to make some notes. There may be some calculations you have made in response to cross-examination. You may want your client-attorney to bring up some points or to define terms such as *the age of retirement*.

Take your deposition transcripts (with corrections) to the stand. If the cross-examiner quotes from it, ask for the page and line. Then take your time reading it, including the paragraph above and below.

On the way to the witness stand, offer your business card to the court reporter. Some experts also drop off a vocabulary list when the case involves difficult terminology. The kindness will be appreciated and your name will be spelled correctly.

Walk to the witness stand with even steps. Carry the folder in your left hand so you won't fumble when raising the right hand to take the oath. It is difficult to regain your composure after dropping the folder contents on the floor. Be confident. Stand upright when taking the oath. Hold your right arm up high with the fingers straight, look the administering officer straight in the eye and say *I do* in a clear voice.

Bring to court only what you need. Everything you bring is discoverable—including the contents of the trunk of your car out in the parking lot. The opposing attorney may make a big deal out of what you bring with you or omit to bring.

As mentioned earlier in Chapter Nine on demonstrative evidence and props, if you have written books on the subject, stack them on the rail of the witness box where the jury can see them.

Sit down in the witness chair confidently. Do not dive into it and do not lean back. Lean forward slightly, keep your hands on the arm rests and look attentive.

Use hand gestures sparingly and only for emphasis. The court reporter can only record words. Count on your fingers to emphasize major points.

First the expert witness must be *accepted* by the judge as an expert in the precise field involved. The technical witness is qualified through skill, training, knowledge or experience. The witness must be an expert, not just someone with experience. You are there to help the jury understand how or why the event happened. Qualifications must be proven to the judge so talk to the judge.

The judge will also determine if an expert is necessary. Cases have been reversed for not allowing an expert to testify but so far none have been reversed for allowing expert testimony.

Presentation during direct examination and cross-examination is made to the jury. Explain to them. Do not talk down to the jury. Be frank and open, as if you were a friend or neighbor. Be sincere, use simple terms. Make eye contact:

watch the jurors, see if they are following you. Do they understand? Are they confused or nodding? If they are not nodding, rephrase and explain again.

People are not used to sitting in one place for hours using their heads. The average education level in the U.S. is less than 10th grade. Use plain language and develop analogies. But do not underestimate the jury. Working together, a jury is pretty smart.

Your client-attorney will present your testimony in three phases. First, he or she will establish who you are and then what you did. This will lay the foundation for your opinion. He or she will:

1. Offer your qualifications as an expert to the judge. Your client-attorney will ask you questions (*voir dire*) about the more relevant portions of your CV. He or she may read right down your CV or may hit just the major points and then weave your credentials into the balance of your testimony.

Present your accomplishments modestly and with a minimum of embellishment. You want to impress the jury, not alienate them. Some of these average people may have an anti-intellectual bias. Review your own CV and be precise about figures and dates. The way you answer these initial questions is important as the jury will be getting their first impression of you.

Q: *Why do you testify?*

A: *I was retained to testify because of my education, experience and expertise in this area.*

A: *To help the jury understand the science and to be part of the judicial system.*

A: *I am the only (sport of) squash expert available. The other*

I WAS VERY STIFF AT FIRST. I WENT TO A DRAMA PROFESSOR WHO ADVISES ATTORNEYS. HE SUGGESTED I PRETEND I HAVE INVITED FRIENDS TO MY LIVING ROOM TO DISCUSS MY OPINION. BE RELAXED. — BRYAN CONLEY, PH.D.

authorities do not wish to get involved. If I did not testify, we would have the blind leading the blind. No one in the courtroom, including the attorneys, would know what really happened. Without my testimony, justice would not be done.

Emphasize pertinent items; do not waste time with non-relevant background. Get to the point and rattle off places and dates. Rehearsing your answers will allow you to speak in sound bites. A good attorney will take the lead on your credentials.

Q: *Don't you have a degree in aeronautical engineering?*

If your client-attorney does not take the lead, if the questions are *open-ended* (i.e. *tell us about your education*), be prepared to count off the relevant schools and degrees.

Slightly understating your qualifications on direct may be advantageous. You may be able to make them more impressive on cross.

Q: *So you have only a bachelor's degree?*

A: *Yes, but I took several graduate courses in my specialty as undergraduate electives.*

The opposing attorney may offer to *stipulate* your qualifications. This means he or she accepts that you are qualified and there is no need to take up court time reviewing your past. In a jury trial, this is a trap. Review of your qualifications is essential to prepare the jury (or judge) for complete acceptance of your testimony.

The judge is usually anxious to get through the qualification issue and hear what you have to say. He or she probably has a copy of your CV and knows who you are.

2. Lay the foundation for your opinions (tests, investigations, facts, etc.) The expert may base his opinion on three sources (Federal Rules of Evidence 703):

a. Acts observed firsthand

b. Evidence presented at trial

c. Data examined outside the court and prepared by a third party (hearsay). The evidence (report) must be of a type reasonably relied upon by experts in the particular field in forming opinions or inferences.

Foundational questions will go something like this:

Q: *Prior to coming to court to testify, did you examine certain documents (equipment, site, etc.)?*

Q: *At whose request was this examination made?*

Q: *When and where did you make your examination?*

Q: *I hand you Plaintiff's deposition, which is identified as Exhibit #1. Is this one of the documents you examined?*

Q: *I hand you (and so on).*

Q: *For what purpose did you examine Exhibit #1?*

Q: *Describe the method of your examination. Is this method of a type used by most experts in your field?*

Q: *As a result of your examination, did you arrive at a conclusion?*

Q: *What is that conclusion?*

Q: *In the course of your work on this case, did you prepare any exhibits to illustrate the basis for your conclusion?*

Q: *Please produce those exhibits, explain how they were made and what they represent.*

Q: *Are these exhibits true and correct reproductions?*

Q: *Using the exhibits, please explain to the court your conclusions.*

Be prepared to count off each thing you did on your fingers: *I visited site; read the depositions of A, B and C; interviewed D, E, and F; researched the following questions, and so on.*

Damage control. If you have a *skeleton* in your closet such as a DUI arrest or a Ph.D. from a mail-order college, be prepared with an answer. Are you an accountant or a CPA? *Board qualified* means you have not passed the test; it is not the same as *board certified*. Tell your client-attorney. He or she will want to defuse the situation by bringing it out on direct examination. Then when the cross-examiner tries to get the admission again and make a big deal of it, your client-attorney may say *Objection, asked and answered.*

If there is a textbook which contradicts some of your claims, it may be presented on cross to your embarrassment. So your client-attorney will defuse the situation by bringing up the matter on direct. During this much friendlier exchange, you will be able to explain why this case is different and an exception. Dealing with difficult questions on direct is much preferable to getting broadsided on cross.

If your skeleton is not related to the question at hand, your client-attorney may ask for a *motion in limine.* If granted, the opposing attorney will not be able to bring up the subject.

3. Ask for your opinion. You will explain what is the general practice in the industry, what caused the accident, etc.

The line of questioning under direct examination proceeds in steps.

(after a line of questioning)

Q: *And based on that, do you have an opinion as to what caused the accident?*

A: *Yes, I do.*

Q: *And what is that opinion?*

A: *(Whereupon you state your opinion.)*

Capsulize your testimony down to three concise sentences. Include your study, finding, conclusions and opinion. Then practice and memorize the statement.

Some experts like to summarize their opinion testimony on one sheet of paper. Their client-attorneys have it entered into evidence and given to the jurors so they may follow along.

Your client-attorney is not allowed to use leading questions or to question you in areas outside your stated expertise. Therefore, the questions will tend to be short, specific and to build on one another.

Demonstrative evidence (enlargements, graphs, tables, charts, X-rays, overlays, models, etc.) show what your opinion is and how you arrived at it. These materials provide interest, clarification and retention to your testimony. Visual aids get attention and stimulate interest. Demonstrative evidence is very effective. Jurors have been socialized to respond to visual aids; they were brought up on television. Your attorney will ask broad questions (such as *explain lift* in an aviation case) to give you an opportunity to teach. Use your demonstrative evidence and elaborate. Present your case point by point.

In working your demonstration, talk to the decision-makers: the jury. Get out of the box with your show-and-tell. Just ask the judge for permission to *approach the jury*. Pass evidence and demonstration materials around to the jury so they can see and feel them. Involve your jury and they will love you.

Stand to one side; do not block the jury's view of your boards. Play to the jury who is your audience. Don't forget that people remember more of what they see, read and do than what they hear. Wake up the jury so they will understand your testimony.

Jurors need visuals to understand something that may be elementary to you. You have studied the entire case; they only know what has been presented to them—and much material has been intentionally withheld. The jury has been confused for several days by the two attorneys. They will love you for making things clear; for making the only interesting presentation. If the jury likes you, they will believe you.

Keep your drawings and models covered until ready for presentation. Build the jury's curiosity, do not distract them during earlier testimony. (See Chapter Nine on demonstrative evidence.)

Try to leave your charts and other demonstrative evidence uncovered when the other side is presenting its case or cross-examining. Leave important pieces of evidence in view so they will make a continuing impression on the jury.

Jurors take demonstrative evidence into the jury room.

JURIES ENJOY BEING AMUSED. THEY ENJOY TAKING PART. PASS YOUR EXHIBITS AROUND. — JUDGE HARVEY HALBERSTADTER

Think of what you want them to have—like the handout for a speech. Put your charts on stiff board so they will stand up against the wall, not slump to the floor out of sight.

The general impression you leave with a jury is more important than answering every question perfectly. Juries go with the expert they find the most believable, the one they trust.

Organization of a trial. The plaintiff (or prosecution) presents its side first. Then the defendant presents its side. You will testify during the presentation made by your side. Expert witnesses usually follow lay (fact) witnesses. For scheduling purposes, some witnesses may be taken out of turn but doing so may interrupt the flow of the presentation and confuse the jury. (See Chapter Eighteen, *A Guide to the Law and the Courts.*)

The judge decides questions of *law* and the admissibility of evidence (what the jury may see or hear). The jury decides questions of *fact*, how much weight to give the evidence (whether to believe you). Therefore, evidence may be allowed by the judge but held to be weak by the jury. Talk to the decision-makers—the jury.

You must know the law governing your field of expertise, but do not offer legal opinions in the course of your testimony. Interpretations of the law are up to your client-attorney and the judge.

Juries normally consist of six, eight or twelve people depending upon the court. There most likely will also be two alternate jurors who will sit through the entire trial in case one of the regular jurors should become incapacitated. The alternates will not be involved in the deliberations at the end of the trial.

In a *court trial* and in suits against the U.S. Government, there is no jury. The judge decides both law and fact. For the purposes of this book, we are going to assume there is a jury.

JUDGES AND JURIES LOVE A CLASS ACT. ALL THEY WILL REMEMBER IS YOUR TIE AND YOUR ATTITUDE.
— JUDGE HARVEY HALBERSTADTER

The lawyer's job is to ask questions. He or she is the *advocate*. The expert witness's job is to answer questions. You are not an advocate for the client, you are an advocate for your opinion. You take an oath to tell the truth, the whole truth and nothing but the truth. The attorney does not.

The expert's role is not to find the truth, or to find the facts, or to find who is right and who is wrong. That is up to the jury.

Address the judge as *Your Honor*. Address the attorneys by title and last name. For example, *Ms. Jones*.

On the stand. Direct *answers* to the attorney and *explanations* to the jury. If your answer is going to be over three sentences, turn to the jury. Limit your answers to ten sentences or the jury will turn off.

Explain your answers clearly so that the least intelligent juror will be sure to understand what you are saying. If you must use technical jargon, be sure to explain each term as you use it. You want to impress the jury but you want them to understand, and you do not want to talk down to them. Also remember that one in ten people over the age of 18 has an *admitted* hearing loss. Some of the rest do not *admit* their impairment. In each jury, one person may not be able to hear you well—and may tune you out.

Powerful language will make you appear more knowledgeable. Say *yes*, not *I suppose so*. Use *93 minutes* not *around an hour and a half*. Say *60 miles per hour*, not *about as fast as a car*. Generalities will make you appear imprecise and/or unsure.

Do not use words you don't use everyday. Using big impressive words may confuse the lawyers while the judge and the jury won't trust you. There are a lot of new terms in the

---

TOO OFTEN AN EXPERT WITNESS BECOMES AN ADVOCATE FOR HIS CLIENT . . . AN EXPERT'S JOB IS TO INFORM THE COURT . . . WHEN EXPERTS TURN INTO ADVOCATES, THEIR CREDIBILITY IS SERIOUSLY WEAKENED AND THEIR EFFECTIVENESS IS SEVERELY HAMPERED. — JUDGE JULIAN JACOBS

legal game and some have peculiar meanings. Make sure you understand them before you use them.

Be a gentle, knowledgeable educator. Avoid buzzwords. Use analogies (*victor airways are highways in the sky*). Be lively and interesting. Practice on a friend. Be direct—don't weasel. Avoid monotone: change the volume, pitch and tone of your voice from time to time. Be confident and self-assured, but not arrogant. Do not memorize testimony. It is best to sound natural and unrehearsed. Take a dose of modesty, good humor and patience with you to the stand. Be yourself.

Some jurisdictions allow the jurors to take notes. If they are writing furiously, slow down.

If you lean slightly against your client-attorney when answering, the jurors will be more likely to believe you are fair, reasonable and competent.

Q: *Would you say...?*

A: *No, but I would say...*

Be careful about taking sides. Do not offer to say whatever your client-attorney wants. Next time, you could find him on the other side and he will ask you about the incident to show you are a *hired gun.*

Your presentation to your client-attorney or to the jury is like a speech. Define your purpose and consider what message you want to leave. Get organized. Be concise. Make every word count. Do not use unnecessarily long explanations or repeat yourself.

There will be times when you will be more effective in getting your point across by using a single dramatic explanation in your testimony to highlight a point you want the jury to remember. Compare the following answers:

IN EVALUATING A CASE, YOU MUST BE IMPARTIAL. IN TESTIFYING, YOU ARE AN ADVOCATE (FOR YOUR POSITION)
— RICHARD SAFERSTEIN

Q: *Do you have an opinion as to whether a reasonably prudent pilot would have attempted a takeoff with this damaged aircraft under those conditions?*

A: *Yes, I do.*

Q: *And what is that opinion?*

A: *I do not think he would have.*

Now consider the same line of questioning with this answer.

A: *I would not have attempted a takeoff under those conditions unless there was a tidal wave coming over the hill.*

As discussed in Chapter Ten on depositions, be very careful in estimating time, speed and distance. Many people cannot estimate these factors accurately, so the opposing attorney may be trying to play upon this. Think about the facts beforehand so you can be accurate. If you are estimating, say so.

Refer to exhibits by number or title. This approach makes you look more polished and credible and helps the court reporter make a clear written transcript of your testimony, which is very important if either side appeals the decision.

The client-attorney is the coach of the team. You are part of the legal system support team. You should support his or her line as long as it is ethically feasible. Do not attempt to take over the lead. He or she is juggling the order of the presentation, timing, which witnesses to call and in what order, and much more. If you try to do something your way, you could botch the case.

If you answer a question incorrectly, correct yourself as soon as possible.

If your client-attorney asks you the same question twice, consider it a signal that your last answer was not what he or she wanted or was not clear enough. When a question is repeated,

DON'T EVER FORGET, YOU WON'T BE ABLE TO GET AWAY WITH MUCH IN FRONT OF THE TWELVE. — MELVIN BELLI SR.

there is an inclination to start with *As I said...* or to simply repeat the answer. Don't. Just answer the question differently. Your client-attorney wants you to rephrase it and elaborate on it. Your client-attorney should signal his or her intent with some different nuance in the question.

When a cross-examiner repeats a question, be careful that your answer does not change or seem to change. If he asks more than twice, your client-attorney should object: *Asked and answered.*

There will be times when it appears that your client-attorney has forgotten to bring out essential facts. You can remind him or her by inserting some key words into the answer for another question. Or say, *That also relates to . . .* He or she may have changed strategy or may simply have forgotten. Your reminder cannot hurt.

Generally, you cannot mention insurance or that a woman has remarried. The revelation of either one may lead to a costly mistrial. In Louisiana, insurers are named parties, sometimes separately represented. They sit in court with everyone else.

Unlike laymen, experts may express opinions relative to matters not observed. Experts may use hearsay evidence if inherently reliable and customarily relied upon by experts in forming their opinion (i.e., a doctor may rely on lab tests).

Be prepared to deal with inconsistencies. Avoid contradicting other technical witnesses on your side.

As said before, the general impression you leave with the jury is more important than answering every question perfectly. Juries often go with the expert they like the best; the one they find the most believable. Do not worry about the things you didn't say. Just make sure the things you did say were well said.

Unless the judge *sequesters* the witnesses (prohibits them from the courtroom), sit through as much of the trial as possible. Listen to the other witnesses. Get to know the players. Sit in back of the courtroom, do not sit with the client's people. You must appear objective.

Industry standards. You may rely on industry or trade association standards in arriving at your opinions. Some standards such as the *Uniform Building Codes*, have been adopted as ordinances by local governments. A standard may help you show (1) a product is defective or free from defects, (2) professional negligence, (3) the failure to provide proper warnings, (4) building and construction defects, (5) the custom and practice of a particular industry, (6) misuse of the product, (7) the compliance with design standards, (8) the proper maintenance of a product, (9) and the correct installation of a product.

Opposing expert. Your opposing expert will be telling the same story, but it has a different ending.

Know what the opposing expert said in court. Try to be there during his or her trial testimony, if permitted. Some experts write furiously on a pad while the opposing expert testifies. The object is to make him or her more careful as well as curious about the notes being taken.

As in the deposition proceedings, it's important to know your opposing expert witness. Find everything he or she has ever published. Investigate his or her background. Find what the expert's teachers have published. A teacher might contradict the expert. If the expert has testified before, contact the lawyers involved and get copies of the depositions and testimony transcripts. Evaluate opposing witnesses' responses. Search for contradictions. Help your client-attorney to discredit or limit testimony of the opposing witness.

Make a few telephone calls to check on the opposing expert's background. Verify each item on his or her CV. Your client-attorney will have an opportunity to attack his or her credibility, and what you find could be very useful.

The opposing expert may be excluded (impeached) if he or she has not faced this specific problem before.

Be restrained in your greeting of the opposing expert during trial, even if you know him or her well. A jury member might see your exchange and your credibility could be damaged. Of course, you should not discuss the case with the opposing expert.

Limiting testimony. It is unlikely you will be able to get enough on your opposing expert to have him *impeached*. Judges do not like to deny an expert to either side. But you may be able to *limit* the expert's testimony.

Q: *Isn't it true you haven't worked on airplanes since 1972?*

A: *Yes.*

(The aircraft in point was manufactured in 1983.)

Q: *Your honor, I move this witness's testimony be limited to aircraft work prior to 1972.*

Q: *Isn't it true that you are an engine mechanic for Lexus automobiles?*

A: *Yes.*

(This case is about a rust-out condition on a Ford.)

Q: *Your honor, since Mr. Expert specializes in engines, he is not fully qualified to render an opinion on body rust. I move this witnesses' testimony be restricted to engines (or to the Lexus).*

Sequestration. While the court is an open proceeding, some judges feel trials move faster and that testimony is less tainted if all witnesses are *sequestered*.

Federal Rules of Evidence: Rule 615. Exclusion of Witnesses:

At the request of a party the court shall order witnesses excluded so that they cannot hear the testimony of other witnesses, and it may make the order of its own motion. This rule does not authorize exclusion of (1) a party who is a natural person, or (2) an officer or employee of a party which is not a natural person designated as its representative by its attorney, or (3) a person whose presence is shown by a party to be essential to the presentation of the party's cause.

It is frustrating for the expert witness to wait in a room or hallway not knowing when he or she will be called or what is going on. It is a handicap to enter a courtroom without knowing the identity and placement of all the players. Is the judge stern? Is the opposing attorney winging it? Or tricky? It is even more difficult when the opposing attorney recounts prior testimony for your evaluation and you do not know if the phrasing is accurate.

Q: *Mrs. Jones (your client) testified that she . . . Do you agree this was her best course of action?*

(This does not sound right to you but you do not know if she did it or didn't do it. To compound your dilemma, your attorney is asleep and fails to jump in to correct the facts and defend you.)

A: *I would have to see the transcript, including the paragraphs above and below her statement, to understand the context of the testimony.*

Never accept the opposing attorney's statement of fact. You need authentication. Ask to read it for yourself. Almost always, the quotation has been taken out of context.

Ask your attorney *not to request* sequestration. In fact, suggest he request you be in court to hear the testimony of one of the witnesses on whom you must rely. If the judge orders it anyway, your client-attorney should object, saying he or she needs you to listen and advise. Your technical help is important to the case. The argument is that experts testify only as to their opinions and must know everything about the case, including witness testimony. It is worth a try.

If you are excluded from the courtroom, visit another trial in the same building to get a feel for the layout and atmosphere. If you do leave the area, make sure your client-attorney knows where to find you.

In very important cases, you may request daily transcripts of the testimony so that you will not be more than a couple days behind.

Being a sequestered witness is like being an airplane pilot: hours and hours of boredom, occasionally interrupted by brief moments of stark terror.

If you are going to be sequestered, arrive at the courthouse early and check out the lay of the courtroom. Many follow the plan of your generic Federal District Court but some are unique. Entering strange territory can throw you off balance.

Cross-examination. The cross-examination is a challenge. Most experts do not like being placed on the spot. It is like being called in by the IRS to explain your tax deductions. But it provides you with an additional opportunity to explain what happened, as well as to influence the jury. Most experts dread the cross; you should treat it as a challenge.

The opposing attorney must show that you are not qualified in this particular area or that you relied on bad data. He or she has three missions during cross-examination:

1. To discredit you. He or she will attack your conduct and character for truthfulness. The cross-examiner will try to show you have little or no theoretical, educational or practical experience or knowledge of the *particular* problem. This experience can be devastating to first-time expert witnesses who have spent a lifetime building a reputation and who are not used to having their integrity or word questioned. You may counter by reciting your credentials from your CV. The cross-examiner will try to show inconsistencies in statements you have made. He or she has reviewed everything you have ever written.

Q: *And you mean to tell the court, you are here to render an opinion and you have only five years experience?*

A: *During those five years, I was able to . . . (Respond to the five, not to the only.)*

2. To discredit the foundations for your opinions. He or she will question whether you have run enough tests, examined enough facts, etc. to be able to form a valid opinion. For example: *how can you be sure if you have not visited the scene of*

MOST LAWYERS VIEW THE CROSS-EXAMINATION OF THE EXPERT AS THE MOUNT EVEREST OF CROSS-EXAMINATIONS.
— JUANITA R. BROOKS

the accident? He or she will try to discredit some of your tests and other evidence and may try to have some or all of your testimony eliminated because you failed to run the right tests.

Q: *Did you do A, B and C?*

(He wants to make you look as though you did not do your homework.)

A: *Of course not. Such a test would not prove anything here. The test was not necessary.*

(He probably will not dare to ask you to explain.)

3. To discredit your conclusions (testimony). The opposing attorney may try to show you are confused and therefore could be wrong. He or she will have to know a lot about the subject to challenge you here. But be careful; he or she may.

The opposing attorney will attack you in two ways. First he or she will attack your credentials with the hope of disqualifying you. Then your opinion will be attacked. He or she wants to appear to be skillful, knowledgeable and fair while making you look evasive, partial and confused: a fool or a liar.

Q: *Are you being paid to testify?*

A: *No sir, I am not being paid to testify. I am being paid for my time, my testimony is my own.*

A: *I am being paid to be here today just as you are.*

You are not being paid for your *opinion*. You are being paid to study the case and form an opinion (come to a conclusion). You are charging the client your normal hourly rate. If you were not here, you would be working somewhere else. Do not be embarrassed to say how much you charge. The higher the amount, the more you are worth. It is the person who is reluctant to tell the jury how much he or she is being paid who can be corrupted by a lot of money.

Of course, you may answer the question this way:

Q: *How much are you being paid?*

A: *My company bills $230 per hour.*

Q: *Did your client pay you for forming this opinion?*

A: *My client paid me for the time I spent and am spending now. My opinion is what the facts, science and logic demand.*

If all your fees have been paid in full prior to your court appearance, all parties will be assured that your opinion and testimony are not contingent on the verdict of the jury. The outcome will not affect your finances.

Q: *Do you often testify as an expert witness?*

A: *Yes.*

Q: *Then you are a professional expert, a hired gun?*

A: *I am a professional pilot and I spend 5-10% of my time testifying as an expert.*

A: *I would like to think that I am being consulted frequently because of my professional competence and reputation.*

Your client-attorney may bring up the compensation question more gently during the direct examination. This is a tactic to defuse the question; to take this offensive play away from the opposing attorney.

This same tactic may be used whenever you think the opposing side will bring up an uncomfortable topic. For example, if you made a statement in your deposition which you wish to alter now, your client-attorney should bring it up on direct and ask you to explain the reason for the change.

When the opposing attorney attacks your credibility, keep calm. His or her actions are not unexpected. You knew what to expect. It is all part of the job, and the best way for the expert

---

WHEN A JURY . . . BELIEVE THAT THE EXPERT IS SIMPLY A PUPPET ON PAYROLL, THEY MAY . . . COMPLETELY DISREGARD THE TESTIMONY.
— RICHARD ANDERSON IN *EXPERTS-AT-LAW* MAGAZINE

to survive is to play the game. The jury is likely to be favorably impressed if you stay cool under pressure.

Do not argue with the opposing attorney and do not defend yourself. Try not to become flustered, stubborn, or recalcitrant; to do so is to concede your point. Use the opportunity to further persuade the jury. Turn to the jury and give a whole new explanation. The opposing attorney will probably be afraid to ask too many questions if he finds he is only opening the door for you. You do not win by slaying your opposing witness, you win when the jury accepts your version of the story.

A good opposing attorney will ask questions on cross that must be answered in the affirmative. The object is to march you down his trail getting you to agree, agree and agree. You can bet you do not want to go down that trail. Try to break up the rhythm by repeating the question and giving more than a one-word answer.

Never look at your client-attorney while you are being cross-examined. Everyone will think you are waiting for a signal. If you really want an objection, and feel it is warranted, make it yourself.

A: *Counselor, I have already answered that question at least three times.*

Trial techniques vary. Professional opponents can be a joy to work with. They let you answer and do your job. They deserve straight answers. On the other hand, if the opposing attorney is nasty, or disruptive, it is OK to slip in a zinger now and then. Just make sure the judge and jury are disgusted with the opposing attorney's conduct first. Some of those *I-wish-I'd-said-that* answers are noted in this chapter.

Some expert witnesses prefer to have a competent attorney on the other side. It is hard to give an intelligent answer to a stupid question.

IN COURT, SURVIVAL IS NOT THE OBJECTIVE. YOU MUST WIN.

Refuse to be brow-beaten. Cross-examinations are limited to matters covered in the examination, but witness credibility may be attacked at any time. Calmly point out where he or she is wrong. The jury recognizes when an attorney is out of line. Think of yourself as being on a television talk show where the host is giving you a hard time.

Remember, opposing attorneys are good at what they do. They cross-examine witnesses for a living. But, as good as they are, they do not know as much about your subject as you do.

Humor. Juries enjoy accidental humor but may be offended by deliberate humor—especially from women. To them, this is serious business. Jurors believe they have an important job. You may laugh at obvious humor but be careful about being the joker yourself.

Q: (Menacingly) *Have you ever been accused of anything?*

A: *Yes, sir, I have been accused of just about everything.*

Q: (Sarcastically) *Well, that is new information. Have you formed any other opinions today?*

A: *Yes sir. I am forming one of you right now.*

Spontaneous humor makes you seem warm, friendly and human.

Unfortunately, humor cannot be used to warm up the jury. However, a good client-attorney will prepare the jurors for you. Here's an example:

I know these blood-alcohol percentages are hard to understand but Dr. David Benjamin is coming on Wednesday. He is not only the noted expert on the subject, he is a caring, sharing teacher who is going to show us how this unfortunate accident occurred.

WHEN YOU COME UP TO THE COURT OF APPEALS, IT IS ALL RIGHT FOR YOU ONCE IN A WHILE TO ACT INDIGNANT. BUT NEVER BE INDIGNANT. (IT WILL DESTROY YOUR OBJECTIVITY AND JUDGMENT UNDER FIRE.) — JUDGE LEARNED HAND

Follow these three basic rules during cross-examination:
1. Look directly at the attorney asking the question. People equate *eye contact* with sincerity. They assume that those who can't look you in the eye must be hiding something.
2. Listen to the question and pause before answering. A short pause allows you to phrase precisely your answer and lets your client-attorney object to the question if it is inappropriate.

If your client-attorney objects, stop talking and wait for the judge to rule. You will be told to answer the question or you will be given a new question.

Analyze the question. It may be *unclear and ambiguous*. Do not guess. Be sure you grasp all the terminology. Do not hesitate to have the question rephrased. If you do not communicate your lack of understanding, it will be assumed that you comprehend the question and that your answer is a whole and complete response to it. You may always rephrase the question yourself.

A: *Are you asking me if I meant . . . (whatever)?*

If you think the opposing attorney is trying to be tricky, ask him or her to reword the question so that the meaning will be clearer.

When a question has more than one part to it, ask to have it rephrased in single elements. Watch out for questions containing the words *or* or *and*.

A: *That was about three questions. Let me take them one at a time.*

The opposing attorney may ask you a question which does not call for new facts. Most likely, he is seeking a different answer. Do not give it to him. The question is considered *argumentative* if he is seeking an explanation of a previous answer.

Watch for questions that inaccurately summarize prior testimony or assume facts that are untrue. Do not accept this characterization of data, assumptions or descriptions of events. Listen carefully and point out each and every inaccurate statement in the summarization.

Assumptions may only be made on facts which are in evidence. *Foundation* must exist or your answer will admit the assumed fact.

3. Turn to the jury and give a complete explanation. By turning, you break eye contact with the questioner. Now speak quickly so the questioner will have trouble reining you in or cutting you off.

If you are interrupted, you have some choices. You may pause respectfully and maintain silence until he or she lets you continue.

Q: *Why are you silent?*

A: *May I continue?*

A: *You interrupted when I was speaking.*

A: *The court reporter can only record one speaker at a time so I am waiting to make sure you are finished so that I may continue uninterrupted.*

Or you may continue talking—even over the questioner's words. He or she will be perceived as the aggressor. Likely, the jurors will feel the opposing attorney is being unfair because you are not being allowed to present your evidence.

Remember that you are the one with the duty to tell the *whole* truth; insist on being allowed to do so. The cross-examiner may love the first part of your answer and hate what he knows is coming next. Make sure the jury hears the part he hates.

The audience is the jury. Do not concentrate on what the opposing attorney is thinking. Consider what the jury is thinking.

Give a responsive answer but do not volunteer additional information. Do not give him or her an opening to another line of questioning. Remember, the longer the answer, the more you are liable to be giving away.

Answer questions with *yes* or *no*, not *un-huh* or with a nod of the head. The court reporter may have difficulty taking down your response. Take turns speaking. The court recorder can only record one person at a time.

It is better to say *I do not know* or *I do not remember* than to make a guess.

Do not use expressions like: *honestly, in all candor, to tell the truth, and I am doing the best I can.* Do not say *always* or *never.* The opposing attorney will jump on adjectives and superlatives. Avoid absolutes unless they are absolutely true.

Q: *Would you swear that is what happened in your tests?*

A: *Yes.*

A: *I was sworn to tell the truth when I took the stand.*

Q: *Have you ever lied?*

A: *Not under oath.*

Be fair and frank. Do not be too anxious to please or too eager to fight. Do not argue or become angry with the opposing attorney. An angry witness is not listening to the questions and is prone to volunteer unasked for information. This is precisely what the opposing attorney is hoping for. It is always better to smile and proceed. Sarcasm, belligerence and loss of composure may lead to careless testimony and they certainly make an adverse impression. Do not undermine your credibility and ability to persuade. Exhibit the same demeanor on cross that you did on direct.

Q: *Do you enjoy being an expert witness?*

A: *I enjoy the challenge.*

A: *I enjoy seeing justice being done.*

Do not resist. Go out of your way to cooperate with the opposing attorney. Show the jury you are impartial. They know you are on one side but express an air of impartiality. Help the

---

THERE IS ONLY ONE WAY TO FIND OUT IF A MAN IS HONEST—ASK HIM. IF HE SAYS YES, YOU KNOW HE IS A CROOK.

— GROUCHO MARX

opposing attorney with pronunciations; give him something. Most judges consider experts to be hired guns; they are surprised when an expert is helpful and truthful. Make admissions quickly and tersely. Do not make the examiner drag them out of you.

Q: *So you admit your client was at least partially responsible for his own injuries?*

A: (If, for example, he assumed the risk) *Yes.*

Concede the obvious.

Q: *If inflation were to rise substantially, would the wages of the plaintiff increase just 2% per year?*

A: *No.*

The jury will like you if you have no apparent bias, good credentials, a pleasing personality, are clear, objective and focused, are not confusing or complex, and know what you are talking about.

Courtroom demeanor. Nonverbal signs may make a greater impression on the jury than your testimony. Studies show that actual words spoken may account for as little as seven percent of a message while the other 93 percent comes from nonverbal elements. In other words, how you say it is more important than what you say. The jury is weighing tone of voice, rate of speech, gestures, posture, eye contact, distance and dress. Do you look and sound like you know what you are talking about? Remember, it is not just what you know that counts, it is what the jury understands and believes you know.

You must play the part. You must sound the part, act the part, look the part and effectively demonstrate the part. You are a professional.

THERE IS A HIGH POSITIVE CORRELATION BETWEEN HOW MUCH WE LIKE SOMEONE AND HOW INCLINED WE ARE TO ACCEPT WHAT THAT PERSON SAYS.
— BETTY BUCHAN, PH.D., USF COLLEGE OF PUBLIC HEALTH

Everything you do around the courthouse is significant; your dress, speech, actions in the courtroom, meetings in the elevators, etc. Jurors are sensitive to behavior on and off the witness stand.

Respond respectfully. Accept counsel's aggression graciously. He or she has a right to question you. If you respond with smart talk or an evasive answer, he or she may jump down your throat or the judge may correct you. Be wary of a nice opposing attorney, too—he or she may be sneaking up on you.

Understand the question. Have it repeated if necessary. Give thoughtful, considered answers.

If the opposing attorney becomes abusive, become more of a gentlemen (or lady). One way to show your concern without revealing your anger is to say *Counsel, your attitude is so offensive, I could not concentrate on the question.* And, remember, your words go on the record which may be useful to you later.

Be polite and keep your answers short. You want to get off the stand quickly without drawing attention to your cross-examination. If you have made any wrong impressions with the jury, your client-attorney will correct them on redirect.

When relaying conversations, indicate whether you are paraphrasing or quoting verbatim.

Your credibility as an expert witness is based on five factors:

1. Your qualifications
2. The accuracy and thoroughness of your investigation and personal observations
3. The accuracy of the hypothetical question or other information supplied to you on cross-examination
4. The validity of your conclusions
5. Your appearance, demeanor and attitude on and off the stand

---

THOSE WHO GOD WISHES TO DESTROY, HE FIRST MAKES ANGRY.
— EURIPEDES

Avoid obscenities, racial slurs and other inappropriate language. Do not refer to the county engineer as a "bureaucrat." Remember, every word is being listened to by the jury and recorded by the stenographer.

Leading questions are those containing the answer, to which you are only asked to agree. They are *leading* because you have been given the answer. Your client-attorney may not be allowed to use leading questions during your direct or redirect examination. However, the opposing attorney is permitted to use leading questions during cross-examination and recross. If any part of the question is not correct, you may say that you cannot *entirely* agree. Then the opposing attorney has to decide if he wants to ask you *why?*

Putting words in your mouth. Beware when the opposing attorney says *Is it fair to say* . . . Phrases such as this mean the attorney is about to put his or her slant on your testimony and you can bet it does not favor you.

Q: *Is it fair to say . . . ?*

A: *It is better to say . . .*

A: *No, it is not fair to say that. What I said was . . .*

Q: *Now you have stated . . .*

A: *No, that is not what I said. What I said was . . .*

Q: *If I can sum up your testimony . . .*

A: *Let me restate my position . . .*

Q: *Isn't it true that . . . ?*

    (If it is not or if any part is not)

A: *No. (If you do not want to explain).*

A: *Not quite. What I said was . . .*

    (If you want to repeat something he hates)

A: *With one exception . . .*

A: *That is almost correct.*

A: *Not exactly.*

Non-questions. If the opposing attorney makes a statement and then pauses for your reaction, do not answer. If the people in the courtroom turn to you expecting an answer, you might try the following to toss the ball back to him and force him to state a question.

Q: *Well, that seems a little hard to believe.*

A: (Take advantage of the opening to illustrate your opinion.) *I know it may seem hard to believe that the plaintiff needs $500,000 when his earnings were only $20,000 per year. The interest on $500,000 at 7% is $35,000 per year but these losses must extend for 40 years and this $500,000 must grow to $700,000 to fund the last 20 years of loss.* (And so on)

A: *If that is a question, sir, I do not understand what it is.*

A: *Is there a pending question? You just made a speech.*

Hypothetical questions combine facts and circumstances and ask you to express an opinion. They are questions in which you are asked to assume that facts and other matters testified to by other witnesses are correct, and to state an opinion based on that assumption. Hypothetical questions must not be misleading or unfair but they are almost always a sign of a mine field. *Suppose this were the case . . . .* or, *Assuming this and that and this, what would you expect a rational person in this area to do?* Keep your eyes open and tread carefully.

The plaintiff is advancing one set of facts and their expert draws a conclusion. The defendant advances another set of facts and their expert draws a different conclusion. The jury has to decide which set of facts to believe and go with that expert.

Hypothetical questions asking you to assume facts must consist of the following. Keep these three rules in mind:

1. Be supported by the evidence (facts which have been admitted into evidence by one side or the other). Therefore, hypotheticals come after all evidence is in.

2. Be factually consistent.

Q: *(Hypothetical question)*

A: *Hypothetically yes, In this case no.*

A: *I do not believe that to be true based on what I know of this case.*

3. Contain enough facts to draw a probable conclusion.

Q: (Hypothetical question)

A: *Yes, but . . .*

A: *That is a great hypothetical question but it does not apply to this situation. So, my hypothetical answer to your hypothetical question has to be...*

A: *That is hard to answer. Using hindsight and sitting here now, I might give one answer but actually being there in an emergency situation, I might have another. I do not know what my mind-set would have been or what I might have been triggered to do.*

A: *Well. That depends.*

Q: *Assume (this and that). Your client testified she. . . (did something). Do you feel this was the most prudent course of action?*

(It does not sound right but you were not present when your client testified.)

A: *I will have to see the record, including the paragraphs above and below that statement to understand the context in which she said that.*

If you counter a hypothetical attempt and it is repeated and reworded, the jurors will lose track of the question and the point. Hypotheticals are only effective when your answer comes right after the question.

Make sure you have enough information to answer the hypothetical question. Listen carefully and be careful what you concede.

Treat the opposing attorney the same way you did your client-attorney during direct examination. You are a professional, you have analyzed the facts, you are there to communicate information to the jury. Know what you said in your deposition and give the same answers, using the same words.

Do not say *that is all that happened.* Say *That is all I remember happening.* Something may trigger additional thoughts later.

Answers on cross-examination should be limited to *yes* and *no,* if possible. Do not say *I think* or *I believe.* It is OK not to know minute details such as exact dates. It is OK to say *I do not remember.* Do not volunteer information or open doors for the opposing attorney to ask more questions.

If the line of inquiry strays from your field, do not stretch your credibility by pretending to know the answer. For example, if you are an expert in parachutes and you are asked if the materials and construction are the same on spinnakers, it is OK to say: *I do not know. I am not a nautical expert. If you can describe the manufacture of spinnakers, perhaps I can compare the materials and construction.* You can always say: *That requires further investigation.* Arrogant people make poor expert witnesses. Be humble.

If the question deals with the subject of your expertise and you do not know, you can always say *I was not asked to research that.*

Yes or No. You can be required to give a simple yes or no answer if the question is proper, but you have a right to explain your one-word answer. On cross, the opposing attorney is looking for short answers; he or she will not ask *open-ended* questions. They do not want to give the jury the impression that you can be trusted to give reliable information. They know you have answers so they are not likely to ask you for them.

One very effective technique for answering questions is to rephrase the question, adding an explanation so that your answer is very clear to the jury. Answer the questions as though you were being interviewed on a television talk show.

Q: *Please answer with a yes or no.*

A: *I can't answer with a yes or no without leaving a false impression with the jury.*

Then if the judge instructs you to answer *yes* or *no*, the jury will know there is something missing. If you answer *well...no* (or *yes*), the opposing attorney probably will not pursue the line of questioning. Or, try:

A: *Yes, with reservations.*

Another choice is to answer *yes, but.* The jurors will know there is more.

If the opposing attorney is persistent and you repeat that you wish to explain why you cannot answer with a yes or no, your client-attorney may object on the grounds that you are being harassed.

If the judge tells you to answer yes or no, it is up to your client-attorney to give you a chance to explain on redirect.

(Later in the testimony)

A: *I gave an incomplete answer in response to an earlier question and would like to correct it.*

If you restate the question prior to answering it, you may turn it slightly to your own advantage.

The long question. The longer the question, the more qualifiers it contains and the more qualifiers, the more opportunities you have to find an exception and disagree.

A: *The question is complex, would you mind breaking it up?* or,

A: *Your question was so long, I got lost.* or,

A: *I am afraid that question is too convoluted. Why don't we take the elements one at a time?*

Do not ask the judge for advice. If the question is improper, it is up to your client-attorney to object.

If your client-attorney objects to a question as being *without foundation, misleading or improper*, take it as a signal that the question is tricky or important. After the judge rules, ask to have the question rephrased.

It is OK to admit you were wrong. If you do not know a fact or circumstance, do not offer to look it up. The opposing attorney will want to know where you plan to look it up, allowing him or her to subpoena records he or she may not have known existed.

Q: *Isn't this possible?*

A: *No sir, it is not possible. Not under the facts of this case. Not from what I have seen.*

Avoid mannerisms. They make you look nervous and the jury will think you are not telling the truth.

Marking exhibits. If you are asked to mark a map, chart or model, make sure you fully understand it. If you are asked to pinpoint something on a map, cover yourself by saying you are not familiar with this particular map (of course, you are familiar with the *area* covered by the map). Then draw a large circle instead of a dot.

Learned treatises are not admissible as substantive evidence but they may be used to contradict and impeach you during cross-examination. Expert witnesses may not quote passages from someone else's book, journal article or other tome. They may, however, base their opinions on standard authoritative texts. If you referred to or considered a passage from a book, you can be cross-examined on the entire text. Do not admit the book is *authoritative*.

Opposing attorneys are allowed to quote passages from a book to try to impeach you as a witness. If you are asked about a passage in a book or article, ask to see it. Read the whole page. You might even ask for a lengthy recess in which to read and digest the entire chapter or article. It is not likely the judge will allow the opposing attorney to press the issue. The passage is probably being taken out of context. Know your field and be prepared to argue for your stand if you disagree with a learned treatise. See Federal Rules of Evidence 803 (18).

Q: *Is this book an authoritative source; a recognized source of professional knowledge?*

A: *If you mean by authoritative, is it perfect? No.*

Q: *Is this book authoritative?*

A: *If you mean by authoritative is this a book with a lot of good information? Yes. But if you mean have I read the entire book recently and do I agree with everything in it? No.*

Q: *Do you agree with this book?*

A: *It is a widely-used reference and is useful but not authoritative. I read this book, and most of the other books on the subject, and based my opinion on the accumulated knowledge.*

Q: *You are not familiar with this article?*

A: *With over 600 journals and 30,000 articles each year, no one can read them all. But I will read it now and give you my opinion.*

Q: *Isn't Dr Guru the universally recognized authority on this subject?*

A: *I am familiar with Dr. Guru's writings but not everyone agrees with every statement she has ever made.*

Quoting from your book or deposition. The most effective manner of impeaching a witness is to find a passage in his or her book or prior testimony which reaches an opposite conclusion to the one professed in court. The opposing attorney may research everything you have ever written and said.

(Opposing attorney reads passage from your book)

Q: *Did you write that?*

A: *Yes, if that was a literal reading of my book.*

Q: *Do you agree with it?*

A: *May I see the page you are reading from?*

If confronted with a passage read out of one of your books, journal articles or past deposition transcripts, always ask to see the entire document before answering. Once you read the page, your memory will be refreshed, the passage will be in context and a good answer will almost always become clear to you. No one is a greater expert on what you have written than you.

Q: HOW DO YOU TELL WHEN YOUR WRITING OR DEPOSITION IS BEING QUOTED OUT OF CONTEXT?

A: WHEN THE OPPOSING ATTORNEY'S LIPS ARE MOVING.

But what if the conclusion in your book is different from the one you are proposing today?

Expert: *Counselor, will you please turn to the reverse of the title page in that book? It should be about page five.*

Attorney: *OK, I have it.*

Expert: *Please read the copyright date on that page.*

Attorney: *1978.*

Expert: *There have been a lot of changes since 1978 and one is the prevalent thought on that subject. Books can only reflect thought up to the day they are printed.*

If you are questioned on any part of a document on direct examination, you may be cross-examined on anything else in it. For this reason, your client-attorney may be reluctant to question you about many documents.

Q: *But didn't you publish this book yourself?*

(He or she is trying to make your book appear to be worthless because it was self-published. He or she is implying that no reputable publisher thought enough of your manuscript to invest in it.)

A: *Yes, I am a publisher too.*

A: *Yes. I publish my own books for three reasons: To keep control of the content, to get to press much faster and to make more money.*
(You may expand on each area.)

Q: *Why didn't you bring these records with you today?*

A: *Because there isn't any information in those records which is inconsistent with my testimony. I didn't need them.*

Q: *How much time do you spend in the practice of your profession as opposed to testifying?*

Remember, you are not a *professional expert witness*. You are a professional, working today as an expert witness. (See Chapter Seven on maintaining competence.)

Q: *Is all your time spent consulting?*
(What if you *are* a full-time expert witness?)

A: *Yes, I am a specialist.*

Q: *Do you always testify for the plaintiff (or defendant)?*

A: *I have a fairly even balance of cases.*

A: *40% of my billings are for the defense.*

A: *75% of my cases are for the plaintiff because they have the burden of proof.*

Check your records. 40% of your billings could come from 10% of your cases or,

A: *Quite often, by the time the defendant hears he is being sued, I have already been hired by the plaintiff.*

A: *Most of my cases have not even gone to trial because I have recommended to my defendant-client that he pay or to my plaintiff-client that he drop the case.*

A: *While I have testified slightly more for the plaintiff, I have an even balance of cases overall. Most of my cases do not go as far as court.*

Q: *Would you agree with the statement "if the student fails to learn, the instructor has failed to teach?"*

A: *Some people learn and still do it their own way.*

Q: *Are (structural engineering) experts 100% correct?*

A: *I do not understand the logic of your question.*

Q: *Well, have you ever been wrong?*

A: *Of course. But not today.*

Q: *Wouldn't it be fair to say...*

A: *What does "fair" mean?*

Q: *Isn't it a fact that ...*

A: *Under all circumstances?*

Q: *Wouldn't you agree?*

A: *On a scale of 0 to 100?*

You might feel it is *somewhat* fair to say it and you do want to be fair so you may be tempted to agree.

A: (Do not agree and explain your reason.)

Some experts like to say *no* if any part is wrong. Then the opposing attorney must decide if he wants to continue pursuing this line of questioning.

Q: *Do you want the jury to understand that...*

Listen closely to this one. Make it clear what you want the jury to understand.

Q: *Do you really believe that position?*

A: *Yes.*

or, you may go on the offensive and take advantage of the opening:

A: *I am glad you asked me that question. Ever since I first heard of this case and discovered what the defendant did to the plaintiff I have felt frustrated and completely disgusted.*

Q: *Don't you think a warning label would have made a difference?*

A: *No sir, warning labels have not stopped people from smoking.*

Q: *Did you discuss your testimony with counsel?*

A: *Of course. I gave him an objective description of where the case stood and he told me some of the questions I could expect to be asked. He also told me to come in here and tell the truth.*

Q: *Have you discussed this case with the opposing expert?*

A: *We are members of the same professional organizations and attend the same meetings. It is difficult to avoid meeting him, talking to*

UNDER CROSS-EXAM, DEMONSTRATE IMPARTIALITY. BE HONEST, COOPERATIVE AND FAIR AND WHAT YOU SAID UNDER DIRECT WILL CARRY MORE WEIGHT. — RICHARD SAFERSTEIN

him and even working with him. The subject came up but I did not volunteer any information.

Watch for this standard cross-examination trick: After your brief answer, opposing counsel pauses and gazes at you expectantly. You will feel an overwhelming pressure to say something more. Stop. If the attorney wants more, he or she can ask for it.

Beware of the opposing attorney who acts dumb. He or she may be trying to convince the jury this is such a complicated area, the client could not have possibly understood what he or she was getting into.

Q: *Skydiving is a very complex subject and I am having difficulty understanding it. What do I have to do to comprehend what happened?*

A: *Allow me to explain again in different terms.*

A: *You could do what your client did: take the First (parachute) Jump Course.*

All of these answers have been used. Some are guaranteed to get the expert into trouble unless the opposing attorney is badgering him.

Q: *Have you ever worked for this law firm in the past?*

(He or she is trying to show you are a *hired gun*.)

A: *Yes, Humpty, Dumpty and Gander is one of the major aviation, more specifically parachuting, law firms and I am one of the major technical experts for parachutes so our paths often cross. In fact, I am probably the only parachute expert they know.*

It may help to study the cases you have worked on for the firm to see how you were initially contacted. You may find good reasons for working so many cases for the same firm. One might be that you were first contacted by other firms and referred to your client-attorney.

The attorney you are working with on this case may have

IF YOU ARE A HIRED GUN, BE A STRAIGHT SHOOTER.
— RICHARD SAFERSTEIN

met you for the first time as an adverse expert and been impressed by your honesty and competence. This can be brought out on direct.

Q: *We have worked together before haven't we?*

A: *Yes.*

Q: *In fact, the first time I met you, you were an expert for one of my adversaries, weren't you?*

A: *That is true.*

You may wish to make up a case log of your work with this firm.

My work for Humpty, Dumpty and Gander

as of September 20, 1998

Chicken v. Fox: First contacted by John Moore of Moore and Moore. He passed me on to H, D & G.

Cat v. Mouse: Contacted by Alan Levin, President of General Mouse. He recommended me to H, D & G.

Smith v. Jones: Larry Knight called me on January 11, 1997. Came to me because of work on previous cases.

Peters v. General Mouse: Recommended by General. Contacted by H, D & G on December 1, 1998. Also worked for Simple, Simon and Pie of Baltimore.

Many lawyers subscribe to the maxim *you can't win the case on direct examination but can lose it on cross.* Don't try to break even but be satisfied if you do.

Redirect examination. The redirect is done by your client-attorney for the purpose of clearing up confusion in the

---

UNLESS THE OPPOSING LAWYER CLEARLY MAKES HIS POINT WITH YOU ON CROSS-EXAMINATION, YOU HAVE PROBABLY WON THE CONTEST.

cross-examination. If you were not damaged in the cross-examination, your client attorney will *have no further questions.* If your client-attorney conducts a re-direct, the opposing attorney will get another shot at you in recross. Questions on redirect are limited to the scope of the cross-examination.

Recross-examination. The recross is done by the opposing attorney. Questions are limited to the scope of the redirect. The recross is usually quite short but can be crucial. Stay on your toes.

Repeat your main theme in both direct and cross-examination if you can. Try to end your testimony on a high note. The attorney will try to get in the last word to exercise his power.

Jury instructions. The jury will receive several instructions from the judge before retiring to the jury room. The instruction regarding your testimony will go something like this:

You have heard evidence in this case from witnesses who have testified as experts. The difference between expert witnesses and the other witnesses is that the expert witnesses may express their opinions. However, an expert's opinion is only reliable when given on a subject about which you believe him to be an expert. Like other witnesses, you may believe or disbelieve all or any part of an expert's testimony.

It is humbling when you realize both how important your testimony may be to the case and how it may be treated by the decision makers.

Ten fundamentals for testifying in court:

☞ Be a real expert. Stick to what you know.

☞ Tell the truth. Never lie.

☞ Listen to the whole question.

☞ Answer the question exactly as phrased. You are being recorded.

☞ Be respectful to everyone, especially opposing counsel.

☞ Do not argue or insult opposing counsel. Let him or her beat up on you.

☞ Show the jury you know what you are talking about.

☞ Help the jury to understand the complex nature of the case. Explain buzzwords and technical words that may not be common to them. Be real. Invite the jury to like you. Be alive and enthusiastic.

☞ Look the jury in the eye.

☞ Speak forthrightly.

Afterwards. When you leave the witness stand, wear a confident expression, and walk directly out of the courtroom unless your client-attorney has instructed you to stay. Do not look triumphant or relieved. Do not stop to talk to the client-attorney or wish the client good luck. You want to look impartial.

Leave the building and get out of the area. You are a busy professional, you must return home to help other clients. You do not have time to sit around to see how the case turns out.

If you are still in the building, you run the risk of being called back to the stand by the opposing attorney.

As long as you are in the courthouse, you are on stage. Be careful. The person you cut off in the parking lot could be a juror. The person you complain to in the elevator could be a juror.

Do not talk to members of the jury outside the courtroom. You will see them in the halls and on the street and there will be a temptation to mention the case. It is okay to offer a simple *good morning* and jurors seem to like this. Do not start a conversation. If a juror starts talking, politely explain this is not permitted. *Excuse me, we are not supposed to talk to each other.* Do not cause a mistrial.

Do not talk to the press until the case is over. Be polite, offer your card but do not pour out your feelings unless you have the express permission of your client-attorney. You

---

EXPERT WITNESSES DO NOT WIN OR LOSE CASES. THEY WORK FOR ATTORNEYS WHO WIN OR LOSE CASES.

have been paid by your side and you have a duty and a relationship to them. They may wish to issue a written news release or to otherwise handle the press themselves. Just say that all statements will be forthcoming from your client-attorney. Remember, the case is not over until the time for appeal has lapsed.

Fatigue. Testifying for any length of time is tiring. Opposing attorneys know this and may try to tire you out so that you will lose your composure and say things that are incorrect or things that hurt you or your testimony. Symptoms of witness fatigue are tiredness, crossness, nervousness, careless answers, willingness to say anything to get off the witness stand, and anger.

Let the opposing attorney hammer away at you. If you are tired, so is the jury. They will side with you. Some attorneys strategize their case to wear down the jury. The hope is that the jury will make a quick decision just to be able to get out and go home.

If you go on the stand after lunch, the opposing attorney may try to keep you on until the end of the day with testimony to continue in the morning. That way, he or she has time to dream up some new questions and you can spend an anxious night worrying about your performance.

Conclusion. The case is not over until the time for appeals has passed. In some jurisdictions, there are rules on file retention. Do not destroy your files, you may need some of the material again.

BEFORE TESTIFYING IN COURT, RE-READ THIS CHAPTER AND CHAPTER TEN ON DEPOSITIONS.

CHAPTER TWELVE

☙

HOW MUCH IS YOUR KNOWLEDGE WORTH?

Expert witnesses generally charge between $800 and $5,000 per day, depending on their type and degree of specialty.

How much you can charge depends upon the going rate as well the amount of competition. If you have developed certain special testing techniques and/or have experience in the field, you can charge relatively more. Fees tend to be higher in California. You want to charge what you are worth but you do not want to price yourself out of the market.

Some experts who work in small towns feel they can't charge as much as similar experts in the big city.

Some experts reduce fees for the indigent, children, and agencies such as the Legal Aid Society, or do a small amount of *pro bono publico* (for the public good or for free) work. They feel that if the attorney is willing to work for less or nothing, they should too.

For examples of fees in many different fields of expertise, send for *Guide to Experts' Fees* published by the National Forensic Center. The address is in the Appendix.

The amount you charge for testifying should be at least as

much as your earnings from your regular work. For example, a doctor who makes $400/hour seeing patients can easily justify charging $400/hour while working on a court case. Some experts argue they should charge more because of the greater effort required and the higher level of aggravation.

Fees charged by lawyers continue to escalate. Even brand new lawyers fresh out of law school charge an hourly rate of $100 or more. And they, presumably, have steadier work than expert witnesses.

Q: *You mean to tell the court you charged over $6,500 for this study?*

A: *Yes, it took a lot of time to read the materials and set up the experiments. The charges also cover travel, hotel, meals and photocopying expenses.*

It must be remembered that consulting is part-time work; you have overhead and you get paid only for the hours you spend on the job. Salaried people earn less per hour but they have many perks and benefits and the work is steady.

A standard fee might be $190 per hour for work done at home. This work might include investigation, research, reading depositions, telephone counseling or visits by the attorney to you. You might charge $1,500 per day plus expenses when hired to leave town to give depositions, do on-site investigation or testify in a trial. That means if you work at home for more than five hours in any one day, you will charge the day rate. In other words, $1,500 is the maximum charge for one day. Some experts disagree and publish only an hourly rate.

Some experts charge time-and-a-half for work on Sundays, holidays and work in excess of eight hours per day.

Do not quote a flat rate for a case. You cannot accurately estimate what it will cost. Charging by the hour is fair to both sides. You might make an exception for creating demonstrative evidence where the time and materials can be accurately estimated.

In very long cases, some experts total the hours and divide by eight to arrive at a (lower) daily rate.

What you are being paid for. This is a sensitive and delicate issue. You are making more than most anyone else in the courtroom, including the judge. You will be asked what you are being paid. If you supply a good answer and do not appear to be apologizing for the amount, the cross-examining attorney probably won't pursue the matter. No one expects you to work for nothing and high-priced consultants seem more important.

In fact, if you charge significantly under the going rate, you may be perceived as not a good expert.

Q: *Are you being paid for your testimony? (are you a hired gun?)*

A: *No, I am not being paid for my time in testimony, I am being paid my regular rate to come to court to explain how this accident happened. Litigation consulting is not my only source of income.*

Q: *Are you being paid to be here?*

A: *Just as you are, sir*

Q: *How much do you charge?*

A: *My office charges $1,800 per day.*

Q: *But, don't you own the business, aren't you the office?*

A: *That money pays for overhead: rent, utilities, office staff, etc. It does not go into my wallet. That is what the company charges.*

Q: *How much have you billed so far?*

A: *I do not know how much my office has billed so far. I am spending my time doing the best job I can for my client. I am not counting the money.*

Q: *What percentage of your annual income comes from expert witness work?*

A: *I do not know. I have never calculated it.*

If you are ordered at a deposition to calculate your income from litigation consulting, quote just the amount for your time, not for your expenses.

Charge from portal to portal. Start the clock when you leave the house or office and stop it when you re-enter (assuming you return straight home). You can justify charging for travel time because it is time you would otherwise spend productively. You can always work on the plane—and you should if you are charging the client for the time. Many litigation consultants like to use travel time to refresh their memories by reading the trial chapter of this book to get in the right frame of mind.

Some litigation consultants charge more for courtroom work than for waiting or travel time. Others use a simplified fee schedule like the sample which follows at the end of this chapter. Some lawyers advise the simple fee plan as they feel it is hard to justify a multi-tiered fee schedule to a jury. If you charge more for testifying than waiting to testify, it sounds as though the expert is *selling* his or her testimony—and at a premium price.

No attorney wants to go into court with the second-best expert, yet some will try to get a lower rate. They should realize that the expert who acquiesces to a lower rate is usually not a professional—someone with experience testifying under pressure.

When a client-attorney asks for a lower rate for a long case, some experts ask for a guarantee and a cancellation clause. That is, they will lower their hourly rate if they are guaranteed a (large) minimum number of hours.

Charge the same rates for each side. You will not appear to be objective if you charge plaintiffs more or less than defendants.

Q: *What was your hourly rate for the* Smith v. Jones *case?*

A: *That is a private matter. I would have to ask my client-attorney on that case before releasing that information.*

Brokerages find cases for you and either take a portion of your fee or mark up your fee. Technical Advisory Service for

---

Attorneys (TASA) is the largest brokerage and they mark up your fee. Many experts are already feeling guilty about their hourly charge and when TASA marks it up, they wince. One way to avoid this apparently excessive fee is to mark the fee down so that TASA is charging close to the same amount you are.

When to start. Any work you do *on* the case is billable. Your initial telephone call and letter are sales time and are not billable.

Depositions. The (opposing) attorney who requested the deposition is responsible for paying you at your usual, published hourly rate and for the deposition expenses. Charge for the actual time used in the examination. Charge travel time and mileage to your client-attorney. Your client-attorney will pay for copies of the transcript. Charge your client-attorney for the time it takes you to prepare for the deposition and to review the transcript. Sometimes the two attorneys will agree to another type of split.

You have an agreement with your client-attorney but not with the opposing attorney. If you are not paid within a reasonable amount of time, bill your client-attorney.

Q: *I note from your billing records that you charged more for your deposition than for other work on this case including this trial. How can you justify charging our side more than your side?*

In some jurisdictions, such as California, you are entitled to be paid *in advance* based on the anticipated length of the deposition. If the examination exceeds the anticipated length, the balance of the fee is due you within five days of receipt of an itemized statement. It is almost impossible to get paid by opposing counsel in a reasonable time after the deposition. If the fee fails to arrive prior to the deposition date, you do not have to appear. However, most experts simply attend the deposition and then send a bill for time and expenses.

If the opposing attorney does not wish to pay your regular rate, he or she may petition the court to set a reasonable fee. Any party, including you, may petition the judge to determine if your fees are reasonable. In some jurisdictions, there is a dollar limit on expert-witness fees.

Terms. Publish your terms by sending your fee schedule to your attorney-client. Stick to the terms you have listed. Some of the terms follow. (Also, see the sample fee schedule at the end of this chapter.):

- Billed monthly and payable net 30 days from date of invoice.

- New accounts shall be initiated with an advance payment of $500.

- All travel expenses shall be paid in advance.

- Fees for depositions shall be paid in advance based on the anticipated length of the examination. Balances due, if any, shall be paid within five days of the deposition.

- Fees for three days' time shall be paid in advance for trials out-of-state, two days in-state.

- Expenses not paid in advance will be surcharged.

- Bills not paid in 30 days will incur interest at the rate of 1.5%/month.

Advance payments or *retainers*. Some experts keep collecting in advance by requiring clients to maintain a minimum account balance. Do not consume the advance, issue a refund at the end of the case.

The term *retainer* is common in business consulting. In expert-witness work, we prefer the term *advance*. Advance makes you appear to be less of an advocate.

Make sure you receive the check for your airfare, estimated hotel expenses and three days of your time (probably $3000-5,000) before you leave town for a trial. If your side loses, you may have a great deal of trouble collecting. Do not lend money to your client-attorney. Let them invest *their* money.

IF AN ATTORNEY CALLS ME LESS THAN 60 DAYS PRIOR TO TRIAL, I QUADRUPLE THE ADVANCE.—IRA RIMSON

Q: *Does your client owe you any money?*

A: *No. My bills have been paid to date and my expenses for this trip were paid in advance. My being paid does not depend on the outcome of this case.*

Expense surcharge. Some experts add a 10% or 15% surcharge to expenses on the theory that they have already paid for the telephone, hotels and air fares and anticipate a long period before they collect. It hurts when you have traveled to court, put in a good effort, finished the job, paid American Express and then have trouble collecting the reimbursement.

Attorneys can avoid these surcharges by providing the tickets for travel and signing for the hotel bill before you arrive.

On-call fees. It is virtually impossible to predict when the expert will go on the stand. You must be available when the court is ready for you. For out-of-town trials, you may use the same daily fee schedule for your time whether you are traveling, waiting or testifying. Your client is paying for your time no matter what you are doing. However, when you are on call for a local trial, a problem arises. If you are a dentist, you may not be able to schedule your patients for tentative appointments. You may not be able to respond to a call to court in the middle of a root canal procedure. Dentists and many other experts have office overhead to pay whether they are working (and being paid) or not. Many expert witnesses deal with this problem by charging an on-call fee which is lower than their regular rate. They stay by the telephone and keep busy with other work, but with work that can be dropped at any time.

Q: *You spent a lot of hours on this case and made a lot of money.*

A: *I believe in being well-prepared so that the jury will have the best information possible.*

Court-hired experts and fee-setting. The judge may appoint an expert to investigate, report and testify (Federal Rules of Evidence. Rule 706). Some 30% of the experts polled by the National Forensic Center have been hired by a court at one time or another. The court set the fees in some 50% of the cases. Compensation in criminal, and some civil, cases is made by the government. In the rest of the civil cases, the court apportions the fee among the parties.

The poll also showed some 30% of the prosecutors set fees while only 9% of hiring insurance companies did.

Contingency fees. The jury is not likely to believe in an expert's objectivity if his or her fee depends on the outcome of the case. Contingency fees are prohibited in some jurisdictions. (California is one.) Some experts have been awarded contingency fees when they worked only on the pre-trial portion of the case as a consultant and did not testify at the trial. Most lawyers do not want experts to get contingency fees, however. They do not want to share.

Ordinary witnesses. *Percipient* or eye witnesses may be compensated as little as $12/day and 20 cents/mile. You may be subpoenaed as a fact or percipient (eye) witness to avoid paying your expert's fee. You will be asked what you saw in your investigation. If this happens, do not be tricked into answering opinion questions.

Your client-attorney must indemnify you against all expenses which you may be forced into in that case. The other side may try to depose you as a lay witness without paying you your fee or may want photocopies of your entire library as part of the discovery process. If you are asked to produce copies of more files or to make up a list of all the articles you have written in the past 30 years, confirm who will be paying for your time.

Who will pay? Clarify whether you will be working for the attorney or the client. You may be paid by the attorney, his or her client, an insurance company, the attorney working for a co-plaintiff or co-defendant, or any party that has a sufficient monetary interest in the outcome of the case. Clients may be harder to collect from. Identify who is going to pay you.

ANY AMBIGUITY IN THE CONTRACT IS LIKELY TO BE HELD
AGAINST THE AUTHOR OF THE CONTRACT.

Throughout this book, we refer to the *client-attorney* when referring to the attorney who hired you.

In October of 1986, Congress passed the Anti-Drug Abuse Act which defined money laundering as knowingly accepting money ($10,000 or more) from someone who earned it illegally. The object was to prevent criminals from benefiting (buying fancy cars or hiring expensive lawyers) from their crimes. This act puts attorneys, experts and others in a difficult position. They may have not only a collection problem, they could be fined and sent to jail for accepting payment for their services from illegally earned sources. When working criminal cases, determine who will be responsible for the bill.

Do not hire subcontractors. If you need help, introduce the new (specialist) consultant or firm to the attorney and let them contract with each other. If you were hired by a brokerage, ask if they can supply a needed expert. Do not become responsible for the work of others or for collecting from one firm and paying another.

Records. Keep accurate, chronologically-written records. If you don't record it, you can't bill it. Whenever you start work, take a break, resume work, finish work or quit for the day, write it down. Make a written record (notes) plus times and date of every telephone call both in and out. Many experts log time by the tenth of the hour or in six-minute increments.

Accounting. *QuickBooks, DacEasy* and some other accounting programs feature time slips to help you keep track of time spent on cases.

Formal understanding. Some experts use a detailed contract but most simply use an engagement letter and append a detailed fee schedule. Some attorneys dislike tightly-written, multi-page contracts; the letter and schedule is softer. But, as always, your experience may be different.

CHECK THE *GUIDE TO EXPERTS' FEES* AND DRAFT A FEE SCHEDULE USING THE FOLLOWING EXAMPLE AS A GUIDE.

Michael J. Maus, R.R.

Technical investigation, consulting and testimony in rodent control cases.

Fee Schedule

January 1998

For work performed in Anaheim.....$190/hour for my time to $1,500/day max.

Includes investigation, research in extensive personal library (consisting of bound magazines, military specifications, videotapes, photographs, training manuals and books), counseling, trial preparation, oral and written reports.

For work performed outside of Anaheim......$1,500/day for my time plus **expenses. (Billed in half days @ $750 each).

Includes investigation, counseling, oral reports, travel, depositions and court testimony. To be followed with a written report, as required.

** **Expenses.**
Actual expenses reasonably and necessarily incurred, such as travel, subsistence and lodging, long-distance telephone charges, the cost of producing documents and materials, professional support requirements, etc., are additional to the consulting fee and will be billed to the client at cost. First Class air travel (Business Class where available) is expected.

Terms:
* Billed monthly and payable net 30 days from date of invoice.

* New accounts shall be initiated with an advance payment of $500.

* All travel expenses shall be paid in advance.

* Fees for depositions shall be paid in advance based on the anticipated length of the examination. Balances due, if any, shall be paid within five days of the deposition. If the opposing attorney fails to pay, then you, the client-attorney, are responsible for the bill.

* Fees for three days' time shall be paid in advanced for trials out of state, two days in state.

* Accounts over 30 days past due shall accrue interest at the rate of 2% per month.

* Payment shall be made to Maus Associates (FEIN #95-1234567).

Mr. Maus is listed as an expert witness by the National Forensic Center; Technical Advisory Service for Attorneys; Expert Resources, Inc.; Maritime & Aviation Consultants; *Lawyer's Desk Reference; Consultants and Consulting Organizations Directory; the Parker Directory;* The *Forensic Register* of the Bar Association of San Francisco; the *Nationwide Expert Witness Directory* from Nova Law Publications and the Aerospace Consultants Directory published by the Society of Automotive Engineers.

Sample fee schedule

CHAPTER THIRTEEN

BILLING AND COLLECTIONS

One of the topics of greatest interest to a technical expert is getting paid. Whenever two or more experts gather, collections is one of the topics most often discussed. Some experts have collection problems, others get their money up-front, some feel they lose clients by being too strict about their terms and many just live with slow payments. About 25% of the expert witnesses polled by the National Forensic Center said they had occasional collection problems.

Payment in advance. Should you demand payment in advance? Ask yourself these questions: Will the plaintiff be able to pay me if he does not recover? Will the defendant be able to pay me if he loses and has to pay a great sum to the plaintiff? Will the defendant be able to pay me if he is in jail?

The same poll showed that 24% require the client-attorney to pay in advance. As justification, many of them argue that they can be more objective about the case if they have already received payment.

What you do depends on the type of clients you are likely to have. For example, if you work for the defense in an industry covered by insurance, you will get your money when the insurance company pays the attorney. This could take several months because insurance companies are often good pay but slow. If you do technical analysis for the defense in drug cases, you want to get all your money up front. Drug runners have money (can pay the bill), are desperate (will pay almost anything you ask), may not have an address (making them hard to find after the trial), are unreliable (why bother to pay after the trial), and may be part of a criminal element (making collection efforts dangerous).

The best advice is to consider the situation and contract with the attorney, not the client.

If your side loses and you are asked to lower your fee, it may look as though you are working on a contingency fee basis. Remember that contingency fees are illegal in some jurisdictions.

Q: *We lost, will you lower your fee?*

A: *No, if my fee depends upon the outcome of the case, then I was working on a contingency basis.*

A: *If you had won, I would not have expected a bonus.*

If the case is taken over by a new attorney, you have a right to have him or her guarantee past fees.

Bill regularly and bill more often as the work mounts. It is easier to pay a small bill than a large one. When payments are slow, some experts use certified mail, return receipt so that the client-attorney cannot claim the bill was not received. If you are billing the Federal Government, note a discount (say 2%) if paid within 30 (or fewer) days. They have to take the discount. You may not get paid in the stated time but most people agree you will get paid sooner.

Enforce collections. Suspend work until you get another advance. If it comes out in court that you have not been paid lately, the jury may think the outcome of the case is very important to you. Your objectivity may be suspect.

Many expert witnesses are charging interest for overdue bills. If you decide to do this, add a notice to your fee schedule so clients will be forewarned.

Many lawyers are not good business people and they keep poor records. So treat the work as a business. Maintain accurate billing records.

Every month, send a detailed billing like the following example. Show precisely what work has been done and what you have charged for it. Include the date, number of hours worked and a short description of the work performed. Itemize all expenses and attach photocopies of receipts. If you have a regular invoice form in your business, you may wish to use it to note *Consultation per the attached* and then include a detailed billing like the one reproduced here.

If you must sue your client-attorney, try small claims court. In small claims court, the debtor will have to represent himself and judges do not look kindly on attorneys who do not pay their bills. You may have to reduce your claim to take advantage of this venue.

COLLECTING FROM AN ATTORNEY IS LIKE COLLECTING FROM ANY OTHER DEBTOR. THERE ARE NO SECRETS TO COLLECTING, ONLY FRUSTRATIONS.

Invoice #4148

<u>Cat v. Mouse, et. al.</u>

1998:	
June 3: Telcon from Mr. Lyon re: case	n/c
Telcon to Mr. Lyon. .15 hours @ $110	$16.50
Telephone charges	$4.50
June 10: Review folder, draft narrative and research in own library. Telcon with Mr. Lyon. 3 hours.	$330.00
Call to Mr. Lyon, telephone charges	$3.00
June 11: Call to Ms. Tiger. .32 hours	$33.00
Telephone charges	$5.50
July 10: Telcon from Mr. Lyon .45 hours	$49.50
July 15: Reviewed answers to interrogatories, called Mr Lyon, researched files, made photocopies for Lyon .95 hours	$104.50
Call to Mr. Lyon, telephone charges	$3.00
Photocopies	$1.30
Postage	$2.40
Subtotal	$553.20
Cheque #7568 rec'd	$500.00
Total due	$53.20

Example of a detailed billing

Chapter Fourteen

Investigation and Testing

To do your job properly, you must run every possible test and thoroughly research every part of your case because the opposing expert may. You must assume the other expert will find what you find.

Q: *What were you trying to prove with these experiments?*

A: *I was not trying to prove anything. I was simply searching for facts.*

If you need more information about the case, tell your client-attorney. The more investigation, analysis, research and testing you are able to do, the more credible, persuasive and comfortable you will be.

Some areas of expertise routinely require detailed testing and lengthy documentation while other areas rarely do.

The American Society for Testing and Materials has published a one-page *Standard Practice for Collecting and Preservation of Information and Physical Items by a Technical Investigator.* It is available from ASTM, Tel: (800) 699-9277; Fax: (313) 930-9088; e-mail: service@cssinfo.com Web site: http://www.cssinfo.com

---

A PRUDENT QUESTION IS ONE-HALF OF WISDOM . . . HE THAT
QUESTIONS MUCH LEARNS MUCH.—SIR FRANCIS BACON

Investigating the site. Visit the site of the accident and write up a report. Your trained eye may pick up relevant facts which were not disclosed in reports. Stand on all corners and become familiar with the place. Close your eyes and try to picture the scene, objects and events. Inspect the site and the equipment as soon as possible. Weather and age may alter the evidence.

Take photographs and/or video of the site and log the shot on a piece of paper. Record the date, time, item being photographed, distance and other pertinent information. After processing the photographs, label, date and sign them. Photograph any labels, placards, signs, warnings or instructions posted on the site or the evidence.

Interview appropriate parties both at and away from the site. You may be able to talk to them in their language and get information other investigators can't. For example, if you are an aviation expert and are investigating a general aviation accident at a small airport, the Fixed Base Operator (FBO) and other airport personnel are not likely to snow you.

Maintain complete records of your investigation; do not rely on your memory. Details which do not seem important at first may be valuable later when new information comes to light.

If you find evidence at the site and remove it, it will require special handling. Make sure it is tagged, identified and dated.

Inspecting the equipment. In many types of cases, you must see the equipment in question. If the other side has it, they will be reluctant to send it to you, since it could get lost. Without it, they would not have a case. They may require your side to give them a hand receipt and a promise to give up the fight if the equipment is lost. You are usually allowed to see the gear in the office of the opposing attorney. During your inspection, he or she may remain in the room. This makes conversations with your client-attorney and inspection difficult.

During your inspection, take a lot of photographs. Once they are processed, identify, sign and date them.

If the opposing attorney, opposing expert or anyone else is

present when you inspect the equipment or site, do not talk with them. All communications should go through your client-attorney.

Chain of custody. Establish a chain of custody for exhibits. Whenever evidence is transferred from one party to another, get hand receipts. You must be able to prove it is the same piece of evidence. If there is tampering, you want to trace the deed back to someone.

If you take evidence into your possession, be very careful. You could be held liable for the amount asked in the case if you lose it. The jury will not be sympathetic if evidence was lost while in your possession. Remember, too, it is illegal to destroy evidence. See the forms at the end of this Chapter.

Spoliation of evidence. Occasionally, in investigating a case, you may find the client-attorney or someone else has tampered with some evidence. If you even suspect this, call your client-attorney. Toss the ball of responsibility into his or her lap. The client-attorney is an officer of the court and has a responsibility to see that evidence is not tampered with. Let him or her decide how to proceed.

Testing. The expert witness interprets scientific and technological facts and renders scientific and technological opinions based on those facts. Quite often, tests are required to establish exactly what those facts are. Your opinion will be particularly persuasive if you have tested your theories and the opposing expert has not. Tests may be conducted by an independent testing facility or you can do them yourself if you are qualified and have the facilities.

Do not perform any test or do any extra investigating until you get approval from your client-attorney. Some have been known to refuse payment on grounds the work was not requested.

Ask yourself why the part failed. Was the failure due to *design, manufacture or usage?*

An expert is only as credible as his data. Be sure to establish the source of all questionable information and the precise procedures performed or not performed.

At the deposition, the opposing attorney will ask for a copy of your file. If he or she determines you are relying on inaccurate or false information, this revelation may be saved for the trial.

You must attend the testing conducted by the opposing expert. Take notes, photograph everything and even consider videotaping the procedure. Sign and date your notes. The other expert is in charge of the testing but you have a right to witness it.

Tests must be conducted under the same or similar conditions as those existing when the accident took place. It is necessary only that the conditions be substantially alike; they do not have to be identical.

Destructive testing may damage or demolish the evidence, so you will have to obtain written consent from both sides in the case before performing tests of this kind. If you damage evidence without permission, you may be accused of *spoliation of evidence* and may not be allowed to testify on your test.

Evaluate the tests. Use recognized standards and specifications wherever possible. If you have to deviate from *real world* tests, be prepared to explain why.

Lab reports should contain:

1. A description of the analytical techniques used in the tests

2. The quantitative or qualitative results with any appropriate qualifications concerning the degree of certainty surrounding them

3. An explanation of any necessary presumptions or inferences that were needed to reach the conclusions

As the expert, you must perform or witness the tests in person. If you use an independent lab, you must guide and control the tests. This means making up a testing procedure or *protocol*. Use standard protocols when they exist.

Q: *Wouldn't you agree a competent expert would have run that test?*

A: *I would agree with the opinion I have expressed.*

Independent laboratory. Some tests are best run by an independent laboratory because the results will appear to be even more objective and/or because you may not have the required measuring devices. You should specifically describe the tests you want performed.

Select the independent laboratory carefully. Do they have the right equipment and personnel and are they properly accredited? When selecting a facility or running a test, think of how you will present the findings to the jury.

Consider your tests carefully before you run them. If they lead to undesirable results, it is difficult, if not unethical, to delete them from your report and testimony.

If your client-attorney contracts with the laboratory, the laboratory report will become his or her work product and be undiscoverable by the opposition. Another personal advantage of having your client-attorney deal directly with the testing facility is that it keeps you out of the billing chain.

Preliminary laboratory reports from the lab to you should be verbal so that other clarifying tests may be discussed. Preliminary results which may be damaging to the case may be embarrassing (and misleading) if committed to paper before subsequent tests are completed.

The testing facility must never communicate with the opposition. They are working for your side. Make sure this is clear.

Many labs and experts destroy their working notes once their final report is drafted. They feel the final report shows everything reflected in the notes and that there is no further need for the working documents.

Machine calibration. All measuring tools should be calibrated regularly and the calibration should be recorded. If your calipers, voltmeters, etc. are calibrated by an independent service and the measurements can be traced to the National Bureau of Standards, your testimony will be more credible.

Q: *When was the machine last calibrated?*

A: *Calibration is not necessary as the measurements are relative (comparative) to each other (if true).*

Legal Evidence Control and Transmittal Form

Case Name:
Client:
Project Number:
Tag Number:
Client-Attorney:
File or Claim Number:
Insurance Company:
Adjuster Company:
Responsible Contact:
Telephone:
Received by:
Received from:
Date:
Witness:
Sampling by:
Description of evidence:

Transferred to:
Date:
Received by:
Witness:
All of above items, only items as follows:

Disposition of evidence:
Not pertinent to case per authority of:
Client contacted for return, rental or disposition by:
Date:
Placed in bonded storage at:
Per authority of:
Date:
Storage number:
Scrapped per authority of:
Date:

If testing is expected to be lengthy, you may wish to request 50% of your testing fee in advance. Once you turn over your report or testify, you are expendable. Your client-attorney does not need you anymore.

After the trial, physical evidence is often secured by the court and cannot be retrieved by the owner or expert. Be prepared to lose anything entered into evidence.

When testing, contact your client-attorney weekly to keep him or her informed.

Evidence Storage/Disposition Form

Case name:

To:

Ladies and Gentlemen:

Apex Testing laboratories maintains locked legal storage space for the retention of evidence while actively pursuing the study identified herein. During our study and prior to making a formal report no charge is made for the retention of evidence.

Upon completion of our study, we prefer to return all evidence to our client. We can retain small samples in our legal storage for a fee of $30 per month, billed quarterly and payable in advance. Large items can be transferred to a bonded warehouse.

Your case or file number:

Lab project number:

Lab report number:

Item(s):

Please notify us within thirty (30) days as to your requirements in the disposition of these materials.

Discard:

Return to the attention of:

Transfer to bonded storage:

Retain per rental defined above. $____   Payment enclosed.

Authorization:

Failure to respond will initiate disposal of the materials mentioned above.

By:

CHAPTER FIFTEEN

YOUR CURRICULUM VITAE

Your curriculum vitae is your resumé. It lists your education, job history, articles or books you have published—everything pertinent to your field of expertise. You send this CV to attorneys who call you about working on a case. They will use your CV to evaluate your qualifications.

Your CV should deal only with one area of expertise. If you are working in two separate and unrelated fields, such as bicycle mechanics and mountain climbing, for example, draft a CV for each.

Some expert witnesses like to use their word processor to tailor their CV to the case at hand. Tell the reader everything you think qualifies you for a particular assignment.

The proper length for your CV is debatable. A long CV makes you look important but leaves more for the opposing attorney to question. Some experts like to publish a long CV for their attorney and a shorter, tailored CV for the opposition. This is not difficult if you maintain a long draft in your word processor and then edit out the extraneous material for a

ATTORNEYS READ EVERYTHING. THEY LIKE LONG CVS BECAUSE OF THE INTIMIDATION FACTOR. MINE IS 12 PAGES LONG AND ABOUT TO BECOME 13 PAGES.
— CHRIS MCGOEY, PREMISES SECURITY EXPERT

customized edition for the deposition. But if the opposing attorney finds and compares the two, be prepared to answer the differences on cross-examination.

Your CV must be honest and accurate. The opposing attorney will probably check your background. You do not want to be exposed as a fraud on the witness stand.

CVs are usually entered into evidence and go into the jury room with the other evidence. You want to leave a lasting impression; your CV should speak for you long after you have left the stand.

Sit down at the keyboard and start building your CV. Place your name and field of specialty at the top and then list your:

- Chronological work experience

- Education and training, formal and on-the-job

- Certifications and licenses

- Publications such as books and articles

- Professional affiliations and memberships

- Patents held, if any

- Awards

- Consulting and expert testimony experience

Use a separate paragraph for each item on the list. Print out the CV on your letterhead.

Then, in a second section of the document, list everything pertinent you have done in this field since leaving school, year by year. As you work on the second section, more ideas will come to you for use in the first section. Keep building, researching and digging into your files. This takes time but the result is very impressive and you will use it again and again.

Print out a clean copy for your file. Reproduce it as

YOU CAN GIVE A CHICKEN A CERTIFICATE THAT HE IS A PEACOCK AND HE MAY THINK HE IS A PEACOCK. BUT THE PEACOCKS KNOW THE DIFFERENCE.

(Letterhead)

Robert A. Katz: Aircraft Accident Reconstruction

Updated January 1,1998

Certifications
Professional Engineer, Safety (California) SF-0002
Certified Safety Professional No. 590062

Education and Training
BS - University of Massachusetts, 1962
MS - University of Southern California, 1965
Pilot training, U.S. Air Force, 1966
USAF Flight Safety School, University of California, 1967
Aircraft Crash Survival Investigation School, ASU, 1968

Professional Affiliations
American Society of Safety Engineers, Member
Systems Safety Society, President 1970-1972
U.S. Parachute Association, Secretary 1973-1974
Professional Experience
1984-Present: Faculty, University of California, Institute of
Safety and Systems Management. Lecturing In Aircraft
Accident Investigation, Safety Engineering, and Safety
Program Management.
1970-1984: vice-president, Engineering, U.S. Aviation Corp.
1968-1970: Chief of Safety Policy and Programs, U.S. Air
Force, Directorate of Aerospace Safety.
1966-1968: Aviation Accident Investigation, Hickam AFB,
Hawaii.

Flying Experience
Pilot. Commercial License. 8,700 hours.
1,200 parachute jumps, Master Parachute Rigger, Instructor.
Professional Papers and Research
Over 400 articles, most in a monthly column in *Aircraft Safety*
Magazine
Five books on flying and aircraft safety including *The Cat and*
Duck Method of Instrument Flying.
Other publications on request.

Curriculum Vitae example

needed, either on a laser printer or a good, clean photocopy machine. Use high quality paper to create a good impression. The hiring attorney wants to know how you will look in court, so include a photo of yourself properly dressed. A wallet-sized photo can be pasted to the CV. They are fairly inexpensive when ordered in quantity. Color always sells better than black and white.

Do not fold your CV, fee schedule and other materials. Mail them in a flat 9 x 12 envelope. Make them easy to handle and file. Pick up some Priority Mail envelopes from the post office. These *flat rate* envelopes look good, go by air at a low rate, and are free.

Faxable one-sheet. In addition to a detailed CV, develop a one-page biography. The bio contains just a summary of the services you offer, areas of expertise, education summary, work summary and a paragraph or two on why you are an expert in your particular field.

Your bio should include a 3 x 3, black-and-white half-toned photograph. When you mail your CV, this bio should be placed on top. It should also be faxed within a few minutes of receiving a telephoned inquiry. Attorneys want quick information when searching for an expert. This faxable one-sheet gives the attorney a quick summary of your qualifications and suitability.

CHAPTER SIXTEEN

❦

YOUR LIST OF CASES

It is useful to maintain a list of the cases you have worked on. The list will reveal several things to you once it starts to grow. How many cases have you taken part in? What percentage went to trial? Do you have a good balance of cases for the plaintiff and defense? Have you worked for the same firm several times? What year did you begin expert witness work?

Generally, your list of cases is for your own use though your client-attorney may be interested in the information. It is not something you want opposing attorneys to find. They could use it to research all your past cases and try to find something with which to impeach you.

A list of all the cases in which you have testified (at deposition or at trial) during the previous four years is required under the amended Federal Rules of Civil Procedure. Now attorneys filing in state courts are asking for the lists too.

Eventually, you will be asked to produce your list of cases at a deposition. When you return home to draft the list, be sure you charge for the time.

This record is easy to maintain. Just keep a running list in your word processing program. This list should include the date hired, name of the case, venue, retaining attorney, deposition and trial testimony.

One aviation safety consultant keeps a computer record in a database management program such as MS-*Access* with the following fields: date the file was opened, title of case, date of accident, type of aircraft, registration of aircraft, plaintiff or defendant, client firm, primary consultant (if there is more than one person working in your firm), court, win/loss/settle, and date case was closed. Kept in the computer, the information is easy to update and print out. Searching and grouping is also simplified.

CHAPTER SEVENTEEN

JURY SELECTION

You probably have more experience in cases in your particular field than your client-attorney. You certainly know more about your subject and how different types of people perceive it. You want a group of jurors who are more likely to identify and sympathize with your side. Brief your client-attorney.

There are consulting firms that specialize in jury evaluation. They perform background checks and observe the reactions of potential jurors during voir dire (the educating and challenging process of selecting a jury). Most of the cases you work on will not have this help. It will be up to you to provide general guidelines to your client-attorney.

Almost every potential juror has some form of expertise. A problem arises when one juror knows something about your area of specialty. The other jurors are more likely to ask this juror-expert for advice and the newly found power could go to his or her head. As a result, you now have a jury of one—and that one may not like you.

For example, in a parachute case, you do not want to include pilots on the jury. Pilots are horizontal aviators while skydivers are engaged in vertical aviation. Many pilots fear and/or dislike air traffic that might collide with their aircraft. Often pilots have a high opinion of themselves and feel that their type of aviation is the only legitimate kind. To compound the problem, other jurors are likely to defer to the pilot for guidance in aviation matters. So, your whole case may turn on the reaction of one juror instead of the social dynamics among several.

On the other hand, female homemakers may make good jurors in parachute cases. Many of them sew. They understand fabric and stitching. When you show them the parachute and point to the construction, they will move to the front of their seats and nod their heads.

Think about your area of expertise and make a list of the types of jurors you would like (and not like) to include. Tell your client-attorney so that he or she will be particularly sensitive to these characteristics in potential jurors during the voir dire.

After the jury is selected. Once your jury is selected, consider what you want to show them. Is this an urban or rural trial? What is the racial makeup? Mostly male or female?

In a rural trial, the jury may not warm up to an out-of-town expert. Many attorneys like to get a local academic type for the lead expert, then call you in for specific expert testimony.

If the jury is largely Latino, suggest the client send the Latino vice-president to represent the company rather than the Anglo sales manager.

In very conservative areas, Utah for example, female experts may find their job more difficult.

For more information, see the excellent book *What Makes Juries Listen* by Sonya Hamlin. (Details are in the Appendix.)

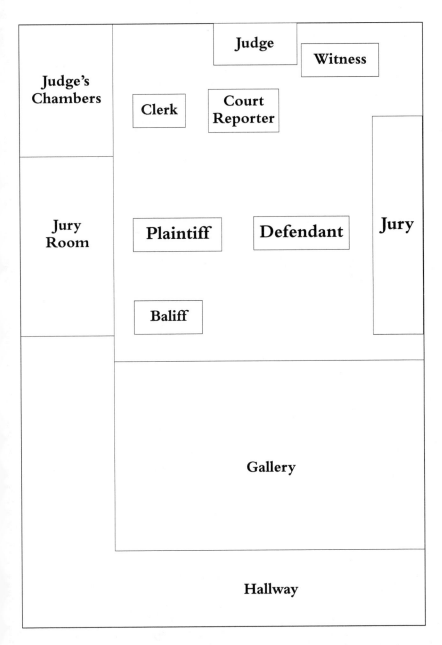

Typical courtroom layout.
Actual layout may vary.

Chapter Eighteen

A Guide to the Law
and the Courts

This chapter will help you understand points of law, courtroom procedures, criminal actions, legal transactions, and arrest procedures. In short, it is a lay guide to the law and the courts. It traces the steps normally involved in a civil case and a criminal case, explaining the procedures most common to most of them. Keep in mind that some variations of procedure exist among the various state courts and even among federal courts.

Civil cases

How a Lawsuit Begins. Court actions fall into two broad categories—civil and criminal. Civil cases are those in which an individual, business or agency of government seeks damages or

This chapter contains a condensation of *Law and the Courts: A Layman's Handbook of Court Procedures*, and is reprinted by permission of the American Bar Association. The complete booklet is available for $2.50 postpaid from the ABA, Circulation Department, 750 North Lake Shore Drive, Chicago, IL 60611. Copyright © 1992, American Bar Association.

relief from another individual, business or agency of government; these constitute the great bulk of cases in the courts. The most common example is the suit for damages arising from an automobile accident. A criminal action is one by the state or federal government against an individual charged with committing a crime.

This section deals with an average civil case. Civil actions generally are brought for breach of contract (*ex contractu*), or for a wrong (*ex delicto*) or tort.

In the early days of the law, courts and lawyers were inclined to restrict the scope of legal actions. Thus, if a set of facts did not fit into an established legal "pigeon hole," the client was without remedy even though he had suffered a wrong to his person or property.

As a consequence, a new system—equity—evolved which provides a remedy that previously was not available. Equity covers such matters as preventing the continuance of a wrong (injunction), and compelling the performance of a contract to sell real estate or unique personal property (specific performance). Ordinarily neither a jury trial nor money damages can be obtained in equity proceedings.

A person who believes that he has been injured or damaged by another person or business firm consults his lawyer and tells him the facts and circumstances which he believes constitute a cause of legal action. The attorney takes the client's statement, interviews possible witnesses, examines applicable statutes and court decisions, and tries to determine whether the client has a case.

If the attorney concludes the client does have a cause of action, he prepares and files a *complaint* or *petition* in the proper court. His client is the *plaintiff* and the person or firm against whom the case is filed is the *defendant*.

The petition states the facts of the plaintiff's action against the defendant and sets forth the damages, judgment or other relief sought. However, the mere filing of a suit is not proof that the plaintiff has a cause of action. Later events may demonstrate that his claim is invalid.

The attorney for the plaintiff also files with the clerk of the court a *praecipe for a summons*. This is a request for the court clerk to issue a *summons* or notice, and to direct the county sheriff to serve a copy of it on the defendant. In some states, a praecipe is not necessary and the summons is issued as a matter of course. In others, the summons may be served in advance of the filing of the petition or complaint. In still others, any person over 21 and not a party to the action may serve the summons.

After the sheriff has served the summons, he returns the original of the summons to the court, with a notation as to whether and, if so, how the defendant was served with the summons. Serving of the summons is the defendant's formal notification of suit. Filing a complaint and serving the summons commences the case.

After service, the defendant is entitled to a certain period of time within which to file his *pleading*, or answer, to the plaintiff's petition.

Jurisdiction and Venue. The attorney must select the proper county or district in which to file the case. A court has no authority to render a judgment in any case unless it has jurisdiction over the person or property involved. This means that the court must be able to exercise control over the defendant, or that the property involved must be located in the county or district under the court's control.

Certain actions are said to be *local*—that is, they may be brought only in the county where the subject matter of the litigation is located. An example of a local action would be an action for the foreclosure of a mortgage on real estate.

Other actions are said to be *transitory*—that is, they may be brought in any county in any state where the defendant may be found and served with summons. An action for personal injuries is an example of a transitory action.

Venue means the county or district where the action is to be tried. Venue may be changed to another county or district upon application or by agreement. Where wide prejudicial publicity has been given to a case before trial, a change of venue is sometimes sought in an effort to secure jurors who have not formed an opinion or to provide a neutral forum not charged with local bias. Venue also may be changed to serve the convenience of witnesses.

A change of venue from the judge usually is granted on an application which claims that the judge has some relationship to the parties, attorneys or facts of the case, which prevents his being completely unbiased during the trial.

Preparation for Trial. The plaintiff and defendant, through their respective attorneys, attempt to marshall all of the pertinent facts bearing upon the case. The defendant may begin his defense by filing certain pleadings, which may include one or more of the following:

Motion to Quash Service of Summons. Questions whether the defendant has been properly served with summons, as provided by law.

Motion to Strike. Asks the court to rule whether the plaintiff's petition contains irrelevant, prejudicial or other improper matter. If it does, the court may order such matter deleted.

Motion to Make More Definite and Certain. Asks the court to require the plaintiff to set out the facts of his complaint more specifically, or to describe his injury or damages in greater detail, so that the defendant can answer more precisely.

Motion to Dismiss. Asks the court to rule that the plaintiff's complaint does not state a legally sound cause of action against the defendant even if, for the purpose of the motion, the defendant admits that all the facts set out by the plaintiff are true. This was once called a *demurrer.*

Answer. This statement by the defendant denies the allegations in the plaintiff's petition, or admits some and denies others, or admits all and pleads an excuse.

Cross-petition or Cross-complaint. May be filed by the defendant either separately or as part of his answer. It asks for relief or damages on the part of the defendant against the original plaintiff, and perhaps others. When a cross-petition is filed, the plaintiff may then file any of the previously-mentioned motions to the cross-petition, except a motion to quash service of summons.

Reply. Either party in the case may file a reply, which constitutes an answer to any new allegations raised by the other party in prior pleadings.

Note: A *plea* or *pleading* refers to an answer or other formal document filed in the action. The words should not be used to describe an argument made in court by a lawyer.

Taking of Depositions. A *deposition* is an out-of-court statement of a witness under oath, intended for use in court or in preparation for trial. Under prevailing statutes and rules in most jurisdictions, either of the parties in a civil action may take the deposition of the other party, or of any witness.

Depositions frequently are necessary to preserve the testimony of important witnesses who cannot appear in court or who reside in another state or jurisdiction. This might be the testimony of a friendly witness—one whose evidence is considered helpful to the plaintiff or defendant, as the case may be. Or it might involve an adverse witness whose statements are taken, by one side or the other, to determine the nature of the evidence he would give if summoned as a witness in the trial.

The deposition may take the form of answers to written questions or of oral examination followed by cross-examination.

A deposition is not a public record, and not available to the press until it is made so by court order.

A state may not compel the presence at a civil trial of a witness who is outside the state or who is in another county of the same state. When the testimony of such a witness is sought, the procedure is for the party seeking the testimony to apply to the court in which the case is pending for the issuance of a commission—commonly called *letters rogatory*. This is directed to an official or attorney in the jurisdiction where the witness is, empowering him to take the witness's deposition and forward it to the court.

In some states, it is not necessary to secure the issuance of a commission, but only to serve notice of the taking of the deposition upon opposing attorneys.

If a witness is absent from the jurisdiction or is unable to attend the trial in person, his deposition may be read in evidence. If a person who has given a deposition also appears as a witness at the trial, his deposition may be used to attack his credibility, if his oral testimony at the trial is inconsistent with that contained in the deposition.

Discovery. In addition to taking depositions in an attempt to ascertain the facts upon which another party relies, either party may submit written questions, called interrogatories, to the other party and require that such be answered under oath.

Other methods of discovery are: requiring adverse parties to produce books, records and documents for inspection, to submit to a physical examination, or to admit or deny the genuineness of documents.

Pre-Trial Conference. After all the pleadings of both parties have been filed and the case is *at issue*, many courts then set the case for a pre-trial hearing. At this hearing, the attorneys appear, generally without their clients and, in the presence of the judge, seek to agree on undisputed facts, called *stipulations*. These may include such matters as time and place in the case of an accident, the use of pictures, maps or sketches, and other matters, including points of law.

The objective of the pre-trial hearing is to shorten the actual trial time without infringing upon the rights of either party.

Pre-trial procedure, used extensively in the federal district courts, frequently results in the settlement of the case without trial. If it does not, the court assigns a specific trial date for the case, following the pre-trial hearing.

Criminal Cases

Bringing the Charge. Criminal charges are instituted against an individual in one of two ways:

1) Through an *indictment*, or true bill, voted by a grand jury, or

2) Through the filing of an *information* in court by the prosecuting attorney (sometimes called the county, district or

state's attorney), alleging the commission of a crime.

In either case, the charge must set forth the time, date and place of the alleged criminal act as well as the nature of the charge.

In most states, crimes of a serious nature, such as murder or treason, may be charged by indictment only. In some states, the prosecutor has the option in any case to proceed by way of indictment or information.

The Grand Jury. The grand jury is a body of citizens (usually 16, but varying in number from state to state) summoned by the court to inquire into crimes committed in the county or, in the case of federal grand juries, in the federal court district.

Grand jury proceedings are private and secret. Prospective defendants are not entitled to be present at the proceedings, and no one appears to cross-examine witnesses on the defendant's behalf.

However, a witness before a federal grand jury is free to describe his testimony to anyone he pleases after he leaves the grand jury room. To this extent, such proceedings are not secret.

Although all states have a provision for impaneling a grand jury, only about half use it as a regular arm of law enforcement. In the others, the prosecutor, on his own responsibility, is empowered to make formal accusation of all, or of all but the most serious, crimes.

In states where the grand jury is utilized, it is convened at regular intervals, or it may be impaneled at special times by the court to consider important cases.

The grand jury has broad investigative powers: it may compel the attendance of witnesses; require the taking of oaths; and compel answers to questions and the submission of records.

Ordinarily, however, the grand jury hears only such witnesses as the prosecutor calls before it and considers only the cases presented to it by the prosecutor.

Nevertheless, a grand jury may undertake inquiries of its own, in effect taking the initiative away from the prosecutor. In common parlance, this is known as a *runaway grand jury*.

The grand jury's traditional function is to determine whether information elicited by the prosecutor, or by its own inquiries, is adequate to warrant the return of an indictment or true bill charging a person or persons with a particular crime. If the grand jury concludes that the evidence does not warrant a formal charge, it may return a *no bill*.

In several states, powers of investigation similar to those of the grand jury are conferred by law upon a single person, a judicial officer or a deputy appointed by him, known as a *one man grand jury*.

Arrest Procedure. When an indictment is returned by a grand jury, or an information is filed by the prosecuting attorney, the clerk of the court issues a warrant for the arrest of the person charged, if he has not already been arrested and taken into custody.

The law usually requires in a *felony* case (generally, a crime for which a person may be confined in the penitentiary) that the defendant must promptly be brought before a magistrate or justice of the peace (in federal cases, the U.S. Commissioner) and be permitted to post bond, in order to secure release from custody, and either request or waive a *preliminary hearing*. When the grand jury indicts, there is no preliminary hearing. In most states, however, persons charged with murder are not eligible for release on a bail bond.

Many jurisdictions permit law enforcement officials to hold a person without formal charge up to 24 hours for the purpose of investigation. But he may not be held for an unreasonable time unless a criminal charge is filed. In addition, the defendant formally charged with a crime is entitled to an attorney at all times. If he is unable to procure an attorney and if he requests counsel, the court will appoint an attorney to represent him, at public expense and without cost to him.

Preliminary Hearing. If the individual charged with a crime requests a preliminary hearing before a magistrate, the court will set a hearing within a reasonably short time. At the hearing, the state must present sufficient evidence to convince the magistrate that there is reason to believe the defendant has committed the crime with which he is charged. The defendant must be present at this hearing, and he may or may not present evidence on his own behalf.

If the magistrate believes the evidence justifies it, he will order the defendant *bound over* for trial in the proper court— that is, placed under bond for appearance at trial, or held in jail if the charge involved is not a bailable offense or if the defendant is unable to post bond. The magistrate also may decide that even without bond the accused will most likely appear in court for his trial and therefore will release him on his *own recognizance*—that is, on his own promise to appear. If he concludes that the state has failed to produce sufficient evidence in the preliminary hearing, the magistrate may dismiss the charge and order the defendant released.

Arraignment. In most instances, a criminal case is placed on the court's calendar for *arraignment*. On the date fixed, the accused appears, the indictment or information is read to him, his rights are explained by the judge, and he is asked whether he pleads *guilty* or *not guilty* to the charge.

If he pleads not guilty, his case will be set later for trial; if he pleads guilty, his case ordinarily will be set later for sentencing. In cases of minor offenses, sentences may be imposed immediately. But in some states, arraignment and plea are separate proceedings, held on different days.

Preparation for Trial. As in civil cases, very careful preparation on the part of the state and the defense precedes the trial. However, the defense may first enter a motion challenging the jurisdiction of the court over the particular offense involved, or over the particular defendant. The defense attorney also may file a demurrer, or motion for dismissal, as in a civil suit.

In preparing for trial, attorneys for both sides will interview prospective witnesses and, if deemed necessary, secure expert evidence, and gather testimony concerning ballistics, chemical tests, cases and other similar data.

Pre-Trial Settlement. Most cases are settled prior to trial.

In civil cases, settlement is one of the objectives of the pre-trial conference. In complex civil cases, special settlement conferences may be held.

Many criminal charges are terminated by plea negotiations in which a defendant enters a plea of *guilty* or *nolo contendere* in the expectation that other charges will be dismissed or that sentence concessions will be granted.

Some communities have experimental programs for removing some controversies from court altogether, as through use of arbitration or mediation in facilities such as neighborhood justice centers.

Trials, Civil or Criminal. While in detail there are minor differences in trial procedure between civil and criminal cases, the basic pattern in the courtroom is the same. Consequently, this section treats the trial steps collectively.

Officers of the Court. The *judge* is the officer who is either elected or appointed to preside over the court. If the case is tried before a jury, the judge rules upon points of law dealing with trial procedure, presentation of the evidence and the law of the case. If the case is tried before the judge alone, he will determine the facts in addition to performing the aforementioned duties.

The *court clerk* is an officer of the court, also either elected or appointed who, at the beginning of the trial, upon the judge's instruction, gives the entire panel of prospective jurors (*veniremen*) an oath. By this oath, the venireman promises that, if called, he will truly answer any question concerning his qualifications to sit as a juror in the case.

Any venireman who is disqualified by law, or has a valid reason to be excused under the law, ordinarily is excused by the judge at this time. A person may be disqualified from jury duty because he is not a resident voter or householder, because of age, hearing defects, or because he has served recently on a jury.

Then the court clerk will draw names of the remaining veniremen from a box, and they will take seats in the jury box.

After twelve veniremen have been approved as jurors by the judge and the attorneys, the court clerk will administer an oath to the persons so chosen to *well and truly try the case.*

The *bailiff* is an officer of the court whose duties are to keep order in the courtroom, to call witnesses, and to take charge of the jury as instructed by the court at such times as the jury may not be in the courtroom, and particularly when, having received the case, the jury is deliberating upon its decision. It is the duty of the bailiff to see that no one talks with or attempts to influence the jurors in any manner.

The court recorder has the duty of recording all proceedings in the courtroom, including testimony of the witnesses, objections made to evidence by the attorneys and the rulings of the court thereon, and listing and marking for identification any exhibits offered or introduced into evidence. In some states, the clerk of the court has charge of exhibits.

The attorneys are officers of the court whose duties are to represent their respective clients and present the evidence on their behalf, so that the jury or the judge may reach a just verdict or decision.

The role of the attorney is sometimes misunderstood, particularly in criminal proceedings. Our system of criminal jurisprudence presumes every defendant to be innocent until proved guilty beyond a reasonable doubt. Every defendant is entitled to be represented by legal counsel, regardless of the unpopularity of his cause. This is a constitutional safeguard.

It is entirely ethical for an attorney to represent a defendant whom the community may assume to be guilty. The accused is entitled to counsel in order that he be protected from conviction on insufficient evidence, and he is entitled to every protection which the law affords him.

Jury List. The trial jury in either a civil or criminal case is called a *petit jury*. It is chosen by lot by the court clerk from a previously compiled list called a venire or, in some places, the *jury array*.

The methods of selecting names of persons for the venire vary among court jurisdictions. The lists in many states are comprised of tax assessment rolls or voter registration lists.

The law in many states requires a preliminary screening by a court official to eliminate persons unqualified or ineligible under the provisions of applicable state laws. In the federal courts, the court clerk is assisted in compiling the list by a *jury commissioner* appointed by the presiding judge.

Some people may be exempted from jury duty by reason of their occupations. These exemptions differ from state to state, but in some jurisdictions those automatically exempted include lawyers, physicians, dentists, pharmacists, teachers, and clergymen. In a number of others, nurses, journalists, printers, railroad, telephone and telegraph employees, government officials, firemen and policemen are among the exempt occupational groups.

On the other hand, many courts are excusing fewer prospective jurors today.

On occasion, the qualification of all jurors may be challenged. This is called a *challenge to the array* and generally is based on the allegation that the officers charged with selecting the jurors did so in an illegal manner.

Selecting the Jury. In most cases, a jury of twelve is required in either a civil or criminal proceeding. In some states, a jury of six may be used for certain trials. In some courts, alternate jurors are selected to take the places of members of the regular panel who may become disabled during the trial. These alternate jurors hear the evidence just as do the regular jurors, but do not participate in the deliberations unless a regular juror or jurors become disabled.

The jury selection begins with the calling by the court clerk of twelve veniremen, whose names are selected at random, to take their places in the jury enclosure. The attorneys for the parties, or sometimes the judge, may then make a brief statement of the facts involved, for the purpose of acquainting the jurors with sufficient facts so that they may intelligently answer the questions put to them by the judge and the attorneys. The questions elicit information, such as the name, the occupation, the place of business and residence of the prospective juror, and any personal knowledge he may have of the case. This questioning of the jurors is known as the *voir dire*.

If the venireman expresses an opinion or prejudice which will affect his judgment in the case, the court will *dismiss him for cause,* and a substitute juror will be called by the court clerk. There is no limit on the number of veniremen who may be *excused for cause.*

In addition to the challenges for cause, each party has the right to exercise a specific number of *peremptory challenges*. This permits an attorney to excuse a particular juror without having to state a cause. If a peremptory challenge is exercised, another juror then is called until attorneys on both sides have exercised all of the peremptory challenges permitted by law, or they have waived further challenges. The number of peremptory challenges is limited and varies with the type of case.

Thus, the jury is selected and then is sworn in by the court clerk to try the case. The remaining members of the jury panel are excused and directed to report to another court in session at the time.

Not all trials have juries. In some cases, due to the subject matter of the trial, there is no right to a jury. Also, the right to a jury trial may be waived in individual cases.

Separating the Witnesses. In certain cases, civil or criminal, the attorney on either side may advise the court that he is *calling for the rule* on witnesses. This means that, except for the plaintiff or complaining witness and the defendant, all witnesses who may testify for either party will be excluded from the courtroom until they are called to testify. These witnesses are admonished by the judge not to discuss the case or their testimony with other witnesses or persons, except the attorneys. This is sometimes called *separation of witnesses* or *sequestration*. If the rule is not called for, the witnesses may remain in the courtroom if they desire.

Opening Statements. After selection of the jury, the plaintiff's attorney, or attorney for the state in a criminal case, may make an opening statement to advise the jury what he intends to prove in the case. This statement must be confined to facts intended to be elicited in evidence and cannot be argumentative. The attorney for the defendant also may make an opening statement for the same purpose or, in some states, may reserve the opening statement until the end of the plaintiff's or state's case. Either party may waive his opening statement if he desires.

Presentation of Evidence. The plaintiff in a civil case, or the state in a criminal case, will begin the presentation of evidence with their *witnesses*. These usually will include the plaintiff in a civil case, although they are not required to testify.

A witness may testify to a matter of fact. He can tell what he saw, heard (unless it is hearsay as explained below), felt, smelled or touched through the use of his physical senses.

A witness also may be used to identify documents, pictures or other physical exhibits in the trial.

Generally, he cannot state his opinion or give his conclusion unless he is an expert or especially qualified to do so. In some instances, a witness may be permitted to express an opinion, for example, as to the speed an auto was traveling or whether a person was intoxicated.

A witness who has been qualified in a particular field as an expert may give his opinion based upon the facts in evidence and may state the reasons for that opinion. Sometimes the facts in evidence are put to the expert in a question called a *hypothetical question*. The question assumes the truth of the facts contained in it. Other times, an expert is asked to state an opinion based on personal knowledge of the facts through his own examination or investigation.

Generally, a witness cannot testify to *hearsay*—that is, what someone else has told him outside the presence of the parties to the action.

Also, a witness is not permitted to testify about matters that are too remote to have any bearing on the decision of the case, or matters that are irrelevant or immaterial.

Usually, an attorney may not ask *leading questions* of his own witness, although an attorney is sometimes allowed to elicit routine, non-controversial information. A leading question is one which suggests the answer desired.

Objections may be made by the opposing counsel to leading questions, or to questions that call for an opinion or conclusion on the part of the witness, or require an answer based on hearsay. There are many other reasons for objections under the rules of evidence.

Objections are often made in the following form: *I object to that question on the ground that it is irrelevant and immaterial and for the further reason that it calls for an opinion and conclusion of the witness.* Many jurisdictions require that the objection specify why the question is not proper. The judge will thereupon sustain or deny the objection. If sustained, another question must then be asked, or the same question be rephrased in proper form.

If an objection to a question is sustained on either direct or cross-examination, the attorney asking the question may make an *offer to prove.* This offer is dictated to the court reporter away from the hearing of the jury. In it, the attorney states the answer which the witness would have given if permitted. The offer forms part of the record if the case is subsequently appealed.

If the objection is overruled, the witness may then answer. The attorney who made the objection may thereupon take an *exception,* which simply means that he is preserving a record so that, if the case is appealed, he may argue that the court erred in overruling the objection. In some states, the rules permit an automatic exception to an adverse ruling without its being asked for in each instance.

Cross-examination. When plaintiff's attorney or the state's attorney has finished his direct examination of the witness, the defendant's attorney or opposing counsel may then cross-examine the witness on any matter about which the witness has been questioned initially in direct examination. The cross-examining attorney may ask leading questions for the purpose of inducing the witness to testify about matters which he may otherwise have chosen to ignore.

On cross-examination, the attorney may try to bring out prejudice or bias of the witness, such as his relationship or friendship to the party, or other interest in the case. The witness can be asked if he has been convicted of a felony or crime involving moral turpitude, since this bears upon his credibility.

The plaintiff's attorney may object to certain questions asked on cross-examination on previously mentioned grounds or because they deal with facts not touched upon in direct examination.

Redirect Examination. After the opposing attorney is finished with his cross-examination, the attorney who called the witness has the right to ask questions on redirect examination. The *redirect examination* covers new matters brought out in cross-examination and generally is an effort to rehabilitate a witness whose testimony on direct examination has been weakened by cross-examination.

Then the opposing attorney may recross-examine.

Demurrer to Plaintiff's or State's Case, or Motion for Directed Verdict. At the conclusion of the plaintiff's or state's evidence, the attorney will announce that the plaintiff or state *rests*.

Then, away from the presence of the jury, the defendant's counsel may *demur* to the plaintiff's or state's case on the ground that a cause of action or that the commission of a crime has not been proven. In many states, this is known as a *motion for a directed verdict*, that is, a verdict which the judge orders the jury to return.

The judge will either sustain or overrule the demurrer or motion. If it is sustained, the case is concluded. If it is overruled, the defendant then is given the opportunity to present his evidence.

Presentation of Evidence by the Defendant. The defense attorney may elect to present no evidence, or may present certain evidence but not place the defendant upon the stand.

In a criminal case, the defendant need not take the stand unless he wishes to do so. The defendant has constitutional protection against self-incrimination. He is not required to prove his innocence. The plaintiff or the state has the *burden of proof.*

In a civil case, the plaintiff must prove his case by a *preponderance of the evidence.* This means the greater weight of the evidence.

The defendant is presumed to be not negligent or liable in a civil case, and not guilty in a criminal case.

The defense attorney may feel that the burden of proof has not been sustained, or that presentation of the defendant's witnesses might strengthen the plaintiff's case. If the defendant does present evidence, he does so in the same manner as the plaintiff or the state, as described above, and the plaintiff or state will cross-examine the defendant's witnesses.

Rebuttal Evidence. At the conclusion of the defendant's case, the plaintiff or state's attorney may then present rebuttal witnesses or evidence designed to refute the testimony and evidence presented by the defendant. The matter covered is evidence on which the plaintiff or state did not present evidence in its *case in chief* initially; or it may be a new witness to contradict the defendant's witness. If there is a so-called *surprise witness*, this is often where you will find him.

After rebuttal evidence, the defendant may present additional evidence to contradict it.

Final Motions. At the conclusion of all the evidence, the defendant may again renew his demurrer or motion for directed verdict. The motion is made away from the presence of the jury. If the demurrer or motion is sustained, the case is concluded. If overruled, the trial proceeds.

Thus, the case has now been concluded on the evidence, and it is ready to be submitted to the jury.

Conferences During the Trial. Occasionally during the trial, the lawyers will ask permission to approach the bench and speak to the judge, or the judge may call them to the bench. They whisper about admissibility of certain evidence, irregularities in the trial or other matters. The judge and lawyers speak in inaudible tones because the jurors might be prejudiced by what they hear. The question of admissibility of evidence is a matter of law for the judge, not the jury, to decide. If the ruling cannot be made quickly, the judge will order the jury to retire, and will hear the attorneys' arguments outside the jury's presence.

Whenever the jury leaves the courtroom, the judge will admonish them not to form or express an opinion or discuss the case with anyone.

Closing Arguments. The attorney for the plaintiff or state will present the first argument in closing the case. Generally, he will summarize and comment on the evidence in the most favorable light for his side. He may talk about the facts and properly drawn inferences.

He cannot talk about issues outside the case or about evidence that was not presented. He is not allowed to comment on the defendant's failure to take the stand as a witness in a criminal case.

If he does talk about improper matters, the opposing attorney may object, and the judge will rule on the objection. If the offending remarks are deemed seriously prejudicial, the opposing attorney will ask that the jury be instructed to disregard them, and in some instances may move for a *mistrial*, that is, ask that the present trial be terminated and the case be set for retrial at a later date.

Ordinarily, before closing arguments, the judge will indicate to the attorneys the instructions he will give the jury, and it is proper for the attorneys in closing argument to comment on them and to relate them to the evidence.

The defendant's attorney will next present his arguments. He usually answers statements made in opening argument, points out defects in the plaintiff's case, and summarizes the facts favorable to his client.

Then the plaintiff or state is entitled to the concluding argument to answer the defendant's argument and to make a final appeal to the jury. The plaintiff or state gets the last word because it has the burden of proof.

If the defendant chooses not to make a closing argument,

which sometimes occurs, then the plaintiff or state loses the right to the last argument.

Instructions to the Jury. Although giving instructions to the jury is the function of the judge, in many states attorneys for each side submit a number of instructions designed to apply the law to the facts in evidence. The judge will indicate which instructions he will accept and which he will refuse. The attorneys may make objections to such rulings for the purpose of the record in any appeal.

The judge reads these instructions to the jury. This is commonly referred to as the judge's *charge* to the jury. The instructions cover the law as applicable to the case.

In most cases, only the judge may determine what the law is. In some states, however, the jurors in criminal cases are judges of both the facts and the law.

In giving the instructions, the judge will state the issues in the case and define any terms or words necessary. He will tell the jury what it must decide on the issues, if it is to find for the plaintiff or state, or for the defendant. He will advise the jury that it is the sole judge of the facts and of the credibility of witnesses; that upon leaving the courtroom to reach a verdict, it must elect a *foreman* of the jury and then reach a decision based upon the judgment of each individual juror. In some states, the first juror chosen automatically becomes the foreman.

In the Jury Room. After the instructions, the bailiff will take the jury to the jury room to begin deliberations.

The bailiff will sit outside and not permit anyone to enter or leave the jury room. No one may attempt to *tamper* with the jury in any way while it is deliberating.

Ordinarily, the court furnishes the jury with written forms of all possible verdicts so that when a decision is reached, the jury can choose the proper verdict form.

The decision will be signed by the foreman of the jury and be returned to the courtroom. Ordinarily, the decision in a criminal case must be unanimous. In some jurisdictions, in civil cases, only nine or ten out of twelve jurors need agree to reach a verdict. However, all federal courts require a unanimous verdict.

If the jurors cannot agree on a verdict, the jury is called a *hung jury*, and the case may be retried before a new jury at a later date. In some states, the jury may take the judge's instructions and the exhibits introduced in evidence to the jury room. If necessary, the jury may return to the courtroom in the presence of counsel to ask a question of the judge about his instructions. In such instances, the judge may reread all or certain of the instructions previously given, or supplement or clarify them by further instructions.

If the jury is out overnight, the members often will be housed in a hotel and secluded from all contacts with other persons. In many cases, the jury will be excused to go home at night, especially if there is no objection by either party.

Verdict. Upon reaching a verdict, the jury returns to the courtroom with the bailiff and, in the presence of the judge, the parties and their respective attorneys, the verdict is read or announced aloud in open court. The reading or announcement may be made by the jury foreman or the court clerk.

Attorneys for either party, but usually the losing party, may ask that the jury be polled, in which case each individual juror will be asked if the verdict is his verdict. It is rare for a juror to say that it is not his verdict. When the verdict is read and accepted by the court, the jury is dismissed, and the trial is concluded.

Motions After Verdict. Motions permitted to be made after the verdict is rendered will vary from state to state.

A motion in arrest of judgment attacks the sufficiency of the indictment or information in a criminal case.

A motion for judgment non obstante veredicto may be made after the verdict and before the judgment. This motion requests the judge to enter a judgment for one party, notwithstanding the verdict of the jury in favor of the other side. Ordinarily, this motion raises the same questions as could be raised by a motion for directed verdict.

A motion for a new trial sets out alleged errors committed in the trial and asks the trial judge to grant a new trial. In some states, the losing party must make a motion for a new trial before appealing the verdict.

Judgment. The verdict of the jury is ineffective until the judge enters judgment upon the verdict. In a civil damage action, this judgment might read; *It is, therefore, ordered, adjudged and decreed that the plaintiff do have and recover the sum of $1,000 of and from the defendant.*

At the request of the plaintiff's lawyer, the clerk of court in such a case will deliver a paper called an execution to the sheriff, commanding him to take and sell the property of the defendant and apply the proceeds to the amount of the judgment.

Sentencing. In a criminal case, if the defendant is convicted, the judge will set a date for sentencing. At that time, the judge may consider mitigating facts in determining the appropriate sentence as well as facts about the defendant developed in a pre-sentence investigation.

In the great majority of states and in the federal courts, the function of imposing sentence is exclusively that of the judge. But in some states the jury is called upon to determine the sentence or make sentencing recommendations to the judge for some, or all crimes.

Rights of Appeal. In a civil case, either party may appeal to a higher court. But in a criminal case, although the defendant has a right to appeal, the prosecution may have no such right or a very limited right to appeal depending upon state law. Appeals in either civil or criminal cases may be on such grounds as errors in trial procedure and errors in substantive law—that is, in the interpretation of the law by the trial judge. These are the most common grounds for appeals to higher courts, although there are others.

The prosecution may not appeal in a criminal case if new evidence of defendant's guilt is discovered after his acquittal. Moreover, the state is powerless to bring the defendant to trial again on the same charge. The U.S. and most state constitutions prevent retrial under provisions known as *double jeopardy* clauses.

Criminal defendants have a further appellate safeguard. Those convicted in state courts may appeal to the federal courts on grounds of violation of constitutional rights, if such grounds exist. This privilege serves to impose the powerful check of the federal judicial system upon abuses that may occur in state criminal proceedings.

The record on appeal consists of the papers filed in the trial court and the court reporter's transcript of the evidence. The latter is called *a bill of exceptions* or *transcript on appeal* and must be certified by the trial judge as true and correct. In most states, only as much of the record need be included as will properly present the questions to be raised on appeal.

Appeal. Statutes or rules of court provide for procedure on appeals. Ordinarily, the party appealing is called the *appellant*, and the other party the *appellee*.

The appeal is initiated by filing the transcript of the trial court record with the appellate court within the time prescribed. This filing marks the beginning of the time period within which the appellant must file his brief setting forth the reasons and the law upon which he relies in seeking a reversal of the trial court.

The appellee then has a specified time within which to file his answer brief. Following this, the appellant may file a second brief, or brief in reply to the appellee's brief.

When the appeal has been fully briefed, the case may be set for hearing on *oral argument* before the appellate court. Sometimes the court itself will ask for argument; otherwise, one of the parties may petition for it. Often, appeals are submitted *on the briefs* without argument.

Courts of appeal do not hear further evidence, and it is unusual for any of the parties to the case to attend the hearing of the oral argument.

Generally, the case has been assigned to one of the judges of the appellate court, although the full court will hear the argument. Thereafter, it is customary for all the judges to confer on the issues presented, and then the judge who has been assigned the case will write an opinion. If a judge or judges disagree with the result, they may dissent and file a *dissenting opinion*. In many states, a written opinion is required.

An appellate court will usually not weigh evidence and generally will reverse a trial court for errors of law only.

Not every error of law will warrant a reversal. Some are *harmless errors*—that is, the rights of a party to a fair trial were not prejudiced by them.

However, an error of law, such as the admission of improper and persuasive evidence on a material issue, may and often does constitute a *prejudicial* and *reversible error*.

After the opinion is *handed down* and time for the filing of a petition for rehearing—or a petition for transfer, or a petition for *writ of certiorari* (if there is a higher appellate court)—has expired, the appellate court will send its *mandate* to the trial court for further action in the case.

If the lower court is *affirmed*, the case is ended; if reversed, the appellate court may direct that a new trial be held, or that the judgment of the trial court be modified and corrected as prescribed in the opinion.

The taking of an appeal ordinarily does not suspend the operation of a judgment obtained in a civil action in a trial court. Thus, the party prevailing in the trial court may order an execution issued on the judgment, unless the party appealing filed an *appeal* or *supersedes bond*, which binds the party and his surety to pay or perform the judgment in the event it is affirmed on appeal. The filing of this bond will stay further action on the judgment until the appeal has been concluded.

Chapter Nineteen

The Rules of the Game

Statutes and rules governing expert witnesses vary from court to court. There are state rules and Federal rules; there are rules of evidence and rules of civil procedure. Some of the more important Federal rules are reproduced here for ready reference. The name and location of the rules for each state are listed.

Ask your client-attorney which court is trying the case; which rules will apply. You will also want to obtain copies of the rules for each state you work in. Visit the *law* library, (probably) in the courthouse of your nearest large town or county seat. If the county seat is too far away, try a University law school.

A list of the statutes and rules governing expert witnesses in Federal Court as well as for each state follows.

The Federal Rules of Evidence.

The rules affecting expert witnesses are contained in Rules 702, 703, 704, 705, 706, and 803 (18). For current wording and comment, see Web site:

http://www.law.cornell.edu/rules/fre/overview.html

Rule 701. Opinion Testimony by Lay Witnesses

If the witness is not testifying as an expert, the witness's testimony in the form of opinions or inferences is limited to those opinions or inferences which are (a) rationally based on the perception of the witness and (b) helpful to a clear understanding of the witness's testimony or the determination of a fact in issue.

Rule 702. Testimony by Experts

If scientific, technical, or other specialized knowledge will assist the trier of fact to understand the evidence or to determine a fact in issue, a witness qualified as an expert by knowledge, skill, experience, training, or education, may testify thereto in the form of an opinion or otherwise.

Rule 703. Bases of Opinion Testimony by Experts

The facts or data in the particular case upon which an expert bases an opinion or inference may be those perceived by or made known to the expert at or before the hearing. If of a type reasonably relied upon by experts in the particular field in forming opinions or inferences upon the subject, the facts or data need not be admissible in evidence.

Rule 704. Opinion on Ultimate Issue

(a) Except as provided in subdivision "b", testimony in the form of an opinion or inference otherwise admissible is not objectionable because it embraces an ultimate issue to be decided by the trier of fact.

(b) No expert witness testifying with respect to the mental state or condition of a defendant in a criminal case may state an opinion or inference as to whether the defendant did or did not have the mental state or condition constituting an element of the crime charged or of a defense thereto.

Such ultimate issues are matters for the trier of fact alone.

Rule 705. Disclosure of Facts or Data Underlying Expert Opinion

The expert may testify in terms of opinion or inference and give reasons therefore without first testifying to the underlying facts or data, unless the court requires otherwise. The expert may in any event be required to disclose the underlying facts or data on cross-examination.

Rule 706. Court-Appointed Experts

(a) **Appointment**. The court may on its own motion or

on the motion of any party enter an order to show cause why expert witnesses should not be appointed, and may request the parties to submit nominations. The court may appoint any expert witnesses agreed upon by the parties, and may appoint expert witnesses of its own selection. An expert witness shall not be appointed by the court unless the witness consents to act. A witness so appointed shall be informed of the witness's duties by the court in writing, a copy of which shall be filed with the clerk, or at a conference in which the parties shall have opportunity to participate. A witness so appointed shall advise the parties of the witness's findings, if any; the witness's deposition may be taken by any party; and the witness may be called to testify by the court or any party. The witness shall be subject to cross-examination by each party, including a party calling the witness.

(b) **Compensation.** Expert witnesses so appointed are entitled to reasonable compensation in whatever sum the court may allow. The compensation thus fixed is payable from funds which may be provided by law in criminal cases and civil actions and proceedings involving just compensation under the fifth amendment. In other civil actions and proceedings the compensation shall be paid by the parties in such proportion and at such time as the court directs, and thereafter charged in like manner as other costs.

(c) **Disclosure of appointment.** In the exercise of its discretion, the court may authorize disclosure to the jury of the fact that the court appointed the expert witness.

(d) **Parties' experts of own selection.** Nothing in this rule limits the parties in calling expert witnesses of their own selection.

Rule 803. Hearsay Exceptions; Availability of Declarant Immaterial

The following are not excluded by the hearsay rule, even though the declarant is available as a witness:

(18) Learned treatises. To the extent called to the attention of an expert witness upon cross-examination or relied upon by the expert witness in direct examination, statements contained in published treatises, periodicals, or pamphlets on a subject of history, medicine, or other science or art, established as a reliable authority by the testimony or admission of the witness or by other expert testimony or by judicial notice. If admitted, the statements may be read into evidence but may not be received as exhibits.

Federal Rules of Civil Procedure: See especially Rules 26-32, 35, and 45. See web site:

http://www.law.cornell.edu/rules/frcp/overview.html

Also check the state statutes and rules governing expert witnesses.

CHAPTER TWENTY

✿

WHERE ARE WE GOING FROM HERE?

THE FUTURE CHALLENGES TO THE EXPERT

The use of expert witnesses and the role of the expert are constantly evolving. Here are some comments, predictions and suggestions.

1. There will be more attorneys. Law schools are turning out lawyers in record numbers. There are 175 accredited law schools in the U.S. Law school administrators say the glamorized image of lawyers on television continues to lure many to law school. Many people, who might otherwise have pursued MBA degrees, have selected law schools. Once they graduate, they select law rather than business. In the early 60s, it was unusual to see female students in law school. Today they make up over half the student body in many schools.

2. Lawyers are becoming more creative. There has been a decline in high-paying legal jobs and law schools are finding it more difficult to place graduates. Lawyers are working harder to scrounge up work. They are becoming increasingly creative with reasons (theories) to sue.

Experts have to be more vigilant about getting paid.

3. Experts will be used more and more. It used to be that if one side hired an expert, the other side had to get one. Now it is a question of how many experts each side will have.

4. Consequently, courts will be more critical of experts. Judges are trying to cut down the number of experts used. Your CV, credentials, brochures and materials must look good so you don't get cut out of the case. Attach a tailored supplemental CV emphasizing your expertise relevant to the case to your full-blown CV. Remember, the CV you take to court must be the same one you produce for discovery (deposition).

5. Competition between experts will be tougher. More and more good people are losing their jobs due to downsizing and becoming consultants. Consultants often become expert witnesses.

6. You must have presentation skills—you must be able to perform. Remember, you are dealing with juries who were raised on TV. Testify in sound bites. You must speak clearly and say things that are understandable, short and memorable.

7. Your demonstrative evidence has to be better and your presentations in court have to be slicker. Consider using video, animation and new presentation technologies; boards and overlays may not be enough.

8. Lawyers are becoming more and more specialized. There are many books, seminars and newsletters on special areas within the bar. As lawyers focus on certain areas of the law, they become experts in their own right and often have libraries and files full of research gleaned from other cases and other experts.

Experts will become more specialized within their areas of expertise too. So, specialize and surround yourself with resource people: investigators, testing laboratories, other experts, etc. Promote a *team* approach. Specialize and provide full service.

9. The stakes are getting bigger. Experts must be familiar with the Federal Rules of Evidence and the Federal Rules of Civil Procedure. You would not play poker without knowing the rules. Do not go into court uninformed.

10. There will be more electronic communication. In some

jurisdictions, it is no longer necessary to haul a criminal from jail to court. Video-conferencing is used for court proceedings. Expert testimony may go the same way to eliminate travel and make better use of expert time. And there will be more video depositions.

11. As court dockets become more crowded and cases take longer to conclude, there will be more opportunities for experts in arbitration and mediation. Many judges are leaving the bench to make more money in alternative dispute resolution.

So the future is bright for expert witnesses; this is a growth industry. As life, science and technology become more complex, consultants will be required to explain them. There is a need for fresh, new experts who want to pursue truth and can work for the plaintiff or defendant with equal ease.

APPENDIX

GLOSSARY OF TERMS

The following definitions of terms are of interest to the expert witness. For further information see the many texts on the subject. *Black's Law Dictionary* provides definitions for thousands of legal terms.

Acquittal: The verdict in a criminal trial in which the defendant is found not guilty.

Action: The formal legal demand of one's rights from another person brought in court. A lawsuit.

Adjudication: The formal pronouncing or recording of a judgment or decree by a court. The court's final order.

Adversary System: The system of trial practice in the U.S. and some other countries in which each of the opposing, or adversary, parties has full opportunity to present and establish its opposing contentions before the court.

Affidavit: A written statement or declaration of facts sworn to by the maker, taken before a person officially permitted by law to administer oaths.

Allegation: The assertion, declaration, or statement of a party to an action, made in a pleading, setting out what he or she expects to prove.

Amicus Curiae: Literally, friend of the court. A party with strong interest in, or views on, the subject matter of the dispute will petition the court for permission to file a brief, ostensibly on behalf of a party but actually to suggest a rationale consistent with its own views.

Answer: The pleading filed by the defendant in response to plaintiff's complaint.

Appearance: The formal proceeding by which a defendant submits himself to the jurisdiction of the court.

Appellant: The party appealing a decision or judgment to a higher court.

Appellee: The party against whom an appeal is taken (usually, but not always the winner in the lower court). It should be noted that a party's status as appellant or appellee bears no relation to his status as plaintiff or defendant in the lower court.

Arbitration: The hearing and settlement of a dispute between opposing parties by a third party who is not a judge. This decision is often binding by prior agreement of the parties.

Arraignment: In criminal practice, to bring a prisoner to the bar of the court to answer to a criminal charge.

Bailiff: A court attendant whose duties are to keep order in the courtroom and to have custody of the jury.

Best Evidence: Primary evidence; the best evidence which is available; any evidence falling short of this standard is secondary; i.e., an original letter is best evidence compared to a copy.

Bifurcation: The splitting of a case into separate issues.

Brief: (1) In American law practice, a written statement prepared by the counsel arguing a case in court. It contains a summary of the facts of the case, the pertinent laws, and an argument of how the law applies to the facts supporting counsel's position; or (2) A summary of a published opinion of a case prepared for studying the opinion in law school.

Burden of Proof: In the law of evidence, the necessity or duty of affirmatively proving a fact or facts in dispute.

Calendar: Can mean the order in which cases are to be heard during a term of court. The *Martindale-Hubbel Law Directory* contains calendars for state and federal courts, and includes the name of the court, the name of the judge, and the date of the term's beginning.

Case in Point: A judicial opinion which deals with a fact situation similar to the one being researched and substantiates a point of law to be asserted. (Also called a *Case on All Fours.*)

Case Law: The law of reported appellate judicial opinions as distinguished from statutes or administrative law.

Cause of Action: A claim in law and in fact sufficient to bring the case to court; the grounds of an action. (Example: breach of contract.)

Cause: A suit, litigation or action—civil or criminal.

Chambers: Private office or room of a judge.

Change of venue: The removal of a suit begun in one county or district, to another, for trial, or from one court to another in the same county or district.

Chattel: Any article of personal property, as opposed to real property. It may refer to animate as well as inanimate property.

Circuit Courts: Originally, courts whose jurisdiction extended over several counties or districts, and whose sessions were held in such counties or districts alternately; today, a circuit court may hold all its sessions in one county.

Circumstantial Evidence: All evidence of indirect nature; the process of decision by which court or jury may reason, from circumstances known or proved to establish by inference, the principal fact.

Citation: The reference to authority (previous cases) necessary to substantiate the validity of one's argument or position.

Civil Law: (1) Roman law embodied in the Code of Justinian which presently prevails in most countries of Western Europe other than Great Britain and which is the foundation of Louisiana law (civil law versus common law); (2) the law concerning non-criminal matters in a common law jurisdiction (civil law versus criminal law).

Claim: (1) The assertion of a right, as to money or property; (2) the accumulation of facts which give rise to a right enforceable in court.

Class Action: A lawsuit brought by a representative party on behalf of a large group, all of whose members have the same or a similar grievance against the defendant. Used when the group is too large for it to be practical to name every member of the group as a party.

Code: By popular usage a compilation or a revised statute. Technically, the laws in force are rewritten and arranged in classified order, with the addition of material having the force of law taken from judicial decrees. The repealed and temporary acts are eliminated and the revision is re-enacted.

Codification: The process of collecting and arranging systematically, usually by subject, the laws of a state or country. The end product may be called a code, revised code or revised statutes.

Commit: To send a person to prison, an asylum, workhouse, or reformatory by lawful authority.

Common Law: The origin of the Anglo-American legal systems. English common law was largely customary law and unwritten, until discovered, applied, and reported by the courts of law. In theory, the common law courts did not create law but rather discovered it in the customs and habits of the English people. The strength of the judicial system in pre-parliamentary days is one reason for the continued emphasis in common law systems on case law (prior decisions). In a narrow sense, common law is the phrase still used to distinguish case law from statutory law.

Complaint: The plaintiff's initial pleading and, according to the Federal Rules of Civil Procedure, is no longer full of the technicalities demanded by the common law. A complaint need only contain a short and plain statement of the claim upon which relief is sought, an indication of the type of relief requested, and an indication that the court has jurisdiction to hear the case.

Condemnation: The legal process by which real estate of a private owner is taken for public use without his consent, but upon the award and payment of just compensation.

Consideration: Something to be done or abstained from, by one party to a contract in order to induce another party to enter into a contract. Usually refers to money.

Contempt of Court: Any act calculated to embarrass, hinder, or obstruct a court in the administration of justice, or calculated to lessen its authority or dignity. Contempts are of two kinds: direct and indirect. Direct contempts are those committed in the immediate presence of the court; indirect is the term chiefly used with reference to the failure or refusal to obey a lawful order.

Conversion: The wrongful appropriation to oneself of the personal property of another.

Conveyance: The transfer of title to property from one person to another.

Corpus Delicti: The body (material substance) upon which a crime has been committed. e.g., the corpse of a murdered person, the charred remains of a burned house.

Corroborating Evidence: Evidence supplementary to that already given and tending to strengthen or confirm it.

Costs: An allowance for expenses in prosecuting or defending a suit. Ordinarily does not include attorney's fees.

Count: A separate and independent claim. A civil petition or a criminal indictment may contain several counts.

Counterclaim: A claim presented by a defendant in opposition to the claim of a plaintiff; it constitutes a separate cause of action.

Cross-examination: The questioning of a witness in a trial, or in the taking of a deposition, by the party opposed to the one who produced the witness.

Damages: Monetary compensation awarded by a court for an injury caused by the act of another. Damages may be *actual* or *compensatory* (equal to the amount of loss shown), *exemplary* or *punitive* (in excess of the actual loss and which is given to punish the person for the malicious conduct which caused the injury), or nominal (less than the actual loss—often a trivial amount such as one dollar) which is given because the injury is slight or because the exact amount of injury has not been determined satisfactorily.

Decree: A decision or order of the court. A final decree is one which fully and finally disposes of the litigation; an interlocutory decree is a provisional or preliminary decree which is not final.

Default: A default in an action of law occurs when a defendant omits to plead within the time allowed or fails to appear at the trial.

Defendant: The person against whom a civil or criminal action is brought.

Demur: To file a pleading (called a *demurrer*) admitting the truth of the facts in the complaint, or answer, but contending they are legally insufficient.

Deposition: A form of oral testimony taken by the opposing attorney in advance of the trial with a court reporter present to record every word. (See Chapter Ten)

Direct Evidence: Proof of facts by witnesses who saw acts done or heard words spoken, as distinguished from circumstantial evidence, which is called indirect.

Direct Examination: The first interrogation of a witness by the party on whose behalf he is called.

Directed Verdict: An instruction by the judge to the jury to return a specific verdict.

Dismissal Without Prejudice: Permits the complainant to sue again on the same cause of action, while dismissal *with prejudice* bars the right to bring or maintain an action on the same claim or cause.

Docket Number: A number, sequentially assigned by the clerk at the outset to a lawsuit brought to a court for adjudication.

Double Jeopardy: Common-law and constitutional prohibition against more than one prosecution for the same crime, transaction or omission.

Due Care: The legal duty one owes to another according to the circumstances of a particular case.

Due Process: Law in its regular course of administration through the courts of justice. The guarantee of due process requires that every person have the protection of a fair trial.

Felony: A crime of a graver nature than a misdemeanor. Generally, an offense punishable by death or imprisonment in a penitentiary.

Fraud: An intentional perversion of truth; deceitful practice or device resorted to with intent to deprive another of property or other right, or in some manner to do him injury.

Garnishment: A proceeding whereby property, money or credits of a debtor, in possession of another (the garnishee), are applied to the debts of the debtor.

Grand Jury: A jury of inquiry whose duty is to receive complaints and accusations in criminal cases, hear the evidence and find bills of indictment in cases where they are satisfied that there is probable cause that a crime was committed and that a trial ought to be held.

Habeas Corpus: *You have the body.* The name given a variety of writs whose object is to bring a person before a court or judge. In most common usage, it is directed to the official or person detaining another, commanding him to produce the body of the prisoner or person detained so the court may determine if such person has been denied his liberty without due process of law.

Hearings: Extensively employed by both legislative and administrative agencies and can be adjudicative or merely investigatory. Adjudicative hearings can be appealed in a court of law. Congressional committees often hold hearings prior to enactment of legislation; these hearings are then important sources of legislative history. Adjudicative hearings are like trials.

Hearsay: Evidence not proceeding from the personal knowledge of the witness, such as a rumor.

Hornbook: The popular reference to a series of textbooks published which reviews a certain field of law in summary, textual form, as opposed to a casebook which is designed as a teaching tool and includes many reprints of court opinions.

Hostile Witness: A witness who is subject to cross-examination by the party who called him to testify, because of his evident antagonism toward that party as exhibited in his direct examination.

Hypothetical Question: A combination of facts and circumstances, assumed or proved, stated in such a form as to constitute a coherent state of facts upon which the opinion of an expert can be asked by way of evidence in a trial.

Impeachment of Witness: An attack on the credibility of a witness.

In Camera: In the judge's chambers; in private.

Inadmissible: That which, under the established rules of evidence, cannot be admitted or received.

Indictment: An accusation in writing found and presented by a grand jury, charging that a person therein named has done some act, or been guilty of some omission, which, by law, is a crime.

Injunction: A judge's order that a person do or, more commonly, refrain from doing a certain act. An injunction may be preliminary or temporary pending trial of the issue presented, or it may be final if the issue has already been decided in court.

Instruction: A direction given by the judge to the jury concerning the law of the case.

Interlocutory: Provisional; temporary; not final. Refers to orders and decrees of a court.

Interrogatories: A series of formal written questions sent to the opposing side. The opposition must provide written answers under oath. Typically the asking side is fishing for information and the answering side is as vague as legally possible.

Intervention: A proceeding in a suit or action by which a third person is permitted by the court to make himself a party.

Irrelevant: Evidence not relating or applicable to the matter in issue; not supporting the issue.

Jurisdiction: The power given to a court by a Constitution or a legislative body to make legally binding decisions over certain persons or property.

Jurisprudence: (1) The science or philosophy of law; (2) a collective term for case law, as opposed to legislation.

Jury: A certain number of persons, selected according to law, and sworn to inquire of certain matters of fact, and declare the truth upon evidence laid before them.

Key Number: Part of the major indexing system devised for American case law, developed by West Publishing Company. The key number is a permanent number given to a specific point of this case law.

Leading Question: One which instructs a witness how to answer or puts into his mouth words to be echoed back; one which suggests to the witness the answer desired. Prohibited on direct examination.

Liability: The condition of being responsible either for damages resulting from an injurious act or for discharging an obligation or debt.

Libel: A method of defamation expressed by print, writing, pictures, or signs. In its most general sense, any publication that is injurious to the reputation of another.

Lein: A claim against property as security for a debt, under which the property may be seized and sold to satisfy the debt.

Limitation: A certain time allowed by statute in which litigation must be brought. Statute of limitations.

Litigate: To bring a civil action in court.

Local Counsel: A local attorney who assists an out-of-town attorney in the litigation of a case.

Malfeasance: Evil doing; ill conduct; the commission of some act which is positively prohibited by law.

Mandamus: The name of a writ which issues from a court of superior jurisdiction, directed to an inferior court, commanding the performance of a particular act.

Mandate: A judicial command or precept proceeding from a court or judicial officer, directing the proper officer to enforce a judgment, sentence, or decree.

Material Evidence: Such as is relevant and goes to the substantial issues in dispute.

Misdemeanor: Offenses less than felonies; generally those punishable by fine or imprisonment otherwise than in penitentiaries.

Misfeasance: A misdeed or trespass; the improper performance of some act which a person may lawfully do.

Mistrial: An erroneous, abortive or invalid trial; a trial which cannot stand in law because of lack of jurisdiction, wrong drawing of jurors, or disregard of some other fundamental requisite.

Mitigating Circumstance: One which does not constitute a justification or excuse for an offense, but which may be considered as reducing the degree of moral culpability.

Moot: Unsettled; undecided. A moot point is one not settled by judicial decisions.

Motion: A formal request made to a judge pertaining to any issue arising during the pendency of a lawsuit.

Negligence: The failure to do something which a reasonable man, guided by ordinary considerations, would do; or the doing of something which a reasonable and prudent man would not do.

Nexus: A connection between groups or series.

Nolo Contendere: A pleading usually used by defendants in criminal cases, which literally means *I will not contest it.*

Nonfeasance: Failure to act. Failure to do what ought to be done.

Objection: The act of taking exception to some statement or procedure in trial. Used to call the court's attention to improper evidence or procedure.

Of Counsel: A phrase commonly applied to counsel employed to assist in the preparation or management of the case, or its presentation on appeal, but who is not the principal attorney of record.

Out of Court: One who has no legal status in court is said to be *out of court,* i.e., he is not before the court. For example, when a plaintiff, by some act of omission or commission, shows that he is unable to maintain his action, he is frequently said to have put himself out of court.

Panel: A list of jurors to serve in a particular court, or for the trial of a particular action; denotes either the whole body of persons summoned as jurors for a particular term of court or those selected by the clerk by lot.

Parties: The persons who are actively concerned in the prosecution or defense of a legal proceeding.

Percipient Witness: One who was there and saw what happened; An eyewitness.

Peremptory Challenge: The challenge which the prosecution or defense may use to reject a certain number of prospective jurors without giving any explanation or reason.

Petit Jury: The ordinary jury of twelve (or fewer) persons for the trial of a civil or criminal case. So called to distinguish it from the grand jury.

Petition: A formal, written application to a court requesting judicial action on a certain matter.

Petitioner: The person presenting a petition to a court, officer, or legislative body; the one who starts an equity proceeding or the one who takes an appeal from a judgment.

Plaintiff: A person who brings an action; the party who complains or sues in a personal action and is so named on the record.

Plea Bargaining: The process whereby the accused and the prosecutor in a criminal case work out a mutually satisfactory disposition of the case. It usually involves the defendant's pleading guilty to a lesser offense or to only one or some of the counts of a multi-count indictment in return for a lighter sentence than that possible for the graver charge.

Pleading: The process by which the parties in a suit or action alternately present written statements of their contentions, each responsive to that which precedes, and each serving to narrow the field of controversy, until there evolves a single point, affirmed on one side and denied on the other, called the issue upon which they then go to trial.

Polling the Jury: A practice whereby the jurors are asked individually whether they assented, and still assent, to the verdict.

Power of Attorney: An instrument authorizing another to act as one's agent or attorney.

Prejudicial Error: Synonymous with reversible error; an error which warrants the appellate court to reverse the judgment before it. Distinguished from harmless error, which does not merit reversal.

Preliminary Hearing: Synonymous with *preliminary examination;* the hearing given a person charged with a crime by a magistrate or judge to determine whether he or she should be held for trial. Since the Constitution states that a person cannot be accused in secret, a preliminary hearing is open to the public unless the defendant requests that it be closed. The accused person must be present at this hearing and must be accompanied by his or her attorney.

Preponderance of evidence: In a civil case, the plaintiff must prove their case and the defendant must prove any defenses asserted by a preponderance of evidence. This is the greater weight of the credible evidence which may be less than the proof beyond reasonable doubt, which would be required in a criminal case.

Presumption of Fact: An inference as to the truth or falsity of any proposition of fact, drawn by a process of reasoning in the absence of actual certainty of its truth or falsity, or until such certainty can be ascertained.

Presumption of Law: A rule of law that courts and judges shall draw a particular inference from a particular fact, or from particular evidence.

Procedural Law: That law which governs the operation of the legal system, including court rules and rules of procedure, as distinguished from substantive law.

Prosecutor: One who instigates the prosecution upon which an accused is arrested or one who brings an accusation against the party whom he suspects to be guilty; also, one who takes charge of a case and performs the function of trial lawyer for the people.

Quash: To overthrow; vacate; to annul or void a summons or indictment.

Reasonable Doubt: In a criminal case, an accused person is entitled to acquittal if, in the minds of the jury, his guilt has not been proved *beyond a reasonable doubt;* that state of the minds of jurors in which they cannot say they feel an abiding conviction as to the truth of the charge.

Rebuttal: The introduction of rebutting evidence; the showing that statements of witnesses as to what occurred is not true; the stage of a trial at which such evidence may be introduced.

Redirect Examination: Follows cross-examination and is exercised by the party who first examined the witness.

Referee: A person to whom a cause pending in a court is referred by the court to take testimony, hear the parties, and report thereon to the court. He is an officer exercising judicial powers and is an arm of the court for a specific purpose.

Remand: To send back for further proceedings, as when a higher court sends back to a lower court.

Resolution: A formal expression of the opinion of a rule-making body adopted by the vote of that body.

Respondent: The party who makes an answer to a bill in an equity proceeding or who contends against an appeal.

Rest: A party is said to rest or rest his case when he has presented all the evidence he intends to offer.

Retainer: Act of the client in employing his attorney or counsel, and also denotes the fee which the client pays when he retains the attorney to act for him.

Rules of Court: Rules that regulate practice and procedure before the various courts. In most jurisdictions, these rules are issued by the court itself, or by the highest court in that jurisdiction.

Slander: Base and defamatory spoken words tending to harm another's reputation, business or means of livelihood. Both libel and slander are methods of defamation—the former being expressed by print, writings, pictures or signs; the latter orally.

Stare Decisis: The doctrine of English and American law which states that when a court has formulated a principle of law as applicable to a given set of facts, it will follow that principle and apply it in future cases where the facts are substantially the same. It connotes the decision of present cases on the basis of past precedent.

State's Evidence: Testimony given by an accomplice or participant in a crime, tending to convict others.

Statute: The written law in contradistinction to the unwritten law.

Statutes of Limitations: Laws setting time periods during which disputes may be taken to court.

Stay: A stopping or arresting of a judicial proceeding by order of the court.

Stipulation: An agreement by attorneys on opposite sides of a case as to any matter pertaining to the proceedings or trial.

Subpoena: A process to order a witness to appear and give testimony before a court or magistrate.

Subpoena Duces Tecum: A process by which the court commands a witness to appear and produce certain documents, records, or other physical things in a trial.

Substantive Law: That law which establishes rights and obligations as distinguished from procedural law, which is concerned with rules for establishing their judicial enforcement.

Summons: A writ directing the sheriff or other officer to notify the named person that an action has been commenced against him in court and that he is required to appear, on the day named, and answer the complaint in such action.

Testimony: Oral evidence given by a competent witness, under oath; as distinguished from evidence derived from writings and other sources.

Tort: An injury or wrong committed, either with or without force, to the person or property of another.

Transcript: The official record of proceedings in a trial or hearing.

Trespass: An unlawful interference with one's person, property, or rights. At common law, trespass was a form of action brought to recover damages for any injury to one's person or property or relationship with another.

Trier of Fact: The jury in a *jury trial*. The judge in a court (no jury) *court trial*.

Venire: Technically, a writ summoning persons to court to act as jurors; popularly used as meaning the body of names thus summoned.

Venue: The particular county, city or geographical area in which a court with jurisdiction may hear and determine a case.

Verdict: In practice, the formal and unanimous decision or finding made by a jury, reported to the court and accepted by it.

Waiver of Immunity: A means authorized by statutes by which a witness, in advance of giving testimony or producing evidence, may renounce the fundamental right guaranteed by the Constitution that no person shall be compelled to be a witness against himself.

Warrant of Arrest: A writ issued by a magistrate, justice, or other competent authority, to a sheriff, or other officer, requiring him to arrest a person therein named and bring him or her before the magistrate or court to answer to a specified charge.

Weight of Evidence: The balance or preponderance of evidence; the inclination of the greater amount of credible evidence, offered in a trial, to support one side of the issue rather than the other.

Willful: A willful act is one done intentionally, without justifiable cause, as distinguished from an act done carelessly or inadvertently.

With Prejudice: The term, as applied to judgment of dismissal, is as conclusive of rights of parties as if action had been prosecuted to final adjudication adverse to the plaintiff.

Without Prejudice: A dismissal *without prejudice* allows a new suit to be brought on the same cause of action.

Witness: One who testifies to what he or she has seen, heard, or otherwise observed.

Writ: An order issuing from a court of justice and requiring the performance of a specified act, or giving authority and commission to have it done.

DIRECTORIES

Write to each directory for information on their services and an application. Some directories offer free listings but most charge. (See Chapter Two) Many bar associations publish a local expert directory.

Forensic Services Directory
National Forensic Center
Betty Lipscher
Hardcover 1,400+ pages $125.50; CD-ROM $195.00
17 Temple Terrace, Suite 401
Lawrenceville, NJ 08648
Tel: (800) 526-5177; (609) 883-0550; Fax: (609) 883-7622
e-mail: forenexpts@aol.com

SAE Consultants Directory ($39.00)
(combined aerospace & automotive directories)
Society of Automotive Engineers
400 Commonwealth Drive, #620
Warrendale, PA 15096-0001
Tel: (412) 776-4970; (412) 776-4841; Fax: (412) 776-0790
Web site: http://www.sae.org

Directory of Scientific & Technical Consultants & Expert Witnesses
Softcover 224 pages $40.00
American Society for Testing and Materials (ASTM)
100 Barr Harbor Drive
West Conshohocken, PA 19428-2959
Tel: (610) 832-9500; Fax: (610) 832-9555
e-mail: service@local.astm.org; Web site: http://www.astm.org

Expert Witness Bank
(45,000 expert files; member only service)
Defense Research Institute (DRI)
750 North Lake Shore Drive, #500
Chicago, IL 60611
Tel: (312) 944-0575; Fax: (312) 944-2003

Register of Expert Witnesses ($15.00)
American Bar Association
750 North Lake Shore Drive
Chicago, IL 60611
Tel: (800) 285-2221; (312) 988-5000; Fax: (312) 988-5568
e-mail: abasvcctr@attmail.com; Web site: http://www.abanet.org

The Legal Expert Pages (California) $100.00
Haslam Publishing
PO Box 270770
San Diego, CA 92198-2770
Tel: (800) 959-7680; (619) 487-6194; Fax: (619) 487-0083
e-mail: haslampub@aol.com

Southwest Directory of Expert Witnesses & Consultants
Texas Lawyer
400 South Record Street, #1400
Dallas, TX 75202-4889
Tel: (800) 456-5484; (214) 744-9300; Fax: (214) 741-2325
e-mail: law.marketing@counsel.com

*Best Directory of Recommended Insurance Attorneys & Adjusters/Expert
Services Section*
A.M. Best & Co.
Ambest Road
Oldwick, NJ 08858
Tel: (908) 439-2200; Fax: (908) 534-1506
Web site: http://www.ambest.com

Expert Pages (on-line)
affiliate of The Seamless Website
300 Enclave Lane
Bedminster, NJ 07921-1916

Tel: (908) 719-2244; Fax: (908) 234-0578;
e-mail: Webmaster@expertpages.com
Web site: http://www.ExpertPages.com

The Noble Internet Directory
PO Box 8208
Foster City, CA 94404
Tel: (800) 640-5959; e-mail: noble@sirius.com;
Web site: http://www.experts.com

The National Directory of Expert Witnesses—online
Claims Providers of America
PO Box 395
Esparto, CA 95627
Tel: (800) 735-6660; Fax: (916) 796-3631;
e-mail: info@claims.com; Web site: http://www.claims.com

Consultants and Consulting Organizations Directory ($525.00)
Darnay & Utener, 16th ed.
Gale Research, Inc.
835 Penobscot Bldg.
Detroit, MI 48226-4094
Tel: (800) 877-4253; (313) 961-2242; Fax: (313) 961-6083

Martindale-Hubbell® Buyer's Guide
Services, Suppliers & Consultants to the Legal Profession
Reed Reference Publishing Company
Tel: (800) 526-4902; Fax: (908) 464-3553

REGISTRIES/BROKERS

Write to each registry for information on their services and an application. Most registries charge a percentage of your fee for each case referred to you. (See Chapter Two) For more registries, usually in more specific disciplines, see *Lawyer's Desk Reference.*

Technical Advisory Service for Attorneys (TASA)
TASA lists more than 24,000 experts in over 6000 categories of expertise.
1166 DeKalb Pike
Blue Bell, PA 19422-1844
Tel: (800) 523-2319; (610) 275-8272; Fax: (800) 329-8272

Technical Advisory Service for Attorneys (TASA)
608 E. Missouri Avenue, Suite D
Phoenix, AZ 85012
Tel: (800) 659-8464; (602) 248-8464; Fax: (602) 274-3720

Forensic Expert Advisers, Inc.
Maureen Shepherd
3305 S. Woodland Place
Santa Ana, CA 92707
Tel: (714) 754-4332; Fax: (714) 754-7432

Maritime & Aviation Consultants
Kirk Greiner
15112 NE 30th Avenue
Vancouver, WA 98686-1669
Tel: (360) 574-1100; Fax: (360) 574-1101;
e-mail: cptkirk@pacifier.com
Web site: http://www.mac-experts.com

Experts Unlimited
Dean C. Dauw, Ph.D.
1212 Lakeshore Drive, #34CN
Chicago, IL 60610
Tel: (800) 432-2083; (312) 644-1920; Fax: (312)649-0588
e-mail: 74514.2152@compuserv.com
American Lawyer Expert Witness & Consultant Referral Service
400 S. Record Street, #1400
Dallas, TX 75202-4889
Tel: (800) 456-5484; (214) 744-9300; Fax: (214) 741-2325
e-mail: law.marketing@counsel.com

Medical Advisors, Inc.
Gary Steinberg
PO Box 1537
501 Office Center Drive, #248
Fort Washington, PA 19034-3220
Tel: (215) 654-0650; Fax: (215) 654-9011

National Consultant Referrals, Inc.
4918 N. Harbor Drive, #103
San Diego, CA 92106
Tel: (800) 221-3104; (619) 523-2188; Fax: (619) 523-2184
e-mail: kline@referrals.com; Web site: http://www.referrals.com

Expert Resources, Inc.
Christina King
4700 North Prospect Road, #1B
Peoria Heights, IL 61614
Tel: (800) 383-4857; (309) 688-4857; Fax: (309) 688-0915
Nationwide database of 3,000+ experts.

Legal Expert Network
Melvin Kramer, M.P.H.
7904 Starburst Drive
Baltimore, MD 21208-3033
Tel: (410) 653-5121; Fax: (410) 484-9515
National general search firm w/ experts & attorneys from Hawaii to
Puerto Rico

Association of Trial Lawyers of America
1050 31st Street NW
Washington, DC 20007
Tel: (202) 965-3500; Fax: (202) 298-6849
Database of concluded cases for locating and assessing
performance of experts

Medi-Legal Services
P.O. Box 1464
El Cajon, CA 92022
Tel: (619) 579-2135; Fax: (619) 444-6473

PROFESSIONAL ORGANIZATIONS AND IMPORTANT ADDRESSES

Here is a list of general forensic and other related organizations. For specific consulting organizations, see the *Encyclopedia of Associations* and *National Trade and Professional Associations*. Ask for them at the reference desk of your public library. You may wish to join some of these organizations and/or contact them about buying membership directories or renting membership mailing lists for promotional mailings.

National Forensic Center
Betty Lipscher
17 Temple Terrace, Suite 401
Lawrenceville, NJ 08648
Tel: (800) 526-5177 (609) 883-0550

American Academy of Forensic Sciences
Anne Warren, Exec. Dir.
410 N. 21st Street
Colorado Springs, CO 80904-2785
Tel: (800) 701-2237; (719) 636-1100; Fax: (719) 636-1993
e-mail: membship@aafs.com; Web site: http://www.aafs.com

Canadian Society of Forensic Science
Fredricka Monti
2660 Southdale Crescent #215
Ottawa, ON K1B 4W5
Canada
Tel: (613) 738-0001 Fax: (613-738-0001)

The American College of Forensic Examiners
Robert O'Block
2750 East Sunshine Street
Springfield, MO 65804
Tel: (800) 423-9737; (417) 881-3818; Fax: (417) 881-4702
e-mail: acfeme@aol.com; Web site: http://www.acfe.com

American Society of Trial Consultants
Ronald J. Matlon, Ph.D.
Dept. of Speech & Mass Communication
Towson State University
Towson, MD 21204
Tel: (410) 830-2448; Fax: (410) 830-3656

National Academy of Expert Witnesses, Inc.
7021 Pheasant Cross Drive
Baltimore, MD 21209-1021
Tel: (800) 296-6239; Tel: (410) 484-1140

Forensic Consultants Association
Margy Grabowski, FCA Administrator
1958 Milford Place
El Cajon, CA 92020
Tel: (619) 685-8043; Fax: (619)593-9989

American Standards Testing Bureau
John L. Zimmerman
40 Water Street
New York, NY 10004
Tel: (212) 943-3160; Fax: (212) 825-2250
Hotline: (800) 221-5170
(21 satellites nationwide)

American Society for Testing and Materials (ASTM)
100 Barr Harbor Drive
West Conshohocken, PA 19428-2959
Tel: (610) 832-9500; Fax: (610) 832-9555
e-mail: service@local.astm.org; Web site: http://www.astm.org

American National Standards Institute
11 W. 42nd Street, 13th Fl.
New York, NY 10036
Tel: (212) 642-4900; Fax: (212) 302-1286
Web site: http://www.ansi.org
Underwriters Laboratories (UL)
Publications Stock
333 Pfingsten Road
Northbrook, IL 60062
Tel: (847) 272-8800; Fax: (847) 272-8129

National Safety Council
1121 Spring Lake Drive
Itasca, IL 60143-3201
Tel: (708) 285-1121; Fax: (708) 285-1315
Web site: http://www.nsc.org\nsc

American Society of Mechanical Engineers
345 East 47th Street
New York, NY 10017
Tel: (212) 705-7722; Fax: (212) 705-7739
(800) 843-2763 Publication Department
Web site: http://www.asme.org

Int'l Society of Air Safety Investigators
5 Export Drive
Sterling, VA 20164
Tel: (703) 430-9668; Fax: (703) 450-1745
e-mail: 73450.2627@compuserv.com

American Bar Association
750 North Lake Shore Drive
Chicago, IL 60611
Tel: (800) 285-2221; (312) 988-5000; Fax: (312) 988-5568
e-mail: abasvcctr@attmail.com; Web site: http://www.abanet.org

Lawyer-Pilots Bar Association
P.O. Box 685
Poolesville, MD 20837
Tel: (301) 972-7700; Fax: (301) 972-7727

National Transportation Safety Board Bar Association
Harry Riggs, President; Tel: 606-283-0515
Mark McDermott, V.P.; Tel: 202-331-1955
PO Box 65461
Washington, DC 20036-5461
National Society of Professional Engineers
1420 King Street
Alexandria, VA 22314
Tel: (703) 684-2880 Fax: (703) 836-4875
Web site: http://www.nspe.org

Defense Research Institute (DRI)
750 North Lake Shore Drive, #500
Chicago, IL 60611
Tel: (312) 944-0575; Fax: (312) 944-2003
e-mail: dri@mcs.net; Web site: http://www.dri.org

Association of Trial Lawyers of America (ATLA)
1050 31st Street NW
Washington, DC 20007
Tel: (202) 965-3500; Fax: (202) 337-0977
800-344-3023 Exchange Plus
Web site: http://www.atlanet.org
Plaintiff or *consumer* association

BOOKS

Books of interest to the expert witness are listed below. For a more complete (though less specific) list, including books aimed at certain area specialties, see the *Catalog of Books* published by the National Forensic Center. Most of these books are available from the National Forensic Center.

Catalog of Books
National Forensic Center
17 Temple Terrace, Suite 401
Lawrenceville, NJ 08648
Tel: (800) 526-5177 (609) 883-0550; Fax: (609) 883-7622
e-mail: forenexpts@aol.com

Guide to Experts' Fees
National Forensic Center
Softcover 50 pages $29.95
17 Temple Terrace, Suite 401
Lawrenceville, NJ 08648
Tel: (800) 526-5177 (609) 883-0550; Fax: (609) 883-7622
e-mail: forenexpts@aol.com

Expert Witness Handbook; Tips and Techniques for the Litigation Consultant
Dan Poynter
Para Publishing
PO Box 8206-P
Santa Barbara, CA 93118-8206
Tel: (805) 968-7277; Fax: (805) 968-1379
e-mail:orders@ParaPublishing.com
Web site: http://www.ParaPublishing.com

How to be a Credible Witness ($10.00)
Katherine Koppenhaver
PO Box 324
Joppa, MD 21085
Tel: (800) 824-3236; Fax: (410-538-8548

Expert Witness Checklists ($160.00)
Douglas Danner & Larry Varn, 1983
Thompson Professional Publishing & Bancroft-Whitney Co.
Lawyers Co-operative Publishing Co.
Aqueduct Building, #660
Rochester, NY 14694
Tel: (800) 848-4000; (800) 527-0430 Fax: (800) 527-0432
Web site: http://www.lcp.com *or* http:///www.bw.com

Expert Witnesses in Civil Trials: Effective Preparation & Presentation
($103.00)
Supplements updated annually $66.00
Mark A. Dombroff
Thompson Legal Publishing & Lawyers Co-operative Publishing
(see above listing for contact info)

Expert Witnesses
Faust F. Rossi
Hardcover, 549 pages, $110.00, 1991
American Bar Association
750 North Lake Shore Drive
Chicago, IL 60611
Tel: (800) 285-2221; (312) 988-5000; Fax: (312) 988-5568
e-mail: abasvcctr@attmail.com; Web site: http://www.abanet.org

Expert Witnesses ($55.00)
Carol A. Jones
Oxford University Press
2001 Evans Road
Cary, NC 27513
Tel: (800) 451-7556; Fax: (919) 677-1303

The Expert Witness and His Evidence ($69.95)
Michael P. Reynolds and Phillip S. King
Blackwell Scientific Publications
238 Main Street
Cambridge, MA 02142
Tel: (800) 215-1000; Fax: (617) 492-5263

The Expert Witness Guide for Scientists & Engineers
Alan E. Surosky
Softcover 222 pages $42.50
Krieger Publishing Co.
Tel : (407) 727-7270; Fax: (407) 951-3671
Web site: http://www.web4u.com

Psychological Experts in Divorce, Personal Injury & Other Civil Actions
Marc J. Ackerman & Andrew Kane
Two vols. 1,032 pages $220.00
John Wiley & Sons, Inc.
Tel: (800) 225-5945; Fax: (800) 597-3299
Web site; http://www.wiley.com

California Expert Witness Guide ($125.00)
Raoul D. Kennedy, 1991
Continuing Education of the Bar
2300 Shattuck Avenue
Berkeley, CA 94704
Tel: (800) CEB-3444; Fax: (800) 640-6994

Effective Expert Witnessing; a Handbook for Technical Professionals
Jack V. Matson, 1994
Hardcover 224 pages $59.95
Lewis Publishers
Tel: (800) 272-7737; (407) 994-0555; Fax: (800) 374-3401
e-mail: orders@crcpress.com

The Expert Witness Survival Manual
Frank J. MacHovec, Ph.D.
Charles C. Thomas, Publisher
Hardcover, 171, pages, 1987, $42.95; paperback $29.95
Tel: (800) 258-8980; Fax: (217) 789-9130

Law for the Expert Witness
Daniel Bronstein
Hardcover 256 pages $64.95
Lewis Publishers
Tel: (800) 272-7737; (407) 994-0555; Fax: (800) 374-3401
e-mail: orders@crcpress.com

Succeeding as an Expert Witness
Harold Feder, JD
Softcover 252 pages $29.95
Tageh Press
Tel: (800) 468-2434

The Vocational Expert Primer
Terry L. Blackwell, Ed.D.
Softcover 117 pages $12.95
Elliot & Fitzpatrick
PO Box 1945
Athens, GA 30603
Tel: (800) 843-4977; Fax: (706) 546-8417

Testifying in Court: Guidelines & Maxims for Expert Witnesses
Stanley L. Brodsky
Softcover 208 pages $19.95
American Psychological Association
Tel: (800) 374-2721; Fax: (202) 336-5502
e-mail: ord@apa.com; Web site: http://www.order@apa.org

Litigation Services Handbook; The Role of the Accountant as Expert Witness
Frank, Wagner & Weil
Hardcover 936 pages $140.00 (supplements updated annually)
John Wiley & Sons, Inc.
Tel: (800) 225-5945; Fax: (800) 597-3299
Web site; http://www.wiley.com

The Consultant's Guide to Litigation Services: How to be an Expert Witness
Thomas Veitch, JD
Hardcover, 240 pages $75.00
John Wiley & Sons, Inc.
(see above listing for contact info)

The Consultant's Proposal
Ron Tepper
Paperback 256 pages $22.95
John Wiley & Sons, Inc.
(see above listing for contact info)

The Deposition Handbook
Dennis R. Suplee & Diana S. Donaldson, 1992
Second Edition 320 pages $125.00
John Wiley & Sons, Inc.
(see above listing for contact info)

Getting New Clients
Dick Connor & Jeff Davidson, 1992
Hardcover, 2nd ed. 304 pages $37.95
John Wiley & Sons, Inc.
(see above listing for contact info)

Expert Witnesses: Direct and Cross Examination
William G. Mulligan
Hardcover 750 pages $140.00 (supplements updated annually)
John Wiley & Sons, Inc.
(see above listing for contact info)

Marketing Your Expert Witness Practice
Charles Martini
Softcover 300 pages $49.95
National Forensic Center
Tel: (800) 526-5177; (609) 883-0550; Fax: (609) 883-7622
e-mail: forenexpts@aol.com

Witness Guide to Testifying in Court ($87.55)
Charlotte Hardwick
Pale Horse Publishing
PO Box 2569
Onalaska, TX 77360
Tel: (409) 646-5590; Fax: (409) 646-5521
e-mail: palehors@indirect.com;
Web site: http://www.indirect.com/www/palehors/

The Art of Cross-Examination
Irving Younger
$25.00, book only; $60.00 book and audio tapes
National Practice Institute
701 Fourth Ave. S, #800
Minneapolis, MN 55415
Tel: (800) 328-4444; (612) 338-1977; Fax: (612) 349-6561

Lawyers' Desk Reference
Technical Sources for Conducting a Personal Injury Action
Harry M. Philo, Esquire
Hardcover, 3 vols. $395.00; (supplements available $195.00)
Forms on disk $160.00
Clark, Boardman & Callahan
155 Pfingsten Road
Deerfield, IL 60015-4998
Tel: (800) 221-9428; Fax: (847) 948-9340
Web site: Http://www.cbclegalinternet

Handling Expert Witnesses in CA Courts ($58.00)
California Continuing Education of the Bar
2300 Shattuck Avenue, Suite 142
Berkeley,CA 94704
Tel: (800) CEB-3444; Fax: (800) 640-6994

What Makes Juries Listen; 2nd ed. (available 1/97)
Sonya Hamlin
Glasser LegalWorks
150 Clove Road
Little Falls, N.J. 07424
Tel: (800) 308-1700; Fax: (201) 890-0042
e-mail: legalwks@aol.com

Qualifying & Attacking Expert Witnesses
Robert C. Clifford
Binder 200 pages $89.98
James Publishing Co.
Tel: (800) 440-4780; (714) 556-0960; Fax: (714) 549-8835

Under Oath: Tips for Testifying
William P. Isele
Softcover 43 pages $19.95
LRP Publications
Tel: (800) 341-7874; (215) 784-0941; Fax: (215) 784-9639
e-mail: custserve@lrp.com; Web site: http://www.lrp.com

Marketing Your Consulting and Professional Services
Richard A Connor, Jr. & Jeffrey P. Davidson
2nd ed., 1990 Hardcover 256 pages $34.95
Wiley Interscience
605 Third Avenue
New York, NY 10158
Tel: (800) 225-5945; Fax: (800) 597-3299
Web site: http://www.wiley.com

The Use of Economists in Antitrust Litigation
Paperback 81 pages $35.00
American Bar Association Press
750 North Lake Shore Drive
Chicago, IL 60611
Tel: (800) 285-2221; (312) 988-5000; Fax: (312) 988-5568
e-mail: abasvcctr@attmail.com; Web site: http://www.abanet.org

The Role of Experts in Business Litigation ($5.00)
American Bar Association Press
(see above listing for contact info)
Expert Witness Handbook: A Guide for Engineers
D.G. Sunar, Ph.D.
2nd ed., 1989, Softcover 73 pages $14.95
Professional Publications
1250 Fifth Avenue
Belmont, CA 94002
Tel: (800) 426-1178; (415) 593-9119; Fax: (415) 592-4519
Web site: http://www.ppi2pass.com

Expert: A Guide to Service as a Forensic Professional and Expert Witness
($65.00)
ASFE, 1995
8811 Colesville Road
Silver Spring, MD 20909
Tel: (301) 565-2733; Fax: (301) 589-2017
e-mail: asfe@aol.com; Web site: http://www.asfe.org

Forensic Engineering
Sam Brown
Hardcover, 1995 656 pages $90.00
ISI Publications
Tel: (713) 441-8989; Fax: (713) 441-7896
e-mail: questisi@gnn.com

An Overview of the Law: A Guide for Testifying and Consulting Experts
Michael E. Sacks, Esq.
Softcover, 1995 62 pages, $19.95
LRP Publications
PO Box 980
Horsham, PA 19044-0980
Tel: (800) 341-7874; Fax: (215) 784-9639
e-mail: custserve@lrp.com; Web site: http://www.lrp.com

Expert Witnesses — Criminologists in the Courtroom
Patrick R. Anderson & L. Thomas Winfree, Jr.
Paperback $29.95; Clothbound $89.50
State University of New York Press
Tel: (800) 666-2211; Fax: (800) 688-2877

The Consultant's Kit ($39.50)
Jeffrey L. Lant, Ph.D.
50 Follen Street #5507-A
Cambridge, MA 02138
Tel: (617) 547-6372; Fax: (617) 547-0061

PERIODICALS

Send for sample copies of, and subscription information on the following periodicals. Some magazines and newsletters accept expert witness advertising. For more listings, check the periodical directories available at the reference desk of your public library.

The Expert and the Law
National Forensic Center
17 Temple Terrace, Suite 401
Lawrenceville, NJ 08648
Tel: (800) 526-5177, (609) 883-0550
e-mail: forenexpts@aol.com

The Testifying Expert ($105.00 per year)
LRP Publications
Frank Diamond, editor
PO Box 980
Horsham, PA 19044-0980
Tel: (800) 341-7874; (215) 784-0941; Fax: (215) 784-9639
e-mail: sdiamond@lrp.com; Web site: http://www.lrp.com

The Forensic Examiner
The American College of Forensic Examiners
2750 Sunshine Street
Springfield, MO 65804
Tel: (417) 881-3818; Fax: (417) 881-4702
e-mail: acfeme@acfe.com; Web site: http://www.acfe.com

Forensic Science International
Elsevier Science Publishers
PO Box 945, MSS
New York, NY 10160-0757
Tel: (888) 437-4636; (2112) 633-3650: Fax: (212) 633-3795
e-mail: usinfo-f@elsevier.com.; Web site: http://www.elsevier.com.

Consultants Report International Magazine
14315 SW Westfall Road
Sherwood, OR 97140
Tel: (503) 682-3317; Fax: (503) 682-0973
e-mail: editor@futurelearn.com;
Web site: http://www.futurelearn.com/~editor

The Expert
Maritime & Aviation Consultants
Kirk Greiner
15112 NE 30th Avenue
Vancouver, WA 98686-1669
Tel: (360) 574-1100; Fax: (360) 574-1101
e-mail: cptkirk@pacifier.com;
Web site: http://www.mac-experts.com

Experts
Texas Lawyer Magazine
Rosalee Hamilton
400 S. Record Street #1400
Dallas, TX 75202-4889
Tel: (800) 456-5484; (214) 744-7738; Fax: (214) 741-2325
e-mail: texas.classifieds@counsel.com;
Web site: http://www.texlaw.com

Scientific Sleuthing Review: A Study of Forensic Science in Law Enforcement
James E. Starrs
GWU Law School
720 20th Street, N.W.
Washington, DC 20052
Tel: (202) 994-6770; Fax: (202) 994-9446

Expert Witness Journal ($95.00 per year)
SEAK, Inc.
Steven Babitsky
PO Box 729
Falmouth, MA 02541
Tel: (508) 548-7023; Fax: (508) 540-8304
e-mail: seakinc@aol.com

Trial Magazine
Assn of Trial Lawyers of America
1050 31st Street NW
Washington, DC 20007
Tel:(800) 424-2725; (202) 965-3500; Fax: (202) 298-6849

ABA Journal ($66.00 per year)
American Bar Association
750 North Lake Shore Drive
Chicago, IL 60611
Tel: (800) 285-2221; (312) 988-5000; Fax: (312) 988-5568
e-mail: abasvcctr@attmail.com; Web site: http://www.abanet.org

California Lawyer
State Bar of California
555 Franklin Street
San Francisco, CA 94102
Tel: (415) 252-0500

The Advocate ($50.00 per year)
Los Angeles Trial Lawyers Association
2140 West Olympic Blvd.
Los Angeles, CA 90015
Tel: (213) 487-1212; Fax: (213) 487-1224

CAOC Forum
Consumer Attorneys of California
(formerly California Trial Lawyers Association)
980 9th Street, #200
Sacramento, CA 95814-2721
Tel: (916) 442-6902; Fax: (916) 442-7734
e-mail: caocforum@aol.com;
Web site: http://seamless.com\consumer

Lawyer-Pilots Bar Association Journal
Jay Rosenbaum
1100 Huntington Building
Cleveland, OH 44115
Tel: (216) 696-2480; Fax: 216-696-2645

Consultants News ($188.00 per year)
Kennedy and Kennedy, Inc.
Templeton Road
Fitzwilliam, NH 03447
Tel: (800) 531-0007; (603) 585-6544; Fax: (603) 585-9555
email: bookstore@kennedypub.com
Web site: http://www.kennedypub.com

Consulting Opportunities Journal ($49.00 per year)
J. Stephen Lanning
PO Box 430
Clear Spring, MD 21722
Tel: (301) 791-9332

AUDIO AND VIDEO TAPES

Preparing & Examining Expert Witnesses in Civil Litigation
Richard M. Bryan, Jack L. Slobodin & Darryl M. Woo
Audiotape $125
Videotape $175
Continuing Education of the Bar
2300 Shattuck Avenue
Berkeley, CA 94704-1576
Tel: (800) CEB-3444; Fax: (800) 640-6994 (orders only)

Expert Witness Challenges is an audio tape by Dan Poynter, author of *The Expert Witness Handbook.* You will learn how expert witness work is changing and how you can adapt to the challenges. Then Poynter will share ten tips and techniques for making your testimony easier and more effective. One 60-minute cassette with resources.
From Para Publishing
ISBN 0-915516-77-2 (Tape E-101) $9.95
Tel: (805) 968-7277; Fax: (805) 968-1379
e-mail:orders@ParaPublishing.com
Web site: http://www.ParaPublishing.com

Marketing Your Forensic Practice is an audio tape by Dan Poynter. You will learn how to select a field of practice, define your geographical area, assemble your promotion package and build a professional image. Poynter will share the ten ways to let lawyers know you are available to assist them. One 60-minute cassette with resources.
From Para Publishing
ISBN 0-915516-78-0 (Tape E-102) $9.95
(see above listing for contact info)

The Deposition
30 minutes $585.00
Commonwealth Films
Tel: (617) 262-5634; Fax: (617) 262-6948
e-mail: commfilms@ids.net
Web site: http://www.ids.net\~commfilm

On The Stand; Testifying in Court
20 minutes $585.00
Commonwealth Films
(see above listing for contact info)

Persuasive Expert Testimony (video)
Two cassettes $195.00
National Institute for Trial Advocacy
Notre Dame Law School
Notre Dame, IN 46556
Tel: (800) 225-6482; Fax: (219) 282-1263
Web site: http://www.nd.edu/~nita

Going to Court
Two Cassettes, 37 minutes, $149.00
Preparing Your Expert Witness
30 minutes, $149.00

Preparing for Your Deposition
20 minutes, $129.00
State Bar of Wisconsin
Law Office Videotape Series
PO Box 7158
Madison, WI 53707-7158
Tel: (800) 728-7788; Fax: (608) 257-5502
Web site: http://www.wisbar.org

Expert Witnesses
Irving Younger
$60.00 audio & book; $195 video & book
National Practice Institute
Tel: (800) 328-4444; (612) 338-1977; Fax: (612) 349-6561

What Makes Juries Listen, 1st ed.
Sonya Hamlin
Audio tapes & study guide, $200.00
Glasser LegalWorks
150 Clove Road
Little Falls, N.J. 07424
Tel: (800) 308-1700; Fax: (201) 890-0042
e-mail: legalwks@aol.com

The Expert Witness
Two videocassettes, $150.00
Court TV Library Service
Tel: (800) 888-4580; Fax: (212) 973-3210

CONFERENCES AND COURSES

Write for descriptions, schedules and prices.
National Forensic Center
17 Temple Terrace, Suite 401
Lawrenceville, NJ 08648
Tel: (800) 526-5177, (609) 883-0550
e-mail: forenexpts@aol.com

The Testifying Expert Conference
LRP Publications
1555 King Street
Alexandria, VA 22314
Tel: (703) 684-0510; Fax: (703) 739-0489
e-mail: lrpconf@lrp.com; Web site: http://www.lrp.com

American College of Forensic Examiners
2750 East Sunshine Street
Springfield, MO 65804
Tel: (800) 423-9737; (417) 881-3818; Fax: (417) 881-4702
e-mail: acfeme@aol.com; Web site: http://www.acfe.com
California Continuing Education of the Bar

Preparing and Examining Expert Witnesses (March 1997)
2300 Shattuck Avenue
Berkeley, CA 94704
Tel: (800) CEB-3444

THE EXPERT WITNESS BOOKSHELF

The following books may be ordered from Para Publishing. See the order blank. Your satisfaction is guaranteed. Order any book, look it over and feel free to return it if not completely satisfied.

The Expert Witness Handbook, Tips & Techniques for the Litigation Consultant by Dan Poynter. (This book). ISBN 0-915516-45-4 Hardcover, 5.5 x 8.5 $39.95

Is There a Book Inside You?, A Step-By-Step Plan For Writing Your Book by Dan Poynter and Mindy Bingham. As an expert witness, your book will validate your expertise and lend credibility to what you say. *Is There a Book Inside You?* will show you how to pick your topic, how to break the project down into easy-to-attack pieces, how and where to do research, a way to improve your material with a step-by-step process that makes writing (almost) easy, and more. Now you can *author* a book whether or not you have the time or ability to be a good *writer*. This book reveals how to find, interview, negotiate, contract and work with writing partners such as editors, researchers, contract writers, co-authors, and ghostwriters. *Writer's Digest Book Club main selection*. Also available on tape. ISBN 1-56860-019-4 Softcover, 5.5 x 8.5 236 pages $14.95

The Self-Publishing Manual, How to Write, Print & Sell Your Own Book by Dan Poynter is a complete course in writing, publishing, marketing, promoting and distributing books. It takes the reader step–by–step from idea, through manuscript, printing, promotion and sales. Along with an in-depth study of the book publishing industry, the book explains in detail numerous innovative book marketing techniques. *The Manual* is a *Bible* for writers and a constant reference for publishers. It is must reading for expert witnesses and consultants. ISBN 1-56860-018-6 Softcover, 5.5 x 8.5 464 pages $19.95

MAKE EACH DEPOSITION AND TRIAL A LEARNING EXPERIENCE.
WRITE DOWN WHAT HAPPENED ALONG WITH THE TOUGH
QUESTIONS.

INDEX

Also see the Glossary

ORDER FORM

Satisfaction guaranteed

🖷 **Fax orders:** (805) 968-1379. Send a copy of this form.

☎ **Telephone orders:** Call 1(800) PARAPUB toll free, (727-2782). Have your credit card ready.

🖃 **Postal orders:** Para Publishing, Dan Poynter, PO Box 8206-978, Santa Barbara, CA 93118-8206. USA. Telephone: (805) 968-7277

💻 **e-mail orders**: orders@ParaPublishing.com

Please send the following Books and/or Tapes. I understand that I may return any of them for a full refund—for any reason, no questions asked.

_____

_____

_____

_____

Please send more FREE information on:
☐ Speaking/Seminars   ☐ Mailing lists,   ☐ Consulting

Company name: _____

Name: _____

Address: _____

City _____ State: _____ Zip:____-____

Sales tax: Please add 7.75% for products shipped to California addresses.

Shipping by air:
US: $4 for the first book or disk and $1.00 for each additional product.
International: $9 for 1st book or disk; $5 for each additional product (estimate).

Payment: ☐ Cheque,   ☐ Credit card:
☐ Visa,   ☐ MasterCard,   ☐ Optima,   ☐ AMEX,   ☐ Discover

Card number: _____

Name on card: _____ Exp. date: ____/____

OPPOSING ATTORNEYS MAKE EXPERTS FEEL GUILTY EVEN WHEN THEY HAVE NOTHING TO FEEL GUILTY ABOUT.

ORDER FORM

Satisfaction guaranteed

🖷 **Fax orders:** (805) 968-1379. Send a copy of this form.

☎ **Telephone orders:** Call 1(800) PARAPUB toll free, (727-2782). Have your credit card ready.

✉ **Postal orders:** Para Publishing, Dan Poynter, PO Box 8206-978, Santa Barbara, CA 93118-8206. USA. Telephone: (805) 968-7277

💻 **e-mail orders**: orders@ParaPublishing.com

Please send the following Books and/or Tapes. I understand that I may return any of them for a full refund—for any reason, no questions asked.

_____

_____

_____

_____

Please send more FREE information on:
☐ Speaking/Seminars ☐ Mailing lists, ☐ Consulting

Company name: _____

Name: _____

Address: _____

City _____ State: _____ Zip:____-____

Sales tax: Please add 7.75% for products shipped to California addresses.

Shipping by air:
US: $4 for the first book or disk and $1.00 for each additional product.
International: $9 for 1st book or disk; $5 for each additional product (estimate).

Payment: ☐ Cheque, ☐ Credit card:
☐ Visa, ☐ MasterCard, ☐ Optima, ☐ AMEX, ☐ Discover

Card number: _____

Name on card: _____ Exp. date: ____/____

NO MATTER WHO IS PAYING YOU, YOUR OBJECTIVE ROLE IS
THE SAME.

ORDER FORM

Satisfaction guaranteed

Fax orders: (805) 968-1379. Send a copy of this form.

Telephone orders: Call 1(800) PARAPUB toll free, (727-2782). Have your credit card ready.

Postal orders: Para Publishing, Dan Poynter, PO Box 8206-978, Santa Barbara, CA 93118-8206. USA. Telephone: (805) 968-7277

e-mail orders: o..ders@ParaPublishing.com

Please send the following Books and/or Tapes. I understand that I may return any of them for a full refund—for any reason, no questions asked.

_____

_____

_____

_____

Please send more FREE information on:
☐ Speaking/Seminars   ☐ Mailing lists,   ☐ Consulting

Company name: _____

Name: _____

Address: _____

City _____ State: _____ Zip:____ ‒ ____

Sales tax: Please add 7.75% for products shipped to California addresses.

Shipping by air:
US: $4 for the first book or disk and $1.00 for each additional product.
International: $9 for 1st book or disk; $5 for each additional product (estimate).

Payment: ☐ Cheque,   ☐ Credit card:
☐ Visa,   ☐ MasterCard,   ☐ Optima,   ☐ AMEX,   ☐ Discover

Card number: _____

Name on card: _____ Exp. date: ____/_____